John Mair

## Nephaleia, or, Total Abstinence from Intoxicating Liquors in Man's Normal State of Health

The doctrine of the Bible, in a series of letters, with addenda to Edward C. Delavan, Esq. With colored plates of the stomach, as affected by strong drink.

John Mair

**Nephaleia, or, Total Abstinence from Intoxicating Liquors in Man's Normal State of Health**
*The doctrine of the Bible, in a series of letters, with addenda to Edward C. Delavan, Esq. With colored plates of the stomach, as affected by strong drink.*

ISBN/EAN: 9783337097592

Printed in Europe, USA, Canada, Australia, Japan

Cover: Foto ©Lupo / pixelio.de

More available books at **www.hansebooks.com**

# NEPHALEIA;

## OR

## TOTAL ABSTINENCE FROM INTOXICATING LIQUORS

### IN MAN'S NORMAL STATE OF HEALTH,

## THE DOCTRINE OF THE BIBLE,

### IN A SERIES OF LETTERS, WITH ADDENDA,

#### TO EDWARD C. DELAVAN, ESQ.

(With Colored Plates of the Stomach, as affected by Strong Drink.)

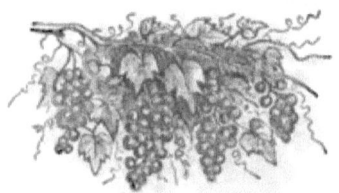

"DESTROY IT NOT, FOR A BLESSING IS IN IT."—[*Isaiah, chap. lxv. v.* 8.

### By JOHN MAIR, M. D., Edin.

*Extraordinary Member of the Royal Medical Society of Edinburgh;
Staff Surgeon, 1st class (Half Pay), to Her Britannic
Majesty's Army.*

---

PUBLISHERS:

*New York*—SHELDON & COMPANY.   *Boston*—GOULD & LINCOLN.
*Philadelphia*—J. B. LIPPENCOTT & Co.
*London, (Eng.)*—TOULNER & Co.
*Montreal*—JOHN DOUGALL.

1861.

Entered according to the Act of Congress, in the year Eighteen Hundred and Sixty-One,

BY CHARLES VAN BENTHUYSEN,

**In the Clerk's** Office of the District Court of the United States for the Northern District of New York.

# INTRODUCTORY LETTER.

St. Catharines, C. W., *September* 18*th*, 1860.

To Edward C. Delavan, Esq., Albany, N. Y.:

My Dear Sir: Understanding that a brief biographical sketch of the esteemed author of the following letters (published under your auspices) was desired by you by way of introduction, and having been requested to undertake this duty, it is with sincere pleasure that I comply. I can honestly say, that during a pastorate stretching over upwards of twelve years, (eight of which were spent in Kingston) I have never met with a more conscientious Christian, or a truer friend—a man of more disinterested benevolence, sterling integrity, and high-toned Christian principle, or one more disposed on the altar of religion and humanity, to present his body a living sacrifice. I can say this with greater confidence, because I do not go the doctor's length in certain departments of the Temperance question, though always cordially appreciating the strength and sincerity of his convictions, the purity of his motives, and the ability, energy and steady consistent perseverance, with which his somewhat unpalatable views have been advocated.

Dr. Mair was born in the city of Aberdeen, Scotland, 7th March, 1798. His father (a man of sound judgment, iron will, sterling worth and noble, independent spirit,) was commander and part owner of vessels trading with North America. His mother (a meek, devout Christian woman) was daughter of Professor John Stewart, of Marischal college, Aberdeen, a most able and acute mathematician, and intimate friend of Dr. Thomas Reid, the celebrated metaphysician, and father of the "Scotch Philosophy." Of the ability and worth of John Stewart, ample evidence is furnished in "Reid's Life" of the renowned Dugald Stewart, and the last edition of his Works and Correspondence, by that prince of mental philosophers, recently deceased, Sir Wm. Hamilton. On the maternal side Dr. Mair is lineally descended from Sir John Stewart, brother to James, 7th Lord High Steward and grandfather to King Robert the IId of Scotland. Sir John commanded a wing of Sir William Wallace's army at the memorable battle of Falkirk, where he fell covered with glory, A.D. 1298.

The doctor's academical education was pursued at the time-honored university of which his grandfather had been an ornament. His degree of A. M. was obtained in 1815; that of M. D. at the University of Edinburgh in 1819. He became an Ordinary and Extraordinary Member of the Royal Medical Society of Edinburgh. He attended the celebrated schools, and walked some of the leading hospitals of London and Paris, perfecting his knowledge of his profession. In the latter city he was a pupil of the distinguished Broussais.

From 1821 till 1852, the long period of thirty-one years, he served as a medical officer in Her Britannic Majesty's army, reaching the rank of staff surgeon, first class. It was in 1847, on my settlement over Chalmers' Presbyterian Church, Kingston, I first became acquainted with Dr. Mair, and I soon discovered in him the living epistle of Christ, known and read of all men. He was then medical officer at that important military post, remaining till 1850, and returning in '53 for permanent residence, on his retirement from the army. He was the centre of a faithful band of Corneliuses of the Vickar's stamp, to which belonged such men as Capt. Hammond, one of the heroes of the Redan of Crimean, but yet more illustrious Christian, fame. In that most interesting of Christian Biographies, "Hammond's Life," "the good physician" obtains honorable mention, and his contribution is not the least valuable. With all those **works** of faith and labours of love into which that most manly and **Christian** soldier threw his whole soul, Dr. Mair had to do. The Bible and tract societies found in him their most efficient practical advocate; of the weekly committee meetings, and the monthly concert for prayer, he was the most regular attender; of the Kingston Sabbath Reformation Society he was the first President, and now fills the office of Secretary. **He** was ever ready to distribute and willing to communicate. His ear was ever open **to the** cry of the needy. Professional advice gratis and pecuniary assistance were most ungrudgingly given to multitudes.

During the fatal emigrant fever of 1847 and the cholera of '49, he followed in the footsteps of the Great Physician who went about continually doing good. The chamber of sickness, the house of mourning—at once the lofty and the lowly were cheered by his presence, and comforted and directed by his prayers and counsel. In our Sanitary Board, and our City Mission, he was very prominent. In addition to his other good works, already enumerated, he has, during this second term of our intercourse, identified himself specially with the management of the public schools and the "sacramental" phase of the temperance question. As a school trustee he has been most energetic and faithful, though subjected not unfrequently to not a little annoyance. With the temperance cause he connected himself in 1843, when in a precarious state of health, influenced by the advice of a brother physician. In 1850, when going home in the ship, two letters by Judge Marshall, of Nova Scotia, brought the sacramental wine question under his notice, and since 1852 he has been decided upon **it**. During the intervening years he has read and written much regarding it, and has been endeavoring to rouse the churches and Christians generally to its consideration. Aside from this subject the doctor has written on others connected with his profession, though from his life having been one of labor and travel, he has not had much time to devote to literary pursuits. We have not seen any of the letters Dr Mair now proposes publishing, but we are certain, from what we know of the man, however much some may call in question his positions, all must admire the honesty and fearlessness with which they are advanced, and the extensive erudition and intimate knowledge of scripture by which their advocacy is marked. Most of the readers of these "Delavan Letters" will be strangers to their author. Let them understand that those who know him best think most of him; and however "peculiar" some may think his views to be, and however fervid, even to fanaticism, others may regard his defence of them, it is the general feeling throughout the entire circle of his acquaintances, that no one has a better right than he to appropriate the eulogium of the patient patriarch—"When the ear heard me, then it blessed me; and when the eye saw me, it gave witness to me, because I delivered the poor that cried, and the fatherless and him that had none to help him. The blessing of him that was ready to perish came upon me, and I caused the widow's heart to sing for joy. I was eyes to the blind, and feet was I to the lame. I was a father to the poor, and the cause which I knew not I searched out."

Believe me, my dear sir,
Very truly yours,
ROBERT FERRIER BURNS.
**Pastor** *Presbyterian Church of Canada*

# LETTERS

FROM

## DR. MAIR TO EDWARD C. DELAVAN.

### LETTER I.

KINGSTON, C. W., March 25, 1859.

MY DEAR SIR,

The Bible, and the Bible only, ought to be the Temperance of the world. Let us heartily adopt this principle as our motto and watch-word, never to be forgotten or forsaken by us. If it had never been lost sight of since the days of the Apostles, or after being for a period neglected, had been again firmly laid hold of by the churches of Christ, some hundreds of years ago, and vigorously maintained in all succeeding ages, down to the present time, there would have been no need of the Temperance or Teetotal movement, for the plain reason that total abstinence from all intoxicating drinks in man's normal state of health, would have been the uniform law and custom in all well governed Kingdoms and Republics, thoroughly incorporated with their civil and religious institutions, and forming the ground-work of their prosperity and happiness.

A triple chain unites the Temperance of earth with the jurisprudence of Heaven, not one link of which can be severed without deranging the whole.

The sum and substance of the two tables of the moral law is expressive of this three-fold love: "Thou shalt love the Lord thy God with all thy heart, and with all thy soul, and with all thy mind, and with all thy strength:" this is the first commandment; and the second is like namely, this: "Thou shalt love thy neighbor as thyself." (Mark xii, 30, 31.) Temperance built upon this immovable foundation, the law of God, in its three-fold character of love to Him, as the **source of** piety or goodliness; love to self, flowing **from the other,** and forming with it the source of self-government or sobriety; **and love** to man flowing from the **two** previous loves, and constituting with these the conjoint source of righteousness or justice, form a temple sacred to Jehovah, which is "as Mount Zion, which cannot be **moved,** but abideth forever." It is at this point **that there** is a necessity for the introduction of the Cross of Christ, for "who (amongst the sinful sons of Adam) is sufficient for **these** things?" But what man could not do has been **perfectly** accomplished by Him, "who, although He was rich, yet **for** your sakes became poor, that ye, through His poverty, might be rich; who magnified the law and made it honorable; who, his own self, bare our sins in His **own** body on the tree, that we being dead to sins should live unto righteousness, by whose stripes ye were healed."

**The** Temperance **of** human, erroneously called Christian expediency, is very different. It must necessarily be lame, impotent, fickle, dishonoring to God, and incapable of bearing the burden, and accomplishing the work laid upon it; because it merely recognizes man's duty **to his** fellows, failing to take into account his paramount duty to God and his prior duty to himself, in which, unitedly, his duty to his neighbor must originate, and by which it must be regulated. In the following words of inspiration, this triune morality (if I may so speak), is beautifully set forth: "The grace of God that bringeth salvation, hath appeared to all men, teaching us that denying ungodliness, and worldly lusts, we should live soberly, righteously, and godly in this present world."

I cannot but reject expediency, then, as the basis or exponent of Bible Temperance. In this sentiment I apprehend you agree with me. You have well said, in your comments on the letter of the Rev. Dr. Yale (p. 24, of the Enquirer), "I have supposed that christian expediency requires that we should give up the use of anything innocent in itself for the good of others; but when the article to be abandoned is known to be positively injurious, by testimony and experience, I have supposed the rule cannot apply; and it then becomes a duty not to use the article at all. St. Paul says, 'It is neither good to eat flesh, nor drink wine, nor anything whereby thy brother stumbleth, or is offended, or is made weak.'

"Now meat is innocent in itself, as a common diet; still we should abandon its use if the good of others require it. It has been taken for granted by some, that St. Paul refers to intoxicating wine; are we sure of this?

"If he referred to the pure, unintoxicating wine, then the rule of expediency with regard to abstinence from wine, rests on exactly the same foundation as on meat; both innocent, both in themselves proper, and right to use; but both, like other good things, liable to abuse, and to be abandoned to prevent a weak brother from stumbling."

St. Paul appears to me to have been most unmercifully dragged out of his true position as the apostle of the Gentiles; who gloried in the cross; the greatest philanthropist that ever lived (second only to Immanuel Himself—the perfect Godman,) to bear the brunt and odium of this dangerous error.

Many will have it, that there is only one kind of wine spoken of in the Bible, and that intoxicating. It is very convenient for such persons to seize upon this saying of the apostle, and try to turn it to account. But it is decidedly a perversion of the passage just quoted, and from this perversion and others of a similar nature, numerous and enormous evils have resulted. To make of alcoholic wine "a good creature of God," like wholesome meat, "not to be refused if it be received with thanksgiving," when it is, in truth, a most dangerous and delusive poison, in the ratio of the alcohol which it contains, must surely be a pestilent error. Thus, men are liable to be misled by their spiritual guides and instructers, and falsely to conceive that there is nothing in the Word of God, which hinders the use of alcoholic drinks, more than of nutritious food, and that there is nothing in these drinks of a deceitful and enticing kind which tends to the formation of an insatiable appetite, which, when gratified, poisons both soul and body. Thus, their minds may be steeled against the reception of those vivid statements of Holy Writ which plainly teach this great lesson, that the use of these intoxicating, or poisonous liquors by man, in his normal state of health, is an abomination in the sight of God. This aberration from the truth sets up, as it were, St. Paul in the place of God, and makes him the antagonist of the Divine law. It excludes, from the temperance movement, God in Christ, Who ought always to have been acknowledged as the founder and law-giver of all genuine temperance, and makes the devoted and heroic apostle the unconscious and unwilling instrument of that exclusion, from which, his noble, generous spirit (were he now on earth) would shrink back with grief and consternation. This doctrine, moreover, as a natural consequence, extinguishes temperance, as a christian grace, and destroys its Divine motives and sanctions; making it seem to be merely a giving up of a good thing, for a longer or shorter period, for the sake of a weak brother, instead of an imperative duty and precious privilege, consisting in the abandonment of an evil thing, alcoholic wine binding upon man, at all times, in his normal state of health; because enjoined by the law of God, as distinctly, (when all the Scriptures upon the subject are considered,) as the sacred observance of the Lord's day, and *as* necessary, to secure and maintain the right worship of Jehovah, and the happiness of the human race.

Meat is a good creature of God: a friend of man, which (as the chameleon changes its tint from the reflected color of surrounding objects), may assume a sombre appearance in the eyes of a superstitious observer, in consequence of its temporary connexion with an evil companion—say an idol—and yet retain all its intrinsic good qualities, unimpaired.

Alcohol (including every alcoholic liquor,) is a poison, which, like the venom distilled from the serpent, is such a sworn friend of Satan, and deadly enemy to man, that it is scarce possible it can be made more hostile, or dangerous by any association which may be formed by it. It may be expedient for me **not** to eat a portion of meat offered to an idol, in the presence of a weak, but conscientious brother, who has lately escaped from the darkness of paganism, and who believes an idol to be something in the world, lest I should prove a snare to him; but I am not likely to meet with such a brother often, and when out of his sight, I need not be so scrupulous, knowing that "an idol is nothing in the world, and that there is **none other God but one**:" the only living and true **God**.

But wine and other strong drink being themselves the basest idols—the most devouring and destroying Molochs, no idolatrous communication with other idols, however intimate, **can** make them more execrable than they now are; neither can any association with holy persons or things, in the least degree improve them, although it will most certainly taint the reputation of their associates. One contingency it is just possible **to** conceive, and only one, to which the language of the apostle (supposing his allusion to have been to alcoholic wine as a good thing) could have been applicable; that is, to the whole family of man, struck down suddenly and simultaneously with typhus fever, or some other asthenic disease of the same class, for the cure of which alcoholic drinks are very generally believed to be a suitable, if not the best, remedy.

Let the advocate of expediency make the most of this argument, and seek support from the following apposite remarks of Professor Miller, of Edinburgh, in his recent work, "Alcohol, its Place and Power." Speaking of alcohol, as a tonic in fever, he says: "But in the trough of fever, dosing goes on without one sign of drunkenness; the brain, on the contrary, growing clearer and clearer in all its functions. Nay, it is perhaps wrong to speak of wine and brandy, when judiciously handled, having a *stimulant* action in such circumstances. They do not excite the brain above the normal standard; they merely bring it up to the normal working, counteracting the state of depression in which they found it sunk, and thus approaching the character of a true tonic.

"In order to do this accurately and thoroughly, however, it is plain that both a careful and skillful management of the remedy is required. *Like other poisons*, it is not to be rashly and empirically prescribed, or the dosing fixed by routine. The case must be suitable; the disease and the necessity for the remedy must be there; the dose must be well adjusted at starting, and its effect must be carefully watched, in order that it may be duly regulated accordingly." Is this the good creature, which, even in disease where its use is beneficial, requires to be so closely watched, and skilfully managed? Can it then be used promiscuously, and at random, in unmeasured quantities, in health, where it is not required medicinally; where it *cannot* nourish, and where it *must* prove poisonous? In future letters, should it be the will of God, that I shall be privileged from time to time to address you upon that department of Bible Temperance which relates to wine and strong drink, I shall endeavor, trusting in the "promises of God, which in Him (Jesus) are, yea, and in Him, amen," to be guided in my researches by the sound views of your distinguished countryman, Jonathan Edwards, who, "being dead, yet speaketh" in the following words of sterling worth and profound wisdom: "The mind and will of God, concerning any duty to be performed by us, may be sufficiently revealed in His word, without a particular precept, in so many express terms, enjoining it.

"The human understanding is the ear to which the word of God is spoken; and if it be so spoken, that the ear may plainly hear it, it is enough. God is Sovereign, as to the manner of speaking His mind, whether He will speak it in express terms, or whether He will speak it, by saying several other things which imply it, and from which we may, by comparing them together, plainly perceive it. If the mind of God be but revealed—if there be but sufficient means for the communication of His mind to our minds, that is sufficient; whether we hear so many express words with our ears, or see them in writing with our eyes; or whether we see the thing which He would signify to us by the eye of reason, and understanding."

I am, my dear sir,

Affectionately yours,

JOHN MAIR.

### LETTER II.

My Dear Sir,

Never was greater injustice done to any book, than has been done to the Bible, in regard to drunkenness, its causes and cure. If hemlock and hellebore, which belong to the same class of poisons as alcohol, had been substituted for wine and strong drink; or in modern phraseology, "wines and spirituous liquors," as dietetic articles of ordinary use, less wonder should have been excited in the minds of impartial judges, than ought to have been produced by the habitual use of alcoholic liquors, by man in his normal state of health; because, neither hellebore nor hemlock is specially spoken against in Scripture; whereas, wine and strong drink are frequently represented there, in the most unfavorable light, that they may be shunned.

It is high time that the errors which prevail in Christendom upon this subject were made manifest, in order to their final destruction; and that justice were done to the word of God, in regard to *alcoholic intemperance*, and *anti-alcoholic temperance*; terms which may be aptly employed, to signify the departments of christian ethics which relate to wine and strong drink, in our future correspondence.

In my letter to you of date 6th June, 1856, which appeared in the Gospel Tribune of July, the same year, there **are certain** apposite remarks, which I now take the liberty of quoting nearly *verbatim :* " It has often been asserted, with apparently some degree of triumph, that there is no command of Scripture against the use of intoxicating wine. How such an assertion could have been made by men intimately acquainted with the sacred volume, it is not easy to explain. The fact is quite the **reverse.** Although the 'blessed Gospel,' as has been well remarked by arch-deacon Jeffreys, 'is not a book of casuistry, nor a statute book of laws;' yet, in the case of wine and strong drink, the general plan of the Divine procedure in leaving specific acts and things, to be judged of by men, with the discerning, intellectual and moral faculties, with which God has endowed them, seems, in a remarkable manner, to have been departed from by Divine wisdom. The Decalogue supplies general laws for man's government, but it does not condescend to enumerate the various modes in which persons may violate these laws.

"Under the 6th commandment, for example, which is: 'Thou shalt not kill,' there is no enumeration of the various means by which murder may be committed; there is no catalogue annexed of the different poisonous substances to be found in the animal, vegetable, and mineral kingdoms, by which life may be destroyed, in a more or less summary manner. You find nowhere in the Bible, any legal prohibition of the use of opium, or arsenic, or any other poison known to the ancients; yet, it cannot be denied, that danger might have been incurred, and may still be incurred, by individuals, and even death be the result from the ignorant, or intentional use of them.

"But the Almighty has acted differently in regard to wine and strong drink. They seem to possess certain qualities which might entitle them to be included in the same category with opium; but universal experience has proved that they are articles which surpass that poison in their power to lead groups of mankind astray from the paths of virtue. They possess peculiarly seductive properties, by which they often irresistibly lure multitudes to destruction; opium-eating being a solitary, while spirit drinking is often a social vice, the prolific parent of innumerable crimes, the destroyer of thousands of souls, the implacable enemy of Jesus and His religion! It is on account of these singularly perverting and destructive qualities possessed by alcoholic drinks, (may it not be safely and reverently believed?) that Jehovah has singled them out and made them conspicuous as objects to be shunned by man; and this He has done in instances too numerous to be recapitulated here, and in a great variety of ways, all calculated to arrest the attention, command the conscience, and regulate the will of those who consent to examine the subject dispassionately, and without prejudice. Is not drunkenness repeatedly denounced as shutting out from the kingdom of God? and is it not true that 'principals include accessaries;' that is, whatever approaches, or comes near to them, or has a tendency to them? Is not the use of alcoholic drinks in man's normal state of health, included under this canon of interpretation, seeing it has been admitted by the physiologist, that it is the nature of these drinks to induce a habit which constitutes 'confirmed drunkenness?'

"Hear what the Rev. Dr. Beecher says, with uncommon power, upon this subject: 'But of all the ways to hell, which deluded mortals tread, that of the intemperate is the most dreary and terrific. The demand for artificial stimulus, to supply the deficiencies of healthy aliment, is like the rage of thirst and the voracious demand of famine. *It is famine*, for the artificial excitement has become as essential now to strength and cheerfulness as simple nutrition once was. But nature, taught by habit, to require what once she did not need, demands gratification now, with a decision inexorable as death, and to most men, as irresistible. The denial is a living death.'

"So far, then, mankind would have had no excuse for tampering with alcoholic, intoxicating drinks, if there had been merely in the Bible such a denunciation as the following: 'Nor thieves, nor covetous, nor drunkards shall enter into **the** kingdom of Heaven;" or even if *this* had been wanting, and their sole, or at least principal instructer, as in other cases, had been the 6th, and other commandments of the Decalogue. But not only is drunkenness denounced in Scripture, but the use of that which produces it, is by name strictly forbidden, thus: 'Look not thou upon the wine when it is red: when it giveth his color in the cup: when it moveth itself aright: at the last, it biteth like **a** serpent, and stingeth like an adder.' Other Scriptural **proofs** are there given, but I do not proceed with them here, as **they** will be brought fully under notice in a future communication.

The following pointed observations, however, may not be out of place: "Would you think it right to make opium your common food, or to use it at all in your normal state of health, if the same epithets were applied to it in the Bible, as are applied to alcoholic wine? or rather, would the testimony of Scripture against it, similar to that against intoxicating wine, induce you to **receive it** into your favor: **although** without that testimony, you keep it at a distance, and eschew the use of it, except as a medicinal agent?—that is to say, would it be right, not only to attach no value to the witness of Scripture and of God against it, but to place that witness to its credit, which ought, according to common sense, grammar, reason and revelation, to militate, in the strongest manner, to its disadvantage and repudiation? Would it be lawful to trifle with *it* **as** men now trifle with **wine and other** alcoholic drinks; not only *if*, but *because* God **had** been pleased to express, in the most authoritative **manner,** His disapprobation of it **as a common** article of diet, **and** stamped it as infamous, over and over again; although, without such Divine interdict, you feel it to be **your** duty to reject it from your daily food? *If so*, then, no doubt it will be perfectly lawful and right for christians to continue, as they have been doing, with intoxicating drinks, for ages past; to treat them with **the same unbounded** confidence, in spite of all **the** awful denunciations of **God against them, and not** only in spite of, but because they **have been so** denounced. For it is obvious that if opium, with its preparations, having only the testimony of man against it, **be** generally **treated as** a **poison,** and therefore avoided **as an** article **of** diet, while alcoholic drinks are so made **of,** which have **the** decided testimony of God against them, in addition **to the** testimony of mankind; were the witness of God super-added against opium, it would not only not corroborate the former evidence to its injury, but altogether neutralize that evidence, and cause it to be received as a good creature, deserving **of the** utmost confidence."

Man believes the testimony **of his fellow** man, that opium is a poison, and acts **in accordance with that** testimony. Shall he not receive "the witness **of God,"** which is greater, and yield implicit obedience to it, for "this **is the witness** which He hath testified" of the wine **which intoxicates;** "**Look** not thou upon the wine when it is **red:** when it giveth his **color in** the cup: **when it** moveth **itself** aright: **at the last, it** biteth like a serpent, **and** stingeth like an **adder."**

Hoping, **in** my next letter, **after** a few further preliminary remarks, to **be enabled by the grace of** God, to sketch out a plan for the Scriptural investigation **of the** great disease— *Alcoholic intemperance,* and the cure thereof: *Anti-alcoholic temperance;* and requesting an interest in your prayers.

I am, Yours affectionately,    JOHN MAIR.

## LETTER III.

My Dear Sir,

One would suppose, from the favor shown by christians generally to the doctrine of expediency, as the basis of modern Teetotalism, that drunkenness was not included under the principles expounded by our Divine Redeemer, **in** His Sermon **on the** Mount, and that anti-alcoholic temperance was a myth, which might in vain be sought for in the Bible; for if a reality to be found there, why should human expediency have been preferred to the Divine law, in all its comprehensiveness and spirituality, in this branch of christian ethics? That, not **only** drunkenness, but everything which has a tendency to it, is **virtually** forbidden by the perfect morality of our Saviour, I **firmly believe.**

I **shall make no** attempt, at present, **to** explain why such a belief **has been so** rare; or why a **lax and** faulty human device should have been preferred to a Divine commandment, perpetually and universally binding upon **mankind.** An effort may be put forth in a future letter to unfold this mystery. I have faith in the Bible, as the only sure and sufficient foundation of all genuine, effective, God-pleasing, God-honoring morality; whether in church, or state; for families, nations, or individuals, **abroad**, or **at home.** I cannot agree with Neal Dow, as he is reported **to have** expressed himself, at the great public meeting in Manchester, when he visited England, in 1857, that legal prohibition is, **or** can be, "the last stage in the temperance reformation." **The** expediency which now views intoxicating wine, &c., as a good creature within **the** sanctuary, but votes it to be **a** nuisance elsewhere, must, I apprehend, give place to the stern, consistent belief, that intoxicating liquor of every kind is an evil thing, as well at the Lord's table as at man's table, ere any prohibitory law, however perfect it may seem, can strike at the root of the Upas tree of drunkenness, **as it flourishes in the church, the family, and the world; and cause it to wither, decay, and die!**

Many temperance reformers, of modern times, seem to have forgotten, or lightly to have borne in mind, that something must go before law, to make it strong and conscience-binding, viz: right principle derived from Divine truth. Arbitrary laws, built on a quick-sand foundation, may be framed, and seem to prosper for a time: but by-and-by they will become powerless and contemptible; or at most, only **extort a base, grudging, outward compliance,** from dread of punishment, **while secret breaches of them will be** committed, and winked at, whenever and wherever men **may find an encouraging opportunity.** How can it be otherwise, if the **church is to have any influence** on her members, **or on the world,** seeing that she consecrates intoxicating liquor, and **pays it the highest** deference, as the symbol of her Saviour's precious, sin-atoning blood, and not alcoholic liquor simply; but (as has been proved in the most clear and convincing manner by you, in your **excellent letters in the** Enquirer, published so far back as **1841, and since, in other** productions of **your pen,** and especially **in your recent work on** adulterations,) "**liquors** sold **as wine, in which there is not a** drop of the fruit of the vine, **but a combination of** poisonous drugs, fit neither **for man nor beast to** swallow, and a perfect disgrace to the communion table!" I apprehend that, although there are many zealous contenders for a Maine-law in America,—and England is fast following her example,—yet a large proportion of them, **if they** were honestly to reveal their secret thoughts and desires, **would** confess that they cherish an inward liking for **strong drink, as** "**a good** creature of God, not to be refused **if received** with thanksgiving;" and that they would be sorely grieved if they **imagined** that they should forever be deprived of the pleasure, and solace derived from it when alone, or in the **bosom** of their families, in the event of a prohibitory law being adopted; and if they had no hope that the reformed customs and habits of society, in consequence thereof, would ultimately lead to the restoration of the traffic. But no such melancholy forebodings need weigh down their spirits by day: no such gloomy visions need haunt their pillows by night. As long as the church continues to patronize alcohol at her sacred altars, happen what may in regard to legal prohibition, they can comfort themselves with the cheering thought that they cannot, and shall not be prevented from turning their apples into intoxicating cider; their grapes into intoxicating wine; or their grain into intoxicating ale or spirits, for domestic use; of which, they may quaff their fill, unawed by the law or its myrmidons, and callous to the warnings of Solomon, inspired by God, so to speak, that poison, like that of a serpent, lurks within the seductive cup! Will it be believed, that an eminent living divine of the Emerald Isle, at a temperance meeting in England, not long ago, broached the fantastic theory (and he seemed serious) that home-liquor-drinking is the legitimate St. Paul-remedy for intemperance; far preferable to a Maine-law, because St. Paul has said, I Cor., xi, 20, 22: "When ye come together therefore unto one place, this is not to eat the Lord's supper: for in eating, every man taketh before other his own supper, and one is hungry, and another is drunken. What? have ye not houses to eat and drink in, or despise ye the Church of God, and shame them that have not," &c.? A flimsy foundation this, surely, upon which to build a goodly superstructure, sacred to temperance; when, according to the Rev. Dr. Bloomfield, Professor Moses Stewart, and other eminent interpreters, there is nothing in the passage to show that the apostle referred to intoxicating wine at all; but that the charges he brings against the Corinthians, were selfish neglect of the poor, on the part of their rich brethren, and carnal, irreverent observance of the Lord's supper, as if it had been an ordinary meal or of the preceding and accompanying love-feast!

But, it is not the question, whether and how far by **means of** fines, prisons, fetters, bolts and bars, a strictly vigilant and efficient police, and all the necessary appendages of a coercive system, or by any other mere human scheme, drunkenness, with its attendant miseries, degradations, and desolations, could be kept within narrow bounds, so as to become a less grievous evil, than at present, that I am desirous should be pondered; but the far nobler question, what ought to be done, by gospel means, to bring not only or chiefly the greatest amount of good to man, but also, and pre-eminently, the richest revenue of glory to God, in the department of anti-alcoholic temperance.

With this sublime object in view, and sincerely desirous, with God's blessing, to contribute somewhat towards its accomplishment, I feel I cannot do better than conclude this letter with the following admirable and apposite remarks from the " Philosophy of the Plan of Salvation," by an American citizen :

"There are two insuperable difficulties which would forever hinder the restoration of mankind, to truth and happiness, from being accomplished by human means.

"The first, which has been already alluded to, is that **human** instruction, as such, has no power to bind the conscience. **Even** if man were competent to discover all the truth necessary for a perfect rule of conduct, yet that truth would have no reformatory power, because men could never feel that truth as obligatory, which proceeded from merely human sources. It is an obvious principle of our nature, that the conscience will not charge guilt on the soul for disobedience, when the command proceeds from a fellow-man, who is not recognised as having the prerogative, and the right, to require submission. And besides, as men's minds are variously constituted, **and of** various capacities, there could be no agreement in such a case concerning the question, 'What is truth?' As well might we expect two school boys to reform each others' manners in school, without the aid of the teacher's authority, *as that men can reform their fellows without the* *sanction of that authority which will quicken and bind the conscience. The human conscience was made to recognise and enforce the authority of God; and unless there is belief of the Divine obligation of truth, conscience refuses to perform its office.*

"But the grand difficulty is this: Truth, whether sanctioned by conscience or not, has no power, as has been shown, to produce love in the heart. The law may convict and **guide** the mind, but it has no power to soften or to change the affections. This was the precise thing necessary, and this necessary end the world could not accomplish. All the wisdom of all the philosophers in all ages could never cause the affections of the soul to rise to the holy, blessed God. To destroy selfish pride, and produce humility—to eradicate the evil passions, and produce in the soul, desires for the universal good, and love for the universal parent, were beyond the reach of earthly wisdom and power. The wisdom of the world, in their efforts to give truth and happiness to the human soul, was foolishness with God; and the wisdom of God—Christ crucified—was foolishness with the philosophers, in relation to the same subject; yet it was Divine philosophy—an adapted means, and the only adequate means to accomplish the necessary end. Said an apostle, in speaking on this subject: 'The Jews require a sign, and the Greeks seek after wisdom; but we preach Christ crucified, unto the Jews a stumbling-block, and unto the Greeks, foolishness; but unto them which are called, both Jews and Greeks, Christ the power of God, and the wisdom of God.'"

I am, with great respect, my dear sir,

Yours affectionately,

JOHN MAIR.

## LETTER IV.

My Dear Sir,

There is nothing more observable in the temperance movement of modern times, than the gradual manner in which fragments of truth, respecting spirituous liquors, have been discovered by successive inquirers, contrasted with the direct and explicit manner, in which the same truth in its simple unity and fulness, though under-varying phases and relations, is authoritatively revealed in the Bible, by its Divine Author. It might be no very difficult, though a most ungracious task for one, aided by the researches and discoveries of the intrepid band of temperance reformers in Europe and America, to detect occasional flaws and slips in some of their doings; and by means of the light which they have kindled, and beyond their own field of vision, it might be possible to discover a fertile region which, to them, seemed enveloped in mist. But a far more agreeable duty than that of a fault-finder invites and constrains me. I rejoice in beholding the admirable harmony which exists between the matured results of scientific investigation, conducted according to Baconian rules—by the slow, but certain method of observation and experiment; by such men as Liebig, Carpenter, Lees, Mussey and Youmans, and the plain statements of Holy Writ, respecting alcohol, the poisonous principle of wine and strong drink—(to the confusion of infidels)—adding another testimony to the cheering and sublime truth, that "the Book of Nature, and the Book of Revelation, have the same author, and whenever rightly interpreted, both declare the glory of God, and show forth his handy-work." It has been beautifully said by Sir David Brewster: "If the God of love is most appropriately worshipped in the christian temple, the God of nature may be equally honored in the temple of science. Even from its lofty minarets, the philospher may summon the faithful to prayer; and the priest and the sage may exchange altars without the compromise of faith, or knowledge."

If, on the other hand, the interpretation given by the opponents of teetotalism of Scriptural language, **in** regard to alcoholic wine and strong drink as good creatures of God, were correct, then, the conclusions of the most eminent, scientific, and practical men of Europe and America, deciding that they are poisonous, and every way injurious to man, in his normal state **of health,** would be opposed to the testimony of Holy Writ, and afford a handle to infidels, to sneer at the Bible as an imposition upon mankind. Instead of referring here to a multitude of authorities, to prove the poisonous nature of alcohol, I need only quote a single passage from the London Times, **which** will be universally allowed to be an echo of the public voice upon **this** subject. **In** the London Times of March 11th, 1857, are to be found these words: "*Opium* is in the same category as *wine*, or gin, or tobacco. Are our distillers enemies to their race? are the planters of Cuba and Virginia to be denounced? are France and Spain no longer to send in the produce of their vineyards, because the people drink and chew more than is good for them? If the moderate use of these is to be justified in health, why should we pour invectives against those who sell the production, which is equivalent to them, (opium) to 300,000,000 of men?" What a debt of gratitude does the world owe (and it will never be paid off till the millennial day,) to Beecher, Hewett, Edwards, Nott, Barnes, Marsh, Burritt and Stewart, Drs. Lee and Sewall, Generals Cocke and Carey, and Hon. Gerrit Smith; and though last, not **least,** Neal Dow, in the United States; to Father Mathew, Livesey, Eaton, Dunlop, Stubbin, Gurney, Buckingham, Gough; to the authors of "Bacchus and Anti-Bacchus," in the British Islands, and a host of other heroic men who have fought manfully in the battle of temperance, and whose names will be handed down to the remotest ages, associated with those of Wilberforce, **Howard and Jenner!** But I must not pass over **your own honored name, which has** occupied so conspicuous a place in the annals of christian temperance, for the last thirty years. In bold defence of the important Scriptural doctrine, that the unintoxicating fruit **of the vine is** the proper emblem of the Redeemer's blood, you, assailed by bitter reproaches and calumnies, meekly **and patiently** persevered, "strong in the Lord, and in the power **of His might."** You have devoted your bodily and mental energies to this glorious cause; you have expended large sums of money upon it; you have zealously and **wisely enquired into the subject** yourself, **and** munificently encouraged others **to do the same; your sole object,** all the while, being to discover **the truth for God's glory and** the good of **the** human **race.**

But the days of superstitious veneration for a vile, traditionary delusion, I trust, are fast drawing to a close. The tables are being turned. It is no longer sacrilegious or pharisaical, frivolous or absurd, to plead for the use of the pure, unintoxicating, *unadulterated* fruit of the vine, **as the Divinely-**appointed symbol of **our Saviour's precious, sin-atoning blood.** In your valuable publications, you have cheered **my heart by** presenting some pithy, seer-like sayings, of **men of note in your** and in other countries, upon this important theme—sayings, which have gushed forth, clear and sparkling, from the deep recesses of their minds, like streams of living water from a perennial fountain, emblematic of the purity of **temperance,** and redolent of unnumbered blessings yet in store for the sin-stained family of man! These apothegms are worthy of being stored up, and **made household words,** by the wise and good **of** all nations.

Thus *you* speak, and this has been your motto for thirty years: "All use of intoxicating drinks, as a beverage in health, is abuse;" and **it** follows from this, " all use of intoxicating drink, in health, is intemperance—the degree regulated by the quantity."

Thus spake the Honorable R. H. Walworth, late chancellor of the State of New York, and first president of the New York Temperance Society—about twenty-five years since: "The time will come when men will as soon be engaged in poisoning their neighbors' wells, as in dealing out intoxicating liquor as a beverage."

"The Rev. Dr. Lyman Beecher, in the following letter, (I quote from your publications,) brings the question of alcohol drinking, as a beverage in health, under whatever cloak it may be disguised to the true test:

'ALBANY, *Aug. 24th*, 1836.

To E. C. DELAVAN,

Dear Sir: Alcohol, taken as a beverage, is always injurious in proportion to the quantity taken, and the frequency of its use. Its use, therefore, is not only *inexpedient* as an injurious example, but is morally wrong, both as it endangers health, and exposes to the insidious dominion of a deadly habit, and countenances its production and use with all its sweeping desolations and woes. The use of alcohol, therefore, as a beverage, is, in my judgment, inexpedient as an example, and morally wrong, as a violation of the obligation to use all lawful means to preserve our own life, and the life of our neighbors. Yours truly, LYMAN BEECHER.'"

"The Rev. Dr. Justin Edwards, now no more, and who, for a long series of years, devoted his best energies to enlighten the public mind as to all the evils flowing from the use of intoxicating drinks as a beverage, in 1832, states in an address: 'It is not needful, or useful. . . . . . It is a poison which injures the body and the soul; it deranges healthy action and disturbs the functions of life; it blinds the understanding, sears the conscience, pollutes the affections, and hardens the heart; it leads men into temptation, and gives evil peculiar power over their minds; it tends to bring those who use it to a premature grave, and to usher all who understand, or have the means of understanding its nature and effects, and yet continue to drink it, or furnish it to be drunk by others, into a miserable eternity.' The present Secretary of State at Washington, the Hon. Lewis Cass, never has tasted ardent spirits, and with Chancellor Walworth was among the first to move in Congress to prohibit the spirit rations in the army and navy. Listen to his noble sentiments, expressed at the capitol at Washington, February 24th, 1833, while advocating the temperance reform: 'This subject becomes unimportant when compared with the ultimate object of those who are prosecuting the warfare against the great enemy of the human race. They seek not only to cure the malady, but to render its recurrence impossible—to save all from the dangers which threaten them: to prevent the abuse, by preventing the use of stimulating liquors, and by preparing the way for the entrance upon life, of a generation not exposed to this fatal temptation. Let, then, one mighty effort be made to banish from our land this bane of national and individual prosperity. Let there be a union of hearts and exertions. Experience and reflection will soon disclose the most practicable plan of effecting the object. Precept and example, when they go together, go far in their operation upon human affairs. Let them be here united. The nature and extent of the evil must be laid open to all. Such an effort would be a crusade far holier than that which sent the nations of christendom to the land of Judea to seek, through battle and slaughter, the tomb of the Saviour. It would be a crusade of virtue against vice; an effort to give tone and strength to public sentiment, and to direct it to the attainment of one of the most important objects which remains to man to accomplish—which would reduce the black catalogue of crimes and criminals, and give an entire new aspect to human affairs.'

"That alcohol, whether found in rum, brandy or wine, is poison, is conceded on all hands. 'It is classed among poisons,' says a learned writer, 'because it is one of those substances which are known by physicians as capable of altering or destroying, in a majority of cases, some of the functions necessary to life.'—[*Dr. Romeyn Beck.*

"Says the Rev. Dr. Wm. Sprague, of Albany: 'Do you make the poison, or do you *use* it, or do you sell it? If you do, never open your lips to pray for the millennium.' He also says, 'the fruit of the vine may be legitimately fermented, or unfermented.'"

"'It is preposterous,' says the Hon. Gerrit Smith, 'to fight against alcohol in other places, and to welcome it at the Lord's table.'

"'As to the communion question, I have no fear but the truth will finally prevail; one great aid to this, undoubtedly, will be the fact, that in all the nation there is not to be purchased a gallon, or bottle even, of the pure fruit of the vine, unless it may possibly be some relict of an old importation.'—[*Hon. Neal Dow.*

"'Do intoxicating drinks add vigor to muscle, or strength to intellect, or warmth to the heart, or rectitude to the conscience? The experience of thousands, and even millions have answered this question. . . . . How many will testify, in each of these respects, that they were sensible gainers from the time they renounced the use of all alcoholic stimulants.'—[*Bishop Alonzo Potter, D. D., LL.D.*

"Father Mathew remarked to a London audience, he had no hesitation in saying that strong drink was anti-Christ; it was opposed to the principles of Christ, His designs, His example, and His reign.

"'The testimony of physicians is uniform and unequivocal. They pronounce alcohol a poison.'—[*Bishop Horatio Potter, D. D.*

"'I believe all use of intoxicating drinks unfavorable to mental effort.'—[*Bishop Wainwright.*

"Says President Wayland, speaking of the sale of intoxicating liquor: 'Would it be right for me to derive my living by selling poison, to propagate the plague around me?'

"Lord John Russell has pronounced his opinion in the following words: 'I am convinced there is no cause more likely to elevate the people of this country, in every respect, whether as regards religion, political importance, literary and moral cultivation, than this great question of temperance.'

"'That pure alcohol is a poison is an admitted fact.'"—[*Rev. Dr. E. Nott, LL.D.*

These oracular sayings were, at least, some of them, the precursors of the great movement, which may be called the Bible-temperance movement. But its consideration must be postponed till a future occasion, should God be pleased to grant it.

Yours affectionately,<br>
JOHN MAIR.

---

### LETTER V.

My Dear Sir,

The first two remedial measures adopted by temperance reformers were merely palliative. They allowed, at the outset, the use of all intoxicating alcoholic liquors in moderation, as they termed it, although moderation in the use of poisonous (the synonyme of intoxicating) drinks, is a solecism in language, carrying contradiction and absurdity in its face. The next step in the movement was also based upon a false principle. By it the use of distilled liquors was wholly prohibited; but, still, the moderate employment of vinously fermented liquors was permitted. When, by scientific research, and accurate observation, the truth began to be discovered that alcohol, in all its forms and combinations, was a poison, and a virulent one too, remedial means of a more radical kind were instituted; and teetotalism, or entire abstinence from all intoxicating alcoholic drinks, as a beverage in health, became the basis of union amongst a large class of temperance reformers. About this period, a temperance convention was held at Albany, February

25th, 1834. At it you introduced the following preamble and resolution:

"*Whereas*, There is so much evidence of the almost universal adulteration of fermented liquors, and of wines particularly, by the use of alcohol, &c., and of the great extent to which the manufacture of factitious wines is carried, as to render it almost, if not quite certain, that the pure **juice of** the grape is seldom procured in this country; and

"*Whereas*, It is now understood, and generally believed, that the reformation of the drunkard is utterly hopeless, so long as he continues to use the smallest quantity of any intoxicating drinks; and

"*Whereas*, It is important to remove all objections against uniting with temperance societies, now urged by a numerous and efficient portion of our citizens: therefore,

"*Resolved*, That those members of temperance societies, who wholly abstain from intoxicating liquors as an ordinary drink, present to the world a consistent and efficacious example, which this meeting would warmly commend to the imitation of every friend of temperance."

You go on to say: "The passage of this preamble and resolution was powerfully, and, I doubt not, conscientiously opposed, not only by a doctor of divinity, but by a doctor of law. Says one: 'The Scriptures permitted and sanctioned the use of (intoxicating) wine. Jesus Christ used it, and consecrated it by making it one of the elements in a religious ordinance instituted by Himself; and more than this, *He manufactured it;* and would gentlemen condemn the Lord of Glory?' Says another: 'We are looking to the great Head of the church for success in this cause. Shall we proceed contrary to His example? If the whole world should go for the preamble and resolution, the speaker would stand by the Bible and the example of our Saviour.'"

Of the document containing these remarks, and others of a

kindred character, the New York State Temperance Society circulated 100,000.

A sermon was preached January 7, 1835, by a very learned clergyman of Albany, *on the danger of being over-wise.* The occasion of this sermon was the dilution of powerful alcoholic wine with water, by certain members of his church, for communion purposes. This was honestly deemed by him an "unhallowed innovation."* This early discussion of this vital question seems to have been instrumental in the good and wise providence of God, in quickening into new life and vigor the minds, and whetting the ingenuity of some true men, who might otherwise have been induced to wait a little longer for a reformatory movement within the church.

But I cannot do better than use your own words to show the effects of the preamble, resolution, protest, and agitation of the wine question generally, upon the temperance movement. You thus proceed : " What were the friends of total abstinence to do in these circumstances ? They were fully convinced that the temperance reformation must either be given up, or that all means of intoxication must be abandoned ; distressed as they were to hear themselves condemned in public assemblies, from the pulpit, and by the press, as inculcating doctrines contrary to the word of God and the example of Christ ; denounced on all sides as fanatics and ultraists, and an almost universal cry that they had ruined the noblest of causes ; yet they felt strong in the *truth* of their position, and persevered in their efforts to sustain it. Here, and there, one and another began to ask : ' Was it really intoxicating wine, that our Saviour made at Cana, and that he used as a symbol of His blood at the institution of the supper ?' Thus they were led to the Bible, and to

---

*A series of articles, in reply to this sermon, appeared in a religious paper published in Boston, from the pungent pen of a distinguished scholar and layman of the Episcopal church, conclusively proving that it was the practice of the early church to dilute sacramental wine with water.

history, to ascertain whether, in fact, they did sanction the use of such wine. Many thanks are due to those who, in the face of persecutions and obloquy, first discussed this question. Among these were Prof. Stewart, Edwin James, M. D., L. M. Sargent, Esq., Mr. Wm. Goodell, Rev. Mr. Duffield, Rev. Dr. Chapin, and others. Those gentlemen appreciated, at that early day, the leading facts and principles which have established the reputation of the valuable essays, known by the titles of 'Bacchus and anti-Bacchus;' and, indeed, there is no doubt that the early discussion of these gentlemen, and others in this country, first induced the authors of these essays to think and write on this subject. A very general excitement was produced by this slight agitation of the question. Many good men were for a time distressed and offended, and walked no more with those so universally denounced as fanatics; but the greatest concern and distress were evinced by makers and venders of factitious drinks. They saw clearly, that if they could no longer plead the example of the Saviour, and its use at the sacrament, good men would soon cease purchasing and drinking their importations and mixtures. We are sorry to declare, but truth demands it, that the clamor, for a while, prevailed; the opposition appeared to triumph, and 'temperance down' was echoed from tavern to grog-shop: from one extremity **of** the nation to another. Still, the friends of total abstinence **held on,** though truth compels me to say—and I say it with deep mortification—they were for a time obliged to suppress in the society's publication the public discussion of the communion question."

"The Enquirer (independent of all organizations,) devoted **to** free discussion as to the *kind of wine proper to be used* at the Lord's supper," began to be published by you at Albany, in December, 1841. From the pages of the first number of that deeply interesting and important work the preceding quotations have been derived. Your letters and comments on them, with other critical, statistical, and scientific documents, contained in its two **first numbers**, afford precious material nowhere else to be found, as data for future reference; while the candid, truth-seeking spirit, which led to the throwing open of its pages to all honorable disputants, whatever **side** they might espouse, is worthy of sincere commendation.

It has been said with great energy and truth, by Youmans, in the following heart-searching words:

"How to deal with crime, committed under the influence of intoxication, has long been a thorny problem for jurists. But the difficulty of government has chiefly sprung from **its double** policy towards the agent which caused intoxication. It has uttered one language to the community, **through the license** system, and another from the bench, through its criminal jurisprudence, which necessarily involved it in inextricable self-contradiction. There is but one way in which it can relieve itself from complicity in this matter, and stand in a just and irreproachable relation to the crime, suffering, and multiform evil which alcohol engenders: and that is, by exerting its utmost power, and bringing all the influence it possesses **to bear against** the drinking practice. All earnest blows **must be struck at** this point, or nowhere. If government really desires **to abate the** evils of intemperance, let it prohibit **their cause.** If it would stand with clean hands to judge those who have **gone into** wrong courses through the agency of liquor, it **must** take an attitude of resolute and unyielding hostility to the system **by** which liquor is furnished. *It has no more right to license this cause of crime than it* **has to sell** *indulgences for the commission of theft, robbery, or perjury.* The only just thing possible for government is to prohibit this cause of crime, **as** thoroughly as it prohibits other crimes and **their causes.**"

But it can hardly be expected that governments will act greatly in advance of public opinion, even on questions manifestly for the general good; nor can it be expected that public opinion will be much in advance of the church of Christ, on the question of right and wrong.

But a step was taken in the right direction: the great work of reformation commenced when the denunciations of a grave ecclesiastic, in the halls of Albany, roused the sacramental host of the Lord from their lethargy, and made them feel that there was a work to be performed **by them**, in searching the Scriptures, to see whether in truth, the Lord Jesus Christ, Immanuel, did make use of poisonous alcoholic liquor, as the symbol of His blood, as had been asserted of Him by the learned divines, when they became alarmed at the adoption of the memorable preamble and resolution at the convention, held in the capitol of the Empire State in 1834.

**It** will be my endeavor, in future letters, with the blessing **of** God upon my labors, to show that the gospel antidote of the lawless mystery of alcohol, at the present time, is the cordial acceptance of the doctrine, that the revealed law of God is against the use of alcoholic liquors, by man in his normal state of health, at his own table, and at the table of the Lord.

I am, my dear sir,
Yours affectionately,
JOHN MAIR.

---

LETTER VI.

MY DEAR SIR,
Alcohol, when taken into the human system, may **be** viewed in relation to man in his normal or abnormal state of health. When viewed in relation **to man in** his normal state of health, it receives the name of poison; when in relation to man in his abnormal state of health, it receives the name of medicine. This is no vain or useless distinction, because the effect of alcoholic liquors differs, according to the healthy or diseased state of persons upon whose constitutions they act, and the nature of the diseases with which they are affected.

Youmans, in his "Scientific Basis of Prohibition," thus speaks of alcohol: "**Of** alcohol itself, **little need** be said. **Its** scientific history has been *thoroughly* canvassed, and no question is better settled than that of its origin and nature. It comes into existence through the chemical destruction of food, and is that common and active principle of all fermented and distilled liquors which gives them the power of producing intoxication. Hence, it is both customary and proper to employ the **term** alcohol, when its various mixtures are referred to." The question of the different effects of alcohol, as acting upon a **healthy or diseased** state of the human body, has **been philosophically** considered in the following words: "**There is a condition in which it is agreed to call** these **agents (poisons) by another name**—that is; when the system **has got into** an abnormal or diseased state, and they are administered with the design of removing the malady; they are then known as remedies, or medicines. It is not to be forgotten, that the word poison is not applied to any physical or chemical qualities of a substance in itself considered. It is the name given to its relations to life—its effects upon the living organization. **Now, though the** agent may not change its properties, the system, **upon which it** acts, may be in such **different conditions that there arises a** difference of effects, **which is** very **properly distinguished by** the **use** of different words. In their remedial **and** restorative influence upon the system, when it is diseased, they are called medicines; in their effects upon the healthy organization, they are poisons. Like other poisons, alcohol may be given as a medicine to combat or extirpate diseased conditions of the system, but the powerful qualities which give it value in these cases, are equally potent upon **the** healthy organism. In the latter case, the change wrought is injurious, and therefore, justly denominated poisonous."*

---

*Alcohol is Poison. New York Weekly Tribune, September 22, 1855.

It is chiefly to the operation of alcoholic liquors upon mankind in their normal state of health, that attention will be directed in these letters. Dr. Carpenter has said: "The term intoxication is sometimes employed, in this country, to designate that series of phenomena which results from the action of all such poisons as first produce stimulation, and then narcotism; of these, alcohol is the type, and the term is commonly applied to alcoholic intoxication alone. It is worthy of notice, however, that the designation is now given, by French writers, to the series of remote or constitutional effects consequent upon the introduction of any poisonous agent into the blood. Thus we meet with the terms 'arsenical intoxication,' 'iodine intoxication,' and even 'purulent intoxication.' In fact, it is there considered an equivalent (as its etymology denotes,) of our word poisoning; and the fact that such a term should be in common use in this country to designate the ordinary results of the ingestion of alcoholic liquors, is not without its significance; for if the classical term 'intoxication' be habitually employed as the equivalent of the Saxon drunkenness, we are justified in turning that classical term into English again, and in asserting that the condition of drunkenness, in all its stages, is one of poisoning."\*

As respects my work, I believe I have been led by the hand of Divine Providence, and the gracious impulse of the Holy Spirit, to turn my attention particularly to the word of God—to search the Scriptures to see whether those things in them which relate to wine and strong drink, were, as they have been generally represented by commentators and critics, and admitted by the church in these last days to be—i. e.: Whether alcoholic liquors were or were not approved of by the all-powerful, all-wise, all-good Governor of the universe, as fit for man's use in

---

\* On the "Use and Abuse of Alcoholic Liquors in Health and Disease." By William Carpenter, M. D. London, 2nd ed., p. 9.

his normal state of health, and enjoined accordingly; or the reverse, in that perfect law which has been mercifully provided by the Bible, for his instruction and guidance in all questions of religion and **morals,** by its Divine author. Its sacred pages then—I am to search. Its testimony—I am to receive. **Its** doctrines, and the fair inferences to be drawn from them—I am to treasure up, and set forth as binding upon mankind at all times, and in all countries, concerning the reception of alcoholic liquors into the human system, and the effects thereof. For this great work, I feel **myself utterly insufficient of myself.** But I ask of Him whose cause it is, to fit me for, and to direct me in, **the prosecution of it,**—**trusting in the promises of the** "**Faithful Promiser,**" **who hath said:** "**If any of you lack** wisdom, let him ask **of God**—**that giveth to all** men liberally and upbraideth not—and **it shall be given him.**" "**Fear thou** not, for I am with thee; **be not** dismayed, **for I am thy God. I will strengthen thee, yea I will help thee, yea I will uphold thee with the right hand of my righteousness.**" "**Ask and it shall be given you; seek and ye shall find; knock and it shall be opened unto you.**" "**Trust in the Lord with all thine heart, and lean not unto thine own understanding. In all thy ways acknowledge Him, and He shall direct thy paths.**"

I solicit your prayers, and those of all good men, that the word of the **Lord** in this department of **Christian morals** may be fulfilled—for **thus hath He spoken:** "**So shall my word be, that** goeth forth out of my mouth: **it shall not return unto me** void, but **it shall accomplish that which I please, and it shall prosper in the thing whereto I sent it.**"

The subject may be treated **of in the following order, and** under the following heads:

I. The teachings of science and the Bible, respecting drunkenness or its **equivalent, poisoning, in** relation to the brain and mind **of man.**

II. The injunctions contained in the Bible, forbidding the use of wine or strong drink to priests and kings.

III. The alarming and opprobrious epithets given to wine and strong drink, in the Bible.

IV. The greatest possible distance, from alcoholic drinks, enjoined by Solomon—in the Bible.

V. The Lord's Supper.

    Believe me, my dear friend,
      Yours affectionately in Christ Jesus,
            **JOHN** MAIR.

### LETTER VII.

My Dear Sir,

  "Poison! What is a poison? Positively, it is any kind of matter which has, in any degree, the quality of disturbing or degrading the natural functions or organs of the human body. Negatively, it is matter which cannot fulfil the purposes **or supply the place of food or** drink—or which can do so in **no** degree innocently or permanently."*

According to the views of Dr. Carpenter, already referred to, it is correct to substitute the word poisoning, for drunkenness, in all its **stages. The** same distinguished authority will justify the employment of the different derivations from the same root, to express the different modifications of poisoning, &c. Thus, **the** men who drink alcoholic liquors, are self-poisoners; those **who** give them to others to drink, are the poisoners of their **fellows**; those who manufacture them, are the manufacturers **of poison**; those who sell them to all and sundry who ask for them, are the venders of poison; or, in the true but frightful language of Wesley, "poisoners general." Those who license the distillation and sale of them, are the encouragers of, and legalizers of poison-making and poison-scattering far and wide, for the sake of money, to the signal injury of mankind. And

---

* Dr. McCulloch. The Alliance Weekly News, March 14, 1857.

those who are, **or** have been the original source whence **the** mass of these evil doings, and of all the pollution, social suffering and domestic wretchedness, connected with these doings, have proceeded: Who are they? where are they to be found? and what name belongs to them? It would be premature to attempt to reply to these questions at present. In the course of this investigation, facts may **be elicited, and revelations made** which may throw light upon the subject.

If alcoholic liquors, when received into the **human system in** a state of health, are always injurious **to man—and when taken** in sufficient quantities, prove fatal—**they ought to be shunned by him.** If otherwise—and a line may be drawn, **up to which they** may be used **without** injury, but beyond **which they cannot** be so used—the question may reasonably be put: What is that line? or, at what degree of the alcohometer is it to be found?

If discoverable, let it by all means be discovered, and made known for the benefit of mankind, as most important for the regulation of their conduct.

For my own part, I believe it to be a matter **of impossibility** for man to discover such **a line as shall clearly denote the** boundary between moderation and excess, **(if such a boundary** there be, except in the imagination); a line which shall rightly proclaim to all: "Hitherto shalt thou **come, but** no farther." Miller, in his late work, mentioned in a former letter,—"Alcohol, its Place and Power,"—says, **when alcohol is** administered as a medicine: "That both a careful and skilful management of the remedy is required. *Like other poisons*, it is not to be rashly and empirically prescribed, or the dosing fixed by routine. The case must be suitable; the disease and the necessity for the remedy must be there; the dosing must be well adjusted at starting, and its effects must be carefully watched, in order that it may be duly regulated accordingly."*

---

* "Alcohol, its Place and Power,"—p. 33.

Moreover, no man, as far as I know, has ever attempted to draw this imaginary line, although many have speculated about it as a possibility. Upon the supposition that it is discoverable in any given case—if such judicious precautions are necessary in the administration of alcoholic liquors as a medicine for the **sick,** where their use may not only be lawful, but proper ; and if all the skill and attention **of a** wise and prudent physician are called into operation for the due adjustment of the dose to the case in hand—what wisdom, discretion, and careful watching would not be needed, in the healthy system, to seize the moment when the magic line should have been reached—a hair-breadth beyond which, a drop of alcohol would prove a poison to the unfortunate wight who should swallow it ? According to this view, a physician would be required for each person, when in **the** act of drinking alcoholic liquors ; and his undivided attention would be indispensable for every individual case ; and every drop of the liquor would need to be measured out most carefully ; **and** every inspiration **of** the air, and every pulsation of the heart to be counted ; and every change of attitude, and feature of the face to be studied ; and every word uttered to be scrutinized, lest, in an unguarded moment, the subtle spirit should have crossed the critical pass, which, by some strange bewitchment, changes a harmless substance into a deadly poison ! A regular staff of qualified, salaried physicians would, therefore, be necessary appendages to every establishment licensed by government to sell spirituous liquors ; and no family, where they were indulged in, could dispense with one or more of the faculty in constant attendance.

In no other way, that I can see, could justice be done to the health of the wine-bibbing community ; but perhaps the tax thus imposed for the support of boards of medical practitioners, might be considered too great to pay for the gratification of an appetite not natural to man or beast ! If so, the only safe alternative would be total abstinence from the perilous stuff

Not to give further play to fanciful vagaries, however, let the question be submitted to the decision of eminent, practical, and scientific men, competent to pronounce a right judgment upon it—whether there is such a thing as moderation in **the use of** alcoholic drinks by man in his normal state of health?

Professor Youmans, in his masterly production, "The Scientific Basis of Prohibition," speaking of alcohol, expresses himself thus: "It is an inveterate foe of the intellectual and moral principle of man. In all its numberless forms, and in every quantity, it is the potent adversary of the **mind.** When alcoholic mixtures are drank, the very **first effect that** we perceive, is a perverted action of the mental faculties. A small quantity does not finish the work, but it begins it. It is the quality of wheat to nourish the body, but a small amount will not completely produce this effect, nor even protect from starvation; still, the nature of all wheat, and in every grain of it, is to nourish and strengthen. So, also, with alcohol—a small quantity may not so poison the brain as to overthrow the mental fabric; still, such are its essential nature and tendency in every form, and every drop. Its inroading effects upon mind are not restricted to the employment of excessive quantities: they follow from its common use. There is much said about the inoffensiveness of liquor, when taken in trifling amount; but all this is little applicable to general practice. People do not take liquors in infinitesimal doses. They drink them to produce a specific and positive alcoholic effect, and they demand and use enough for the purpose. Whatever may be said about 'flavor,' 'aroma,' 'fruitiness,' 'body,' 'nutriment,' or other secondary properties of intoxicating liquor, if alcohol be absent, it is mockery to offer these in substitution.

"We must bear in mind, that when a small portion **of liquor** is taken—as a glass of wine—it is not mingled with the mass of the blood, and lost in the general system. This result is forbidden by the law of local affinity. The alcohol is drawn out of the circulation into the nervous tissue, and the single dose, therefore, ceases to be insignificant. Although minute, **when** compared to the whole body, it becomes powerful when concentrated upon a single part. In the quantity, therefore, necessary to produce the agreeable exhilarating and stimulant effect for which it is used, alcohol so deranges brain action as to violate the harmony of the mind. The feelings become excited, the temper irritable, so that the individual is easily "touched," and provoked to acts of impropriety and violence, by causes which, under other circumstances, would be unheeded. Long before the speech thickens, and the motions falter, there is a firing of irascible passions which leads to the commission of numberless offences, from two-edged utterances that wound the spirit, to homicidal thrusts that destroy the body."

Thus Dr. Carpenter speaks upon this subject: "The state of mental excitement just described, is very similar to the incipient stage of phrenitis or mania. It is not a *uniform exaltation* of the mental faculties, but in some degree a perversion of them; for that voluntary control over the current of thought, which is the distinguishing character of the sane mind of man, is considerably weakened, so that the heightened imagination, and the enlivened fancy have more unrestricted exercise; and whilst ideas and images succeed each other in the mind with marvellous readiness, no single train of thought can be carried out with the same continuity as in a state of perfect sobriety. This weakening of all voluntary control over the mental operations must be regarded, then, as an incipient stage of insanity."

The following were the views of the late celebrated Dr. Gregory, professor of Chemistry in the university of Edinburgh, endorsed by the Rev. William Reid, editor of the well-known British Messenger: "The argument from science was entirely in favor of the temperance movement, because, while on the one hand they had the mere possibility that alcohol might not be injurious in certain conceivable, but rare circumstances; on the other hand, in these circumstances, even where they did occur, alcohol was not the best agent, and they could always supply its place by other **and better** materials which were entirely free from its injurious qualities."

He (Mr. Reid,) took the ground thus given him by Dr. Gregory, and contended that the poison should be dealt with simply as other poisons were being dealt with. Arsenic, for example, was found some years **ago to be the instrument** of many murders and suicides; an act was passed to prohibit its sale, except under very stringent regulations, and the **result**, according **to** the Lancet, (no friend to our cause,) was, that "murders and suicides by arsenic have become extremely rare."*

The following admirable remarks are from the report of the speech of Dr. McCulloch, versus Dr. Laycock, delivered by him, at Edinburgh, March 6th, 1857.†

"What is temperance, and moderation? We can correctly use these terms only in regard to what is wholesome, appropriate and good—physically, morally and religiously. **To** speak of the moderate, or dietetic use of a poison, is an abuse of language that would be scouted and ridiculed, if applied to anything save the use of these popular intoxicants. Poison is the name of an *intrinsic quality*, and has no reference **whatever** to quantity, quantity being only considered in regard to extent of its *poisonous effects*. One grain of opium, or one drop of alcohol, therefore, is as much, and as truly a poison, as a pound, or gallon. Food and drink are not poisons, and poisons never can be food or drink, in the true meaning of the terms. To hear men, then, who ought to know better, speak of them in **reciprocal** terms, betrays a pitiable ignorance of the logical definition and nature of the things indicated.

---

* The Alliance Weekly News, January 17th, 1857,—p. 311.
† Id. March 14th, 1857.

"Allow me to illustrate this analogically. First, take it morally. What would you think of a man who attempted to palliate or defend his falsehood and dishonesty, by pleading that he was a temperate liar, or a moderate thief? Take it physically. What would you think of another, who bragged that he ate arsenic and strychnine, and drank prussic acid and laudanum, temperately and moderately, as diet and refreshment?

"If these shock your sense of propriety, and are evidently absurd, how is it that many of you are blind to the equal absurdity in regard to these poisonous drinks? Is it habit, custom, conventionality and fashion, which cause you to see the mote in the eye of the opium-eater, but blind you to the alcoholic beam in your own? *Alcohol is a poison; total abstinence from the dietetic use of these drinks in any shape, form,* **or** *quantity, is the only true—the only logical temperance and moderation in regard to them.*"

These authorities, to which many more could be added, (with what has been said previously upon the subject in preceding letters,) may suffice to supply an answer to the question, " Whether there is such a thing as moderation in the use of alcoholic liquors by man in his normal state of health?"—in the negative.

That being done, it will require no fresh argument to show, that even a regular staff of well informed, conscientious physicians attached to every tavern, would not be sufficient to prevent poisoning; and that no medical science or skill in the domestic circle, would avert a similar result. Alcohol is the arch poison —the poison of poisons—which, at its first outset, aims at, and seizes upon the highest and noblest faculties of man's nature, which **have** God's **image** stamped upon them—with relentless grasp; **and** afterwards invades those powers which he has, in common with the lower animals, in definite succession.

" Physiologists are agreed that different parts of the brain are devoted to different uses. The first effect of alcohol is upon **its** higher and frontal portion, which is the seat of the intellectual and moral faculties. This part of the brain is excited by a small quantity of liquor, and **when** more is taken it becomes more deeply perverted, and the hinder and lower portion of the organ, which controls the nerves of motion, is attacked, and the individual loses the faculty of perfectly governing or regulating the bodily movements. When a still greater quantity is drunk, the action of that part which is devoted to the **higher** sentiments, seems utterly suspended, the power of voluntary motion is lost, and the poison passes downward to the extreme lower portion of the organ, which is connected with the spinal cord, and has charge of the respiratory process. The breathing is thus interfered with, and becomes heavy and labored, as we see in dead-drunkenness. The mind cannot serve two masters; just in proportion as it is surrendered to the influence of an external force, which invades it through the brain, it ceases to be in its own keeping. With the sparkles and effervescence of alcoholic excitement, there is a weakening of the regulating and restraining forces by which the mind manages its own **movements**—a partial loss of that voluntary control over the mental operations, which, as Dr. Carpenter remarks, '**must be** regarded as **an** *incipient stage of insanity.*' **At the same time,** the lower passions and propensities are aroused to inordinate activity. In healthful mental conditions, these press powerfully upon the higher controlling sentiments, and from their reaction results moral equilibrium of character. The influence of alcohol is thrown entirely in the scale of the animal impulses against the reason, judgment, and conscience; and it is evident that where these are just able to hold the baser passions in subjection, and maintain the mind's equipoise, the effect of the disturbing agent must be to destroy the mental balance, and tell disastrously upon the conduct. That when liquors are taken in sufficient quantity to produce their characteristic and desired effect, the mind is some way jostled and disturbed, no observing person can doubt; and that this disturbance, however trifling it may be, consists in replacing the reasoning and voluntary powers by blind passional forces in the mind's government, is proved by the fact, that if more of the stimulant be taken, the revolution becomes complete; reason is entirely prostrated, and brute **impulse** is in the ascendant. In intoxication, the action of the brain is so deeply perverted as to completely unhinge the mind; thought is confused and bewildered; self-directing power is lost; the passions are stimulated to unrestrained fury, and the whole mental fabric is swamped amid the surges of delirium. Intoxication is universally admitted to be a state of temporary insanity. To 'intoxicate,' says Webster, is 'to excite the spirits to a kind of delirium; to elate to enthusiasm, frenzy, or madness.' That such is the effect of *alcoholic* liquors, is shown by the fact that they are universally known as '*intoxicating* liquors.' Thus, the common term by which they are designated, connects them at once with man's mental constitution, as a cause of frenzy, delirium, and madness."\*

It is this affinity of alcohol for the brain of man, (as Dr. Percy would call it,) and especially its predilection for the seat of the exalting, and self-governing powers of reason, conscience, and will, which renders it a poison so much to be dreaded and denounced by all who seek the glory of God, and desire not only to preserve unharmed, but to improve and *strengthen* these noble faculties.†

Here, it may be proper to introduce the following clear and concise account of the laws of narcotic poisons, from the pen of Dr. McCulloch: "The physiological laws of narcotic poisons, are principally four in number:

---

\* Youmans' Scientific Basis of Prohibition.
† Prize Thesis. "An experimental inquiry concerning the presence of alcohol in the ventricles of the brain." By John Percy, M. D. p. 104.

"1st. That **after** using them for some time, the quantity of the dose must be increased in order to produce the same effect:

"2d. That **the** time between the doses **must** also be diminished, for the **same** reason:

"3d. That the depression and exhaustion which follow, are exactly equivalent to the amount **of** excitement or exhilaration caused by the quantity used:

"4th. **That** they—many of them—tend to create an artificial appetite **or craving,** which renders **the** person so using them, a slave **to the habit."**

Having **thus** endeavored to show that alcohol is a brain-poison, first perverting **the** noble and self-governing **powers of** man, viz: reason, **conscience** and will, and then exciting to undue **action the passions and** propensities **which** he has, in common with the lower animals—destroying the mental balance, and impelling to acts of outrage and infamy; and further, that if small portions could be taken with impunity (which cannot be proved, and is rendered improbable by the experiments of Dr. Percy, indicating that the substance of the brain has a particular affinity **for** alcohol, and receives a larger proportion of it than the other parts of the body, attracting **it to** itself **as** the magnet does iron), there is no possibility of **drawing a line** between the harmless and injurious effects thereof, upon man in his normal state **of** health,—and **as there is no instinct** which will warn him *when* to stop—as in **the case of** wholesome food or drink—but **on the** other hand, as has been pointed out above, the cry which it has a tendency **to emit is** like that of **"the** horseleech's two daughters: give, give," continually; therefore, no general rules can be laid down by which it can be safely administered to man in his normal state of health; and **as it** is impossible that all men can have physicians to watch over them day and night, therefore its prohibition becomes a practical necessity, for man's well being and well doing.

So much for the scientific argument against alcohol, and common sense would return the same just verdict, if common sense were not biased and restrained by the alcohol drinking habit, so firmly rooted in the corrupt soil **of** traditionary, superstitious veneration for that poison; because **it has** been erroneously (as I believe,) supposed, that the Holy Scriptures are favorable to its use. Let **it then** be assumed, for **the sake** of argument, **that** science **and** common sense heartily unite in condemning the employment **of** alcohol for ordinary purposes, and only tolerate its use **when** cautiously administered under judicious medical **superintendence—in peculiar** cases of disease—as is done with deadly nightshade, wolfsbane, and other poisons of the same class. Would it not thus be rendered probable, nay, certain, that God would ratify this two-fold testimony, concerning alcohol, in His written word **(if** true, and if He should prescribe rules concerning it there), according to the well established principle before referred to, that the God of nature and of **grace is** one, and *therefore* **cannot** contradict Himself; **so that the law** discovered by science, and corroborated by common sense, should be found essentially to correspond with the word which **perfect wisdom** has graciously provided as "a lamp unto the feet, and **a light unto the path**" of His straying children, whom He originally created in his own image? In future letters, God willing, this principle will be illustrated.

In the meantime, believe me to be,

Yours affectionately,

JOHN MAIR.

---

LETTER VIII.

**My Dear Sir,**

Having, in my last letter, I trust, made it plain by competent evidence, that alcohol is an active brain-poison, laying hold of the seat of the noblest intellectual and moral faculties of man, and perverting them; and that common sense if free to speak, and unrestrained by prejudice, tradition and superstition, would chime in with this conclusion; and having, moreover, shown that all use of alcoholic liquors ought **to be avoided by** man in his normal state of health, either because—as seems probable from the nature of the case, and the experiments of Dr. Percy—the smallest quantity may prove injurious to him; or, because no line of demarcation can be drawn between **the** harmless and hurtful effects of alcohol, **I** now beg **you to** accompany me into the Scriptural inquiry, regarding alcoholic liquors, bearing in mind that I intend to make free use of the term poisoning, interchangeably with drunkenness; **and, as** poisoning can proceed from no other cause than the application of poison, I shall also feel justified in substituting **the term** poison, or brain-poison for alcohol, and poisonous liquor **for** any liquor which contains a notable quantity of the same.

In approaching the sacred precincts of the house of God, to inquire in His temple about temperance, we may, I apprehend, safely intrust ourselves to the guidance of that immortal allegorist, John Bunyan, the dreamer, whose dreams far excel most men's waking thoughts. What, then, does he say, in his racy, vigorous, homely style, **about our duty in regard to eating and drinking?**

He thus speaks through the mouth of Discretion: "Only this general rule ought to be observed, that we forbear eating and drinking such things as we find **by experience, or** know by common observation to be prejudicial to health, impediments to virtue and devotion, spurs **to vice and** passion, by intoxicating *the brain*, **heating the blood, disordering** the spirits, **or by any** other **way being** subservient to the **works of the flesh, or the** temptations **of the Devil. In so** doing, we shall do well."

Let it be remarked here, that "decidedly the first of allegorists"—**as the** historian Macaulay calls him—was, perhaps, the first of toxicologists to make use of the term "intoxicating the brain," or poisoning the brain; a term so frequently and justly applied **to** alcohol, in recent times, **by those who have** gone most fully and scientifically into the consideration of that direst of poisons.*

Let us notice, however, that he appeals to experience and observation only, as our teachers. He does not refer "to the law and the testimony of God" as affording specific instructions in **regard to** brain-intoxicating, or poisonous alcoholic drinks. But, were John Bunyan to arise from the dead *now*, and make himself acquainted with the science and statistics of alcohol of our day, would not the words uttered by him, as given above, seem to him to have been prophetic of its evil effects as they have since transpired in the world? Would not the words "*intoxicating the brain*," appear to him aptly to designate its action upon that vital organ? and would not numerous passages of Scripture flash at once upon his enlightened mind, which would convince him that God had expressly forbidden the use of that poison by man in his normal state of health?

**One** step more, and we are within the sacred precincts, where the Most High God, with a voice like thunder pealing from the clouds of heaven, or as "the sound of many waters," gives forth the lively oracles for the moral government of men. And now, let us "put off our shoes from off our feet, for the place whereon we stand is holy ground." (Exodus iii, 5.)

"Their wine (that of idolaters,) is the poison of dragons, and the cruel venom of asps," (Deut. xxxii, 33,) contrasted with "the pure blood of the grape," (Deut. xxxii, 14,) one of the

---

* Perhaps the striking remarks of Cyrus, to his grandfather, Astyages, when he was acting as his cup-bearer, ought to give him the precedence in this matter, as the first, in profane history, to notice the poisonous nature of alcoholic drinks. The reason he assigned for not tasting the cup, was, because he apprehended **there** was poison in the liquor. "Poison, child!" exclaimed the astonished grandsire, "How could you think so?" "Yes, poison, papa; for not long ago, at an entertainment you gave to the lords of your court—and after the guests had drank a little of this liquor, *I perceived all their heads were turned;* and when you would have danced, you could not stand upon your legs."—[*Rollin's Ancient History.*

blessings held out to the Israelites in the Holy Land. Now it is worthy of remark, that this is the only passage of Holy Scripture, as far as I know, where a deadly animal poison, of **the** reptile tribe, is made use of to illustrate the nature of another material poison, viz : alcohol, the product of the decomposition of " he fruit of the vine."

All the other passages enumerated by Eadie, in his Concordance, where the term poison is figuratively used, have immediate reference to the judgments of God, or moral evil. I **give a** list of the same, that they may be examined, by those **who are** interested in the question : Job vi, 4 : xx, 16 ; Psalm lviii, **4 ;** Psalm cxl, 3 ; Romans iii, 13 ; James iii, 8.

Is there not something to be gathered from this singular fact ? Does it not tend to show that alcohol is no ordinary poison, but that it possesses qualities assimilating it to the poison of serpents, which render it peculiarly the enemy of man, to be shunned by him, as venomous reptiles are, almost instinctively ? Are we not thus forcibly reminded of the Seducer of our first parents—that Evil Spirit

> "Who brought death into our world
> And all our woe,
> With loss of Eden ;"

and who has made more havoc of the human race, in a physical, intellectual, moral and spiritual point of view, probably by this one poison, alcohol, than by all the other poisons of the animal, vegetable, **and** mineral kingdoms, heaped together into one vast, putrid mass, rankling with corruption, and sending forth noxious exhalations to blast and to destroy ! Would it not seem by this, (one of the earliest notices **of** alcohol in Scripture,) to have had the brand of infamy purposely stamped upon it by the Almighty, when the **human** race were still in their pupilage ; that by its persistent association with the "great Dragon, that old Serpent, called the Devil, and Satan, which deceiveth the whole world," alcohol might forever after retain its place in the memories of all mankind, exciting horror, detestation, and disgust in their breasts, and causing them to shrink from it as a most cruel and treacherous enemy?

If these observations be correct, then it follows that alcohol, in the Scripture sense, is a terrific poison; and thus we have an additional reason for using the phrase poisoning, instead of drunkenness, when it seems meet, in our future inquiries.

Let us now turn our attention to Ephesians v, 18: "Be not drunk (poisoned,) with wine, wherein is excess; (asotia—alcohol—insalvability,) but be filled with the spirit:" which, in plain English, amounts to this,—have nothing to do with drink containing the poison alcohol; or, do not drink of any liquor containing alcohol, which is the deadly enemy of man's salvation. I give this interpretation for the following reasons: It is in the spirit of the original, but without a tithe of its power. Who will not admit this, who has read the passage just quoted, **from** the mouth of the great lawgiver of the Jews—Moses? Who has ever inhabited a region infested with poisonous serpents and other poisonous reptiles, and has not been upon his watch lest he should unawares, tread upon one of them, and have his flesh transfixed with its fangs, and die a miserable death? And, should not the man, who knows the body-and-soul-destroying nature of alcoholic poison, in this age of wide-spread, accurate knowledge regarding it, be still more on his guard, lest, like the fabulous serpent, it should allure him to his temporal, and not only that, but to his eternal ruin also?

Science gives its support to the same honest interpretation of the passage, and so would common sense, if she had not herself been intoxicated with the fumes of alcohol, sent forth from christian altars, kindled by the sparks from the strange fire of pagan incense!

But other portions of Scripture can be brought to strengthen this argument: "Ye are all the children of light, and the children of the day; we are not of the night, nor of darkness.

Therefore, let us not sleep as do others, but let us watch, and be sober;" (*nephomen, abstinent*, especially in respect to wine*); I Thess. v, **5, 6**: "For they that sleep, sleep in the night; and they that be drunken, (poisoned,) are drunken (poisoned,) in the night." "But let us who are **of the** day be sober, (abstinent from wine,) putting on the breast-plate of faith and love; and for an helmet, the hope of salvation:" I Thess. v, 7, 8. "Wherefore gird up the loins of your mind, be sober (abstinent from wine,) and hope to the end," &c.: I Peter i, 13. **"But** the end of all things is at hand; be ye therefore sober (abstinent from wine,) and watch unto prayer:" I Peter iv, 7. "Be sober, (abstinent from wine,) because your adversary, **the Devil,** as a roaring lion, walketh about seeking whom he may devour:" I Peter v, 8.

The following beautiful quotation, from Coleridge, may be aptly introduced here: "A language will often be wiser, not merely than the vulgar, but even than the wisest of those who speak it; being like amber in its efficacy to circulate the electric spirit of truth, it is also like amber in embalming and preserving the relics of ancient wisdom, although one is not seldom puzzled to decipher its contents. Sometimes it locks up truths which were once well known, but which, in the course of ages, have passed out of sight and been forgotten." May it not be said of the word *nepho*, **e** *ne et pio—non bibo*—I **do** not drink the "wine wherein is excess"—that it belongs to this class; that it has locked up a truth which was well known to the Jews and Christians, in apostolic times, "but which, in the course of **ages,** has **passed out of sight** and has been forgotten," viz: that total abstinence from alcoholic liquors is the explicit doctrine of the christian religion?

If so, is it not full time **that** it should **be unlocked**; and

---

* Greek and English Lexicon of the New Testament. By Edward Robinson, D. D., etc. A new edition, carefully revised and corrected by S. T. Bloomfield, D. D. London, 1839.

that the truth, so long concealed, should be disclosed for the admiration and hearty reception of all lovers of genuine temperance, and of mankind; and, that the knowledge of that truth should spread, with electric speed, "from sea to sea, and from the river to the ends of the earth;" and, that an anthem of praise and rejoicing be sung by all nations, ascribing "blessing, and honor, and glory, and power, unto Him that sitteth upon the throne, and to the Lamb forever and ever?" "Alleluia, for the Lord, God Omnipotent reigneth." "Grace unto you, and peace be multiplied."

    I am, my dear brother,
      Yours affectionately,
        In christian bonds,
          JOHN MAIR.

## LETTER IX.

My Dear Sir,

  A few more comments may be offered upon I Thess. v, 5-8. I have ventured to give a perfectly anti-alcoholic interpretation of Ephesians v, 18; and I now proceed to adduce additional reasons for interpreting the following passage in the same manner: "Ye are all the children of the light, and the children of the day; we are not of the night, nor of darkness. Therefore, let us watch and be sober: (abstinent from wine, wherein is excess): For they that sleep, sleep in the night; and they that be drunken, (poisoned,) are drunken (poisoned,) in the night; but let us, who are of the day, be sober;" (abstinent from wine, wherein is excess): I Thess. v, 5-8. According to the ordinary, popular sense of the terms "drunk" and "sober," quoted above; or, of the abstract terms corresponding to them, "drunkenness" and "sobriety," the one **is** contrary to the other; but, if we attempt anything like scientific accuracy, we must view them as only different degrees of intoxication, the one constituting an incipient, and **the other an advanced stage of alcoholic poisoning ;** or, at least, **sobriety,** according to the common acceptation of the term, may co-exist with an abnormal change wrought **upon the person by alcohol.**

To illustrate this—a man, in vulgar estimation and parlance, would be considered sober, who should be able to stand or move in a becoming manner, in obedience to the word of command; (if a soldier, to go through his facings); **whose speech** should not be inarticulate, or incoherent; his face **not flushed ;** and **whose natural and** animal functions should present no marked perversion, obvious to the beholder, &c., ; and **he would only** then be judged drunk, when his face should appear flushed, or swollen ; his eyes vacant and blood-shot ; **his expression sottish ;** his speech inarticulate, **or incoherent ; his walk unsteady, or** zig-zag — his behaviour eccentric **and** at variance with his natural character, either **by unwonted** sullenness and silence, **or by** vivacity and talkativeness; or he should present more, or fewer of this group of symptoms, &e. ; and yet, in the former case, as truly, though not so intensely **as in the latter, the man** *would* have been poisoned by **alcohol, if from its use, his** circulation had become hurried, **his** imagination excited, his self-control lessened, so that he could not prevent wild, or vicious fancies **from** running their course ; **make nice and** accurate distinctions between **delicate shades of good and evil,** and act accordingly ; give judgment on any difficult point at issue ; feel devoutly inclined, **and** capable of engaging in prayer to God, with faith, fear **and fervor, and** of faithfully observing His ordinances, **as** he otherwise could (*cæteris paribus*,) have done : **all** of which duties, in their proper season, **are,** or may be required, and ought **to be performed by** all men according to the Divine law, which **is** equally binding upon all men. Now all who know the deceitful and insidious nature of alcoholic poison, and are familiar **with** its effects, know, full well, that the condition **just described as a sober** condition, precedes the condition previously sketched, which is commonly called drunkenness, and slides into it by imperceptible degrees. But we cannot possibly conceive of the man who is thus sober, *alias*, in vulgar phraseology, *not drunk*, being in that sound state of mind which the Scripture, above quoted, as emanating from the Holy Spirit, demands—whatever popular opinion may be upon the subject; but we must believe, that if he acted voluntarily, when he brought himself into that state, that he poisoned himself, violated the Divine law, and sinned in God's sight; and this, we maintain to be the doctrine of natural religion—but how much more of revelation; for the apostle Paul, as moved by the Holy Spirit, has said: "Let us watch and be sober:" (or rather abstinent from wine, wherein is excess—insalvability:) "For they that sleep, sleep in the **night**; and they that be drunken, (poisoned,) are drunken (poisoned,) in the night; but let us, who are of the day, be **sober,** (abstinent from wine, wherein is insalvability.")

We conclude, then, (for I trust I have your concurrence in the argument,) that both natural and revealed religion condemn the use of alcoholic liquor by man in his normal state of health, whatever may be said to the contrary notwithstanding; and we are of the opinion that the terms "drunken" and "sober," respectively, should be exchanged for poisoned and abstinent, **(from** wine, wherein is excess,) to prevent ambiguity. The term drunk, may originally have expressed all that was wanted, with *precision;* but it has lost its strict, genuine meaning, from corrupt association with false and untenable, **so** called Scriptural doctrines, concerning alcohol, or wine containing it; doctrines which represent that poison as **a** "good creature of God," and lead **its votaries** impiously to call it **by the** holy name of "water of life," and to consider it a panacea for all the ills which flesh is heir to; doctrines, which, instead of deterring from the use of alcoholic drinks in the smallest quantity, have served to lull asleep all suspicions of danger **at** the outset, (when real danger exists, and when alone it can be arrested,) and instead of restraining, have encouraged and afforded the most powerful motives to indulgence in these poisonous drinks, by awarding to their use, the dignity of a **social virtue,** if not a christian grace. Moreover, to the man in the *intermediate* states—between the first sensible impressions made **upon** the stomach and the brain by the poison, and the succeeding condition of bestial drunkenness,—attractive and imposing epithets have been given, such as being comfortable, exhilarated, invigorated, refreshed, and so forth ; all tending to lead poor, sinful human nature, far, far away from God and happiness ; to build **up** Satan's kingdom, and undermine the kingdom of our Lord **and** Saviour Jesus Christ !

The same principles apply to the term "sober," as to "drunk." They both, in their accredited popular sense, permit the moderate use of alcoholic liquors, and consequently give free license to drink the first glass. Nevertheless, "*Ce n'est que le premier pas qui coûte:*" "*Principiis obsta:*" "Stop at the beginning :" "Look not thou upon the wine when it is red :" "Behold how great a matter a little fire kindleth." In plain language, total abstinence is the only true philosophy, and sound Bible morality in regard to alcoholic drinks. That **it** is sound Bible morality, will hardly be denied by any unprejudiced person, who will candidly examine the argument contained in this and preceding letters ; and that it is the only true philosophy concerning alcoholic drinks, has been clearly and ably taught in the following admirable passage, by Youmans, in the "Scientific Basis of Prohibition," which may be said, in a few words, to contain the pith and marrow of anti-alcoholic temperance :

"It is in vain to urge that government lends its sanction only to the moderate employment of alcoholic beverages, and reprobates their excessive **use.** *This is impossible. Government cannot fix the magic line, up to which, indulgence is safe* *and commendable, and beyond which, it is dangerous and to be prohibited. Government must either consent to the habit through all its imperceptible degrees of growth, or it must entirely interdict it. In this case, the beginning is every-* **thing.** Put out your shoot in the soil, and the forces of nature will take care that it becomes a tree. Start your drinking habit, and the laws of nature will see to it, that it shall grow and bear fruit of its kind. It is preposterous to attempt a defence of government, by saying it only justifies a commencement of drinking practices. As well might the culprit on trial for arson, plead innocence on the ground that he did not burn the dwelling, but only fired a train of combustibles **that** led to it."

I trust it has been made sufficiently plain, that the mind of the Spirit, in I Thess. v, 5–8, as in the passage previously quoted from Ephesians v, 18, is, that by "drunken," is to be understood, one, in any degree, under the influence of alcoholic poison; and by "sober," one who is a total abstainer from "wine, wherein is excess," or any kind of alcoholic liquor, except in that state of the constitution where it can be used medicinally, i. e., beneficially under altered circumstances, or in a diseased, or abnormal condition thereof; and as these words "drunken" and "sober" do not convey that meaning, as above explained, it seems proper that they should be discarded, **and** the words "poisoning" and "abstinent," substituted for them. "How immense is the difference as to the light in which we shall learn to regard a sin, according as we have been wont to designate, and to hear it designated by a word which brings out its loathsomeness and deformity; or by one which conceals these; as when in Italy, during the period that poisoning was rifest, nobody was said to be poisoned; it was only that the death of some was assisted (*aiutata*); or again, by one who seeks to turn the edge of the Divine threatenings against it by a jest, as when in France a subtle poison, by which impatient heirs delivered themselves from those who stood between them and the inheritance which they coveted, was called "*poudre de succession.*"\*

Do not these emphatic words apply to deaths, of daily occurrence, from alcoholic poison? How are these deaths represented, in most instances, in the papers? Do not coroners and their juries frequently return poisoning with alcohol, as deaths "by the visitation of God?" How dishonoring to Jehovah is this! How blasphemous to screen human guilt under the broad covering of Divine Sovereignty, instead of bringing the crimes home to the perpetrators of them—in most cases, the licensed dealers in wines and spirituous liquors, who bask in the sunshine of royal or republican indulgence.

The following extracts from the Alliance Weekly News, March 14th, 1857, tend to illustrate and confirm the truth of these observations:

824. John Knowles dies suddenly whilst "very drunk;" was much in the habit of drinking rum, and used to suffer much after fits of drinking; yet the coroner's jury return a verdict: "Died from natural causes, by the visitation of God," February 25.

825. John Davis staggers home from the public house, quite drunk; while undressing, he falls backward and injures his spine, so that he dies from the effects. Verdict: "Accidental death," February 26.

When death is caused by neglect or carelessness, our juries make their verdict with a note of censure; but when grog-selling has been the real cause, they are mostly willing to charge the blame on "accident," or any other "scape-goat."

The doctrine being, I trust, established upon the basis, both of science and Scripture, that total abstinence from intoxicating drinks is the law of God, (as far as the portion of

---

\* "On the Study of Words." R. C. Trench, B.D. Published, &c., New York, 1855. p. 60.

revealed truth, already examined, have to do with it,) a glance may now be **taken of** some **other** portions of Holy Writ, relative to drunkenness. "He **(Noah,)** drank of the wine, and was drunken, (poisoned,) and he **was** uncovered within his tent:" (Genesis ix, 21.) After uttering a memorable prophecy, in **which** Canaan was cursed, and Shem and Japhet blessed, Noah's light was extinguished; he is no more **heard of in the** Mosaic narrative, although he **lived three** hundred and fifty years after the flood. **It appears, from the** statement **of the** inspired historian, (verse **24,) that** "Noah **awoke from his** wine, and knew what his *younger* son had done unto him." **Are we** not to understand by this that Canaan, his grandson, **was** the individual who gave to him the poisoned cup?

May he not have been trained to wickedness by his father, **Ham? He,** evidently, had a very different character from the **two other brothers,** Shem and Japhet,—for he saw the **nakedness of his father, and told** his two brothers without; while, in contrast **to his indecent** and unfilial conduct, **they** "took a garment **and laid it upon both** their shoulders, **and went** backwards and covered **the** nakedness of their father, **and** their faces were backward and they saw not their **father's** nakedness:" (verse 23.) In connection with this, **see** Hab. ii, 15, where it is written: "Woe unto him that giveth his neighbor drink: that puttest thy bottle to him, **and** makest him drunken **also, that thou mayest** look upon his **nakedness." Is** not this **the key to the** explanation of **the conduct of Noah,** and his wicked son **and** grandson, **Ham and Canaan? The curse** came upon the descendants of **both, and no doubt both took** part in this **base** transaction.

**It is here** worthy of remark, that African slavery took its rise in an **act of** drunkenness! How many fathers, since those days, have taught their sons to **be** drunkards, and to revel in sensual indulgence, after the **example** of Ham and Canaan? How few, alas! have been imitators of Jonadab, **the** son of Rechab, and have inherited a blessing from the Lord, because they obeyed the voice of their sire, and abstained from wine and strong drink according to his commandment. (Jeremiah xxxv, 5–8.) "They reel to and fro, and stagger like a drunken (brain-poisoned,) man:" (Psalm cvii, 27.)

"This is the effect of alcoholic poison, **when** taken in such quantity as to impair the functions of the deeper and posterior parts of the brain, connected with special sense and muscular power: "Thus sight **and** hearing are affected, the **limbs grow** weak and tottering, the head swims, the tongue refuses distinct articulation,—at the **same** time, intellectual excitement becomes more and more decidedly intellectual perversion, partaking **of** the nature of delirium; reason is at discount, and voluntary control placed more and more in abeyance."*

"Drink ye and be drunken, (poisoned,) and spue, and fall, and rise no more:" (Jeremiah xxv, 27.) How many wise, mighty, noble, yea, and religious men also, have fallen, never to rise again, beginning with the so-called moderate use of alcoholic liquors; and yet, men are found, and scientific men too, **who** hesitate not, with a face of no ordinary effrontery, **to** affirm, that "the drinking just so much as promotes **the comfort** and well-being **of** an individual, at any particular time, **of which,** each person must **be his** own judge, is temperate drinking." I envy not the man who could thus speak. I cordially concur with you, "That there is no such thing as 'temperate drinking.' That alcohol, in all its forms, is poisonous; that alcoholic drinks when taken (in health,) are always injurious; consequently there **can be no temperance** in the use of them (as a beverage in health,) any more than of arsenic; or, in other words, **all** use (as beverage in health,) is abuse."

May the following eloquent words of truth and soberness, which you have uttered, prove a salutary warning to all who

---

* "Alcohol, its Place and Power." By James Miller, F. R. S. E., p. 15.

are disposed to listen to false—however palatable and specious—doctrines of the advocates of moderate drinking, according to Dr. Hun's definition of it :

"The advocacy of downright drunkenness, in its most disgusting forms, would not be half so much to be deprecated as the advocacy of such moderate use of intoxicating poisons as you have authorized; which use imperceptibly, and by a necessity of nature, leads to drunkenness; and not half so much to be deprecated, because the advocacy of the former would not be half so full of danger, either to the risen or the rising generation, as the advocacy of the latter.

"It is not the example of the ragged, squalid drunkard, who wallows in the gutter by day, and returns in the spirit of a fiend, at night, to his hovel, to beat his children, and inflict on her who bore them a still severer vengeance; it is not the example of this man that allures the young and inexperienced to criminal indulgence. Such example carries its antidote along with it, in those attributes of degradation, and wretchedness, and loathing, by which it is accompanied. Not so the example of the elegant, fashionable, temperate and moral wine-drinker. Here there is, at the outset, nothing to shock or revolt; here temptation is presented in covert and alluring forms, and hence in forms most dangerous to virtue. Thus assaulted, many a young man of purity and promise has already been induced (abandoning the secure position of total abstinence,) to take the inceptive step in that downward path of temperate drinking, which leads, by imperceptible degrees, to drunkenness and degradation.

"Not a sot can be found in Christendom, whose career did not commence with moderate drinking; and thus will terminate the downward movement of many whose career has already thus commenced.

"What, then, is not to be apprehended from an attempt to bring the counsels of science to bear in aid of the incentives of pleasure? What, when the pen and the press are employed, not in raising new barriers at the entrance of this road to death, **but in** breaking down those which have already been planted there? What, when in view of the banquet already bedecked with flowers, and accompanied by the fascinations of music, a voice (professing to be the voice of Wisdom) is uttered, not to inform the ignorant that poison is contained in the inebriating chalice; not to inform the wavering that safety lies in abstinence; in one word, not to warn away the unsuspecting from temptation; but uttered, on the contrary, only **to give** assurance **to all** that 'temperate drinking consists in drinking just so much as promotes the comfort and well-being of the individual, at any particular time, without producing any subsequent injury; and that each person must **judge** for himself **how** far he can go with safety.'

"Amid all the 'follies of this charlatan age,' to which you allude with so just a feeling of disapprobation, no announcement has been made, I apprehend, so full of peril as this, or so precisely calculated to disappoint the hopes of the parent, to corrupt the virtue of the **child, to** embitter the **life of woman,** and send a moral blight over the moralities of the entire community.

"Let a young man, of convivial habits and feeble resolutions, adopt and follow out the counsel you have given, and his doom is certain; and unless the course of nature changes, he will reach a dishonored end, and fill a drunkard's grave. Nor will even age secure, from such a doom, those who shall follow out such counsel.

"It is wise to listen to the teachings **of** experience. And what, I ask, has, in times gone by, been the consequence of moderate drinking, and the history of moderate drinkers?

"The physician's diary, and the ages of the dead, chiseled on monumental marble in the graveyards which adjoin our city, will answer this interrogation. In view of these records of what has been, who can look upon a family, however full of promise, where temperate drinking is tolerated, without shuddering at the thought of what awaits some, perhaps all of its members in future.

"If the temperate use of the wines of France, with whose drinking usages you have become familiar, have induced, to **such an** extent, disease in the human stomach as Broussais, from actual dissections, declares, what must be expected from a similar use of the intenser poisons contained in the fabricated liquors manufactured and sold, and drank in this Republic? Or, what must be thought of the wisdom of promulgating the license for their use, which you have promulgated? and (unless counteracted,) what must be the consequence of its promulgation?

"Especially, what must be the consequences of its promulgation, by one charged not only with the duty of watching over the lives and the health of our citizens, but with the still graver duty of watching over the morals, and forming the characters of others to sustain elsewhere, and in future times, the same high office.

"What must the millions of total abstinence citizens in this Republic think of an **institution, planted at** the capital of the Empire State, for the education of youth in the healing art, in which institution the salutary restraints, which an enlightened public opinion has recently imposed on the rising generation, are to be removed; in which institution the efforts to banish the entire use of intoxicating poisons are to be counteracted, and in which those destined hereafter **to stand at** the side of the sick bed as sentinels, to watch those crises **of** disease on which the issues of life and death depend, are to be taught, in place of preserving that clearness of intellect and firmness of nerve which total abstinence secures, that it will be befitting for them to indulge in the moderate use of intoxicating liquors, and, that in place of considering that there is any fixed limit to that use that must never be transgressed, that each '**must** judge for himself how far he can go with safety.'

" Who, that is interested in the character of our institutions, the health of our citizens, the **morals** of our youth, or the best interests of the human race, can fail to be afflicted at such an apparent retrograde movement **in morals, as well as** science, as the promulgation of such a license among us would seem to imply.

" You say, 'One who crosses a river, runs some risk of being drowned;' and you ask, 'will you therefore say that the act of crossing the river produces a state of incipient asphyxia?' I answer, I would not; still, if that **river were** deep **and rapid,** and had proved fatal to thousands who had undertaken to ford it, I should advise all travelers to cross on the total abstinence bridge, where there was no danger of drowning, rather than encounter the current of the treacherous, moderate drinker's stream which flowed beneath; and the children, too, sporting on the verge of its excavated banks, I should warn away, rather than encourage them to see how far they could wade out from the shore with safety.

" Far be it from me to impute to you any design, by the advocacy of moderate drinking, to encourage inebriation. **I doubt** not you would shrink from the idea of corrupting, by your counsels, the rising generation ; or confirming the risen generation in habits that must prove ruinous. Still, it is my deliberate and solemn conviction that your writings tend, and only tend, to do both. And an earnest anticipation of what they will hereafter effect, is furnished in the estimation in which they are held alike by the drunkard and the drinker, and in the encouragement they have imparted **to the** hopes, and the confirmation they have given to the habits of both.

" Trusting that the evils deprecated as the consequence of what you have already written, will, through the good providence of God, be prevented ; and hoping that you will, ere long, yourself perceive that you are in a false position, and, changing that position, come to the aid of total abstinence—a practice safe and salutary, and worthy to be defended by the loftiest talents, and full of promise both to the church and the world."—*The Enquirer, No. 3, vol. I, p.* 127.

. . . . "But now I have written unto you, if any man that is called a brother be a fornicator, or covetous, or an idolater, or a railer, or a drunkard, (alcoholic poisoner,) with such an one no not to eat:" (I Cor. v, 11.) "They are not all Israel who are of Israel:" (Romans ix, 6.) How many persons ought to be ejected from the church of Christ, (if the views given above, of drunkenness, be Scriptural,) whose society is now courted, and who form a very large proportion of those who frequent the house and table of the Lord?

"Now the works of the flesh are manifest, which are these, adultery, fornication, murders, drunkenness, (poisoning,) revellings and such like : of the which I tell you before, as I have also told you in times past, that they which do such things shall not inherit the Kingdom of God :" (Gal. v, 19, 21.)

If the views, above mentioned, be correct, is there not reason to fear that many of those who are now confident that they are "fellow citizens with the saints, and of the household of God," may come short of the promised rest, and never tread the golden streets of the New Jerusalem—drink of the water—or eat of the bread of life ? "There shall in no wise enter into it, anything that defileth, neither whatsoever worketh abominations or maketh a lie, but they which are written in the Lamb's book of life :" (Rev. xxi, 27.)

My dear brother,<br>
Yours affectionately,<br>
JOHN MAIR.

## LETTER X.

My Dear Sir,

The first Bible interdict of wine and strong drink, is to be found in Lev. x, 8–11. The words are: "And the Lord spake unto Aaron, saying, Do not drink wine nor strong drink, thou, nor thy sons with thee, when ye go into the tabernacle of the congregation, lest ye die: it shall be a statute for ever throughout your generations: and that ye may put difference between holy and unholy, and between unclean and clean; and that ye may teach the children of Israel all the statutes which the Lord hath spoken unto them by the hand of Moses."

The awful event which was the occasion of the promulgation of this law, is recorded in the preceding verses of this chapter. Nadab and Abihu, the sons of Aaron, the High Priest, were destroyed by the igneous element (probably electric fire,) for offering strange fire before the Lord, thus disobeying the commandment (Exod. xxx, 9) which forbids the offering of strange incense upon the altar of incense.

This crime seems to have consisted chiefly in contempt of God's way of receiving intercession for sin. The **fire they used** was their own fire, "sparks of their own kindling." But what was the cause of this misconduct? Evidently the use of some intoxicating liquor, which had impaired their mental soundness, clouded their judgments, blunted their senses, inflamed their passions, and impelled them, in an infatuated and inebriated state, to rush impetuously into the holy place with *strange fire*, and draw down upon their guilty heads the **fire of Divine** vengeance! The command, "Do not drink **wine**," &c., in connexion with the sudden and awful death inflicted upon these priestly transgressors, and the reasons assigned for the specific prohibition, then for the first time published, cannot be otherwise accounted for. No doubt these anointed Priests knew that Noah had fallen **into** the sin of drunkenness, and Lot after him, and they should have been rigidly on their guard not to drink anything intoxicating, when about **to** engage in the sacred services of the tabernacle, so that they might have all their senses about them, and their moral and intellectual faculties clear and unimpaired when approaching the Most High God; for He had said, "I will be sanctified in them that come nigh me, and before all the people I will be glorified:" (Lev. x, 3.)

They committed two evils: 1st, they failed to distinguish between the wine, or liquor, which, in its nature, is "a mocker," and that which is innocent, and drank of that poisonous wine, or liquor; and 2d, as the consequence of the preceding crime, they fell into the grievous sin of confounding things holy and profane, even the righteousness of Jesus, as symbolized by the sacred fire of the altar of burnt offering, and His all-prevailing intercession, as emanating from it, with their own inherent and acquired vileness and sinfulness! To prevent the recurrence of these evils, Jehovah ordained the law above referred to, viz: "Do not drink wine," &c.

In considering this passage, a distinction should be made between the part of the law which is judicial, and applicable to the Jewish theocracy only, and that which is moral, and therefore of perpetual obligation. The punishment of death was **of** the former class. The reasons assigned, for the declarative part of the law, prove that it belonged to the latter class.

The very essence of the sin of drunkenness is here brought out by implication, viz: obscuration of the intellect, destruction, or depravation of the moral sense, and paralysis of the heart, or that state of mind (using the term in its widest sense,) where the man is rendered incapable of distinguishing between holy and unholy, clean and unclean, and of teaching the precepts of God. The chain of causation is complete, 1st, the use of wine, or strong drink; 2d, the obscuration and depravation of the moral sense and intellectual powers; **and** 3d, inability to teach the Divine statutes.

But these are states of mind not peculiar to the **Jewish** priests, or people—not confined to any class, or nation. They are **states** of mind which exist everywhere, under the same circumstances, where the same causes are in operation; and it may fairly be presumed, that it was because the duties of the priesthood were of immeasurably greater importance than those of the ordinary vocations of human life; and because dishonor done to Jehovah, by that order of men, as exemplified in the inebriety of Nadab and Abihu, with its fatal consequences, must have been far more displeasing to Him, than any common breach of the Divine law; that this statute was, at this time (B. C. 1490,) enacted, with special reference to Aaron and his lineal descendants. This does not hinder, however, the intelligent and spiritually minded reader of Scripture from applying the terms of the law to all men, especially to christians; for it is plainly the duty of all men, everywhere, to aspire after the highest degree of intellectual and moral improvement of which they are capable; for God says, "Be ye holy, for I **am holy**," and "Be ye perfect, even as your Father in Heaven is perfect."

But to be somewhat more particular in our examination of this remarkable law, in its immediate application to the Aaronic priesthood:—By the words "Do not drink wine nor strong drink, thou, nor thy sons with thee, when ye go into the tabernacle of the congregation, lest ye die: it shall be a statute for ever throughout your generations: and that ye may put difference between holy and unholy, and between unclean and clean; and **that ye may teach the** children of Israel all the statutes which the Lord hath spoken unto them by the hand of Moses;" we are to understand, 1st, that the use of all intoxicating drinks was forbidden to the priests of Aaron's line, when going into, or officiating in the tabernacle, upon pain of death; 2d, that the use of all intoxicating liquors was forbidden to them, at all times, outside of the tabernacle, in order to their being able to put difference, or to distinguish between holy and unholy, and unclean and clean; and to teach the children of Israel, all the statutes which the Lord had spoken unto them **by the** hand of Moses.

A very meagre and unsatisfactory interpretation of this passage seems to have been given by eminent expositors. Thus, in a "Commentary upon the Holy Bible, from Henry and Scott;" published by the Religious Tract Society of London— notes on this chapter, 8–11,—under the head of "Wine forbidden to the priests when in the service of the tabernacle," it is said: "Observe here the prohibition, 'Do not drink wine, or strong drink.' At other times the priests were allowed it, but during the time of their administration they were forbidden it." We cannot assent to this interpretation, but must adhere to that given above, for the following reasons. The design of the Almighty, in enacting and publishing this law, seems to have been five fold:

1st. To prevent the priests of Aaron (holy persons,) from being injured and polluted by alcohol, when entering upon the duties of the tabernacle, (the holy place.)

2d. To prevent the commission of crimes, liable and likely to proceed from alcoholic intoxication, such as presenting strange fire before the Lord, &c.

3d. To prevent the admission of any unclean person, or thing, into the tabernacle.

4th. To prevent the priests from teaching otherwise than as prescribed in "the statutes spoken unto the children of Israel by the hand of Moses."

5th. To prevent the manifested purity and glory of God from being tarnished, by irreverent, or insolent approaches to Him, by the priests who were specially consecrated to His service, in any or all the ways before mentioned.

If the two first of these ends could have been accomplished

by mere abstinence from intoxicating liquors by the priests, *when going into the tabernacle of the congregation*, we do not see how the other three ends could have been accomplished by such abstinence *alone*, if they had previously availed themselves of the license granted to them according to the interpretation of the Tract Society Commentary, of drinking wine or strong drink outside the tabernacle. But we do not see how, even the first end could have been accomplished, if the letter of the statute only, was observed; for, although the priests did not drink intoxicating liquor, in the act of going into the tabernacle, or while in it; still, if they had previously been drinking wine or strong drink, so as to be intoxicated when going into the tabernacle, or serving in it, the intention of the Divine Lawgiver, as expressed in the two first paragraphs, would have been defeated.

But admitting, for the moment, that the first two ends proposed could have been accomplished, we do not see how abstinence *merely*, when going into the tabernacle, could have sufficed to secure the accomplishment of the other ends proposed; and

1st. We do not see how such abstinence could have sufficed to prevent the introduction of unclean persons, or things, into the tabernacle. Let us take the leprosy, for an example. The priests, if they had drunk of alcoholic liquors outside the tabernacle, (according to the license granted to them in the view of this Commentary,) might thus have been rendered incapable of accurately discriminating between cases of real leprosy, and cases bearing only the semblance of it, and have mistaken the former for the latter, (Lev. xiii, 14,) and thus allowed leprous persons to enter into the tabernacle and defile it. All this time, too, they might have been unsuspicious of being intoxicated, or in any way rendered unfit for the correct performance of this sacred duty—as we often find persons accustomed to the *moderate* use of intoxicating liquors, perfectly self-confident that all is right with them, when, in reality, they are incapable of discharging the duties of their calling, because their judgments have become impaired, and other faculties of their minds perverted, by that most delusive and dangerous of poisons—alcohol.

2d. We do not see how such abstinence, in the act of going into the tabernacle, or within it, could have prevented the priests from teaching *otherwise* than prescribed in "the statutes which the Lord had spoken unto the children of Israel by the hand of Moses," for similar reasons to those adduced above; that is to say, they might have had the balance of their minds disturbed, their imaginations excited, at the expense of their judgments, and their whole mental economy so disordered by the previous *moderate* use of alcoholic liquors, as to have been rendered totally unfit, rightly to divide the word of truth, and to expound the Scriptures in a manner profitable to their **hearers.** And it ought to be borne in mind, that the priests were, at all times, liable to be called upon to give instruction in the law: (Malachi ii, 5–9.) "They were not *mere* sacrificers as their posterity had become; but they were sensible that the priests ought *ever* to be ready to speak upon any part of sacred knowledge, and, as the messengers of God, to instruct the people from his Word." (Scott.) "It is required of the priests of God's sanctuary, that they should be men of knowledge and heavenly wisdom, so as their hearts should keep, and their lips should express to the people, the right understanding of Divine things." (Bishop Hall.)

3d. The fifth great reason for the enactment and promulgation of this prohibitory liquor law, may be said to comprehend all the rest, for the grand intent of the Divine Lawgiver as set forth in the 3d verse of the 10th chapter of Leviticus, was to prevent the tarnishing of His purity and glory, by any act or thing, contrary, in spirit or letter, to the mode of worship which He had established for His chosen people, according to the Mosaic ritual.

So far as the law was violated in any of the previous particulars, so far was the plan of salvation of sinful men, by the righteousness of the Saviour to come, foreshadowed in the priestly and sacrificial types and symbols of His atonement and intercession, soiled and made light of, by his professed worshipers.

According to these views, if correct, it must be evident that the interpretation given in the Commentary of the Religious Tract Society, upon this passage, must be unsound, and, therefore, ought to be rejected; for how could the infinitely wise God have enjoined the use of means for the attainment of ends, which could not be attained by the use of these means? and, we trust it has been made plain in the preceding remarks, that by the employment of these means, the ends proposed could never have been accomplished.

Some have been of opinion that the expression, "When ye go into the tabernacle of the congregation," should be taken in a periphrastic sense, to signify the assumption of the priestly office, by entering upon the duties thereof. We would merely remark, that this does not appear to us to be the natural sense of the passage.

We might now return to the first part of the interpretation which we have adopted, viz: that the use of all intoxicating drinks was forbidden to the priests when going into, or officiating in, the tabernacle, or temple, upon pain of death. But, as this view is not objected to, we proceed to the consideration of the second part, viz: that the use of all intoxicating drinks was forbidden to them, at all times, outside of the tabernacle, in order to their being able "to put difference between holy and unholy, and between unclean and clean; and to teach the children of Israel all the statutes which the Lord had spoken unto them by the hand of Moses."

According to this view, the passage will read thus: "And the Lord spake unto Aaron, saying, Do not drink wine nor strong drink, thou, nor thy sons with thee: that ye may put difference between holy and unholy, and between unclean and clean; and that ye may teach the children of Israel all the statutes which the Lord hath spoken unto them by the hand of Moses." Here it will be observed, that the whole of the clause, "when ye go into the tabernacle of the congregation, lest ye die: it shall be a statute for ever throughout your generations," is unnecessary,* according to the particular view of the subject we are now taking; and may, therefore, be considered as parenthetical, in relation to what follows. But if expressed, there will be a necessity for repeating a second time, the 8th, and part of the 9th verse, so that after giving the passage just as it stands in the 10th chapter of Leviticus, 8th to 11th verse, it would have to be read a second time, thus beginning with the 8th verse; omitting " when ye go into the tabernacle of the congregation, lest ye die: it shall be a statute for ever throughout your generations," and then supplying the words after "and," in the 10th verse, from the 8th and 9th verse, in this manner: "*And* the Lord spake unto Aaron, saying, Do not drink wine nor strong drink, thou, nor thy sons with thee: that ye may put difference between holy and unholy, and between unclean and clean; and that ye may teach the children of Israel all the statutes which the Lord hath spoken unto them by the hand of Moses."† According to this method of

---

* Referring, above, to the Ceremonial and Judicial aspects of the law, we say the whole of the clause "When ye go into the tabernacle of the congregation, lest ye die:" down to "generations," "is unnecessary," because the Jewish types and ceremonies have given place to the great antitype, and every true worshipper is a temple of the Holy Ghost, and a king and priest unto God; but, while there appear to us, valid reasons for not regarding the law in its judicial and ceremonial phases, they cannot affect it in its moral bearing upon the church, which must be ever the same.

† It will be well for the reader to have his Bible in hand, turn to the passage, and adhere to the directions given above, in examining it.

construction, the only true interpretation of this passage (as we believe,) is naturally, rationally, and spiritually brought out; that interpretation which reduces it into harmony with other portions of Holy Writ, the purity, spirituality, and extent of God's law, the claims of Christ's sermon on the mount, the perfections of all Jehovah's attributes, the laws of alcohol, and the analogies by which it is excluded, as a poison, from both the animate kingdoms of nature.

What a paradox would it have been, if God (according to the rejected interpretation which has occupied so much of our attention,) had sanctioned the use of alcohol by his priests, under any circumstances, in their normal state of health, when, by a law of their organization, the irrational and morally irresponsible tribes of nature, shrink from it with abhorrence! But other modes of testing the truth of our interpretation, may be resorted to, under the heads of synthetic and analytic experiments.

1st. *Synthetic Experiments.*—We have the synthetic experiments presented to us, in the conduct of the priests, as graphically described by the prophets Isaiah and Ezekiel, in the following words: "But they also have erred through wine, and through strong drink are out of the way; the priest and the prophet have erred through strong drink, they are swallowed up of wine, they are out of the way through strong drink: they *err in vision*, they *stumble in judgment*:" (Isaish xxviii, 7:) Compare Isaiah lvi, 9-12.

"Her priests have violated my law,\* and have profaned

---

\* Might not Hophni and Phinehas, sons of Belial, be included in the same category? Is it not highly probable from their father, Eli, accusing Hannah of being intoxicated, that he was apt to be peculiarly suspicious of others, from familiarity with drunken outbreaks in his wretched sons and their infamous paramours, at the door of the tabernacle? How is it possible to account for such abandoned, shameless profligacy, as is described I Samuel ii, 12, 17, 22, upon any other supposition than that of intoxication by alcohol, or some kindred poison?

mine holy things: they have put no difference between the holy and profane, neither have they shewed difference between the *unclean* and the *clean*, and have hid their eyes from my sabbaths, and I am profaned among them:" (Ezekiel xxii, 26.)

These experiments plainly speak this language, in confirmation of the interpretation we have given, of the great doctrine proclaimed by Jehovah, (Lev. x,) that alcohol, which, to use modern phraseology, is the essence of wine and strong drink, when received into their living, human bodies, caused the priests to *err in vision*, so that they could not put difference between holy and unholy, and between unclean and clean, and to "*stumble in judgment*," so that they could not "teach the children of Israel all the statutes which the Lord had spoken unto them by the hand of Moses."

In chemico-physiological language, it might be said that these priests, by introducing alcohol, contrary to God's law, into their stomachs, placed *it* in conditions to come within the sphere **of** the elective attraction of their brains, (referring **to** Dr. Percy's opinion, that the cerebral substance seems to have a peculiar affinity for alcohol,) so that by combining with that part of the organ of intelligence which is related to *vision*, that function had become impaired; and with the part which is related to *judgment*, that function had become perverted, and they were thereby rendered incapable of performing the duties **of** the sacerdotal office, to which they had been solemnly set **apart** by their Sovereign, and their God.

2d. *Analytic Experiments.*—We **have** the analytic experiments **set** before us, in the character and conduct of those two tried servants of God, Samuel, and John the Baptist, both priests, in the highest and holiest sense of the term, "the circumcision, which worship God, in the spirit;" both abstainers from wine and strong drink, although only one of them, the immediate forerunner of our Lord, was a priest by hereditary descent. Men, they were, of dauntless courage, elevated piety, uncompromising integrity, richly gifted with heavenly wisdom, "stedfast and immovable, always abounding in the work of the Lord." In their blameless lives, and in the faithful and self-denying performance of all their sacred duties, we possess the analytic proof of the truth of the interpretation, that total abstinence from alcoholic liquor qualified them for the discharge of their duties outside the tabernacle of the congregation. In chemico-physiological language, it might be said of these illustrious men, that by keeping alcohol out of their stomachs, they prevented *it* from contaminating their blood, and thus from coming within the sphere of attraction of the seat of their heaven-born intellectual and moral faculties—the brain. By a bold figure of speech, they, as the blessed guides and instructers of the people, might be said to have decomposed and neutralized what may appropriately be named *alcoholic crime*, (nine-tenths of the whole, in modern **Christendom**,) by separating between its elements—alcohol, on the one part, and the cerebral substance, on the other, and keeping them forever at a distance, according to the will of God; while their *antipodes*, the wicked priests—the sons of Belial—might be said to have called that astounding and overwhelming class of crime into existence, by bringing kindred elements into combination in the living laboratories of their bodies, when they first drank of the intoxicating cup; and to have given *it* a mighty impulse for the destruction of mankind, by their habitual use of it, in opposition to God's holy law.

We think we are now justified in arriving at the conclusion, from the results of the synthetic and analytic experiments, recorded in Scripture, to which we have directed attention; the absurdities and contradictions involved in the other doctrine, which we have endeavored to expose, and the harmony of the views we have enunciated with the fundamental doctrines of natural and revealed religion, and deductions of science—that the interpretation adopted by us, is that which is according to the mind of the Spirit, and, therefore, the only true interpretation. That interpretation is this, that the use of all intoxicating drinks was forbidden to the priests, at all times, outside the tabernacle, in order to their being able to put difference, or to distinguish between holy and unholy, and between unclean and clean; and to teach the children of Israel all the statutes which the Lord had spoken unto them by the hand of Moses If we have erred, in any particular, in this discussion, we shall be glad to have our errors pointed out, as, we trust, our sincere desire is, the establishment of the truth, and *that* only.

The consideration of the duty of the christian priesthood, in regard to wine, and strong drink, must be deferred till a future opportunity, should God be pleased to grant it.

I remain, my dear friend,
Yours affectionately,
JOHN MAIR.

### LETTER XI.

My Dear Sir,

We maintain that the grounds, upon which the Divine law, against the use of wine and strong drink by the Aaronic priesthood, was established under the Jewish economy, were moral principles of permanent obligation, and, therefore, applicable to those who hold a similar relation to the Divine Lawgiver, under the Christian economy. It will be for those, **who** hold contrary sentiments, to show that they are right, and that we are in error, in this matter. If God saw it fit and necessary to enact a law prohibiting the use of alcoholic liquors, by the priests of Aaron's line, the only foundation upon which we can imagine the possibility of His permitting such a law to become obsolete, in regard to the christian priesthood, consistently with the inviolable nature of all His attributes, would be the establishment of one or more of the following propositions, as undeniable truths, viz: that the nature of man has so changed, since the commencement of the Gospel Dispensation, that his system is no longer susceptible of injury from alcoholic poison; that alcohol has lost its deleterious qualities, as regards man, and is no longer a deadly poison to him; or, that Jesus has less love to those whom he hath made priests and kings unto God and His Father—all true christians—than he had to the Jewish priesthood, or than He even now cherishes to irrational animals; so that he could allow those, for whom He died upon the cross, to be exposed to dangers from which he has carefully shielded the latter, by a law of their organization!

To all of these absurd, and even blasphemous conjectures, an unconditional negative must be given. They are utterly at variance **with all** His attributes and laws, **upon** the inviolability and stability of which, not only all our plans and purposes depend, but the supremacy and universality of the Divine government rests, as its sole foundation. The nature of man is now essentially the same as it ever has been, since the fall of Adam. It was a fact in the time of Moses and Aaron, it is **a** fact still, and **ever** will be, while the present constitution of things lasts, that vinously fermented grape-juice, &c., **contains** more or less of the poison alcohol, (which our immortal **bard**, Shakspeare, so inimitably describes, as follows: "O thou invisible spirit of wine, if thou hast no name to be known by, let us call thee Devil! O that men should put an enemy to their mouths to steal away their brains!") that fearful brain-poison, which, when taken into the body in sufficient quantity, transforms man, as man—however dignified and sacred his office may be—into a beast; and the natural tendency of which, is to gender an incontrollable appetite, or craving; terminating, often, in a slavish habit, from which no one, who has begun to tamper with it, can claim exemption, **or** discharge.

But, not only can no sufficient reason be assigned why the law against alcoholic liquors, given to the Aaronic priesthood, should not extend to Christ's royal priesthood; we proceed a step further, and fearlessly affirm that there are paramount reasons why it should comprehend them in its embrace, and why it should be more strictly observed by them. Let us take a glance at a few passages of Holy Writ, confirmatory of this proposition:

"And suddenly there was with the angel a multitude of the heavenly host praising God, and saying, glory to God in the *highest*, and on earth peace, good will toward men:" (Luke ii, 13, 14.)

"Verily I say unto you, among them that are born of women there hath not risen a greater than John the Baptist: notwithstanding he that is least in the kingdom of heaven is greater than he:" (Matt. xi, 11.)

"Who also hath made us able ministers of the new testament; not of the letter, but of the spirit: for the letter killeth, but the spirit giveth life. But if the ministration of death, written and **engraven in** stones, was glorious, so that the children of Israel could not steadfastly behold the face of Moses for the glory of his countenance; which glory was to **be** done away: how shall not the ministration of the spirit be rather glorious? For if the ministration of condemnation be glory, much more doth the ministration of righteousness exceed in glory. For even that which was made glorious had no glory in this respect, by reason of the glory that excelleth. For if that which is done away was glorious, much more that which remaineth is glorious:" (II Cor. iii, 6–11.)

"But ye are come unto mount Sion, and unto the city of the living God, the heavenly Jerusalem, and to an innumerable company of angels, to the general assembly and church of the first-born, which are written in Heaven, and to God the Judge of all, and to the spirits of just men made perfect, and to Jesus the mediator of the new covenant, and to the blood of sprinkling, that speaketh better things than that of Abel. See that ye refuse not Him that speaketh. For if they escaped not who refused him that spake on earth, much more shall not we escape, if we turn away from Him that speaketh from Heaven:" (Hebrews xii, 22–25.)

"And that servant, which knew **his lord's will and** prepared not himself, neither did according **to his will**, shall be beaten with many stripes. But he that knew not, and did commit things worthy of stripes, shall be beaten with few stripes. For unto whomsoever much is given, of him shall be much required: and **to** whom men have committed much, of him **they will ask the** more:" (Luke xii, 47, 48.)

"Ye also, as lively stones, are built up a spiritual house, an holy priesthood, to offer up spiritual sacrifices, acceptable to God by **Jesus Christ:" (I Peter ii, 5.)**

"But ye are a chosen generation, a royal priesthood, an holy nation, a peculiar people; that ye should shew forth the praises of Him who hath called you out of darkness into His marvellous light:" (I Peter ii, 9.)

Who so blind as not to perceive what the design and import of these and similar portions of Scripture is? **and they could** easily be multiplied.

Do they not vividly demonstrate that the day has **dawned,** and the shadows have **fled away; that** "the darkness **is past,** and the true light now shineth;" that the sun of righteousness is in the meridian; that he has **arisen upon** us "with healing in his wings;" that we have not only far greater insight into "**the mystery of** Godliness," **than our Jewish** predecessors had—"beholding, as in a glass, the glory of the Lord," "God having shined in our hearts to give the light of the knowledge of the glory of God in the face of Jesus Christ," the promise, that He would "send the Comforter," having been fulfilled; **and** that, therefore, we shall be far more guilty than the **priests of** Aaron were, if we, forgetting the apostolic encomium, "Ye are all the children of light, and the children of the day," ignore and despise the obligation laid upon us, as "kings and priests unto God"—to abstain from wine, wherein is excess, (asotia, insalvability,) and to "walk honestly as in the day, not in rioting and drunkenness, not in chambering and wantonness?"

But to have done with general reasoning, let us now proceed **to show** that there is direct Scriptural testimony to the fact, that the use of alcoholic liquors is forbidden, to the spiritual priesthood, under the new testament dispensation.

We now request attention to Ezekiel xliv, 21–24, omitting the 22d verse. It is thus written: "Neither shall any priest drink wine, when they enter the inner court. And they shall teach my people the difference between the holy and profane, and cause them to discern between the unclean and the clean. And in controversy they shall sit in judgment; and they shall judge it according to my judgments: and they shall keep my laws and my statutes in all my assemblies; and they shall hallow my sabbaths."

**The verses** just quoted **form** part of Ezekiel's prediction concerning the temple, continued from the 40th chapter to the end of the book. It has generally been considered one of the most obscure and ambiguous portions of Scripture. We are of opinion that the temple, with its priests and sacrifices, as seen by Ezekiel, in vision, are emblematic representations of pure, undefiled Christianity, as never altogether extinct, but especially as it will be displayed in greatest perfection, in the latter days —during the millennium;—and, in support of this view, we offer the following arguments:

1st. In the words of Lowth, "Nothing is more common than for the prophets to describe the state of the Christian church by representations from the Jewish temple and service."

2d. The plainness and simplicity of Christian ordinances, contrasted with the complexity and gorgeousness of the Jewish rites and ceremonies. In the former, gold and silver are altogether wanting, or, at least, are not enjoined in the Word of

God—and neither of them is mentioned in the construction of Ezekiel's temple—while of the tabernacle, and temple at Jerusalem, they constituted essential parts; and the priestly garments were richly ornamented, not only with gold, but also with precious stones, according to Divine appointment. Compare Exodus xxv to xxviii, I Kings vi, with Ezekiel xli, xliv, 16.

3d. The spiritual worship of genuine Christianity is indicated by the statute, "Thus saith the Lord God; No stranger, uncircumcised in heart, nor uncircumcised in flesh, shall enter into my sanctuary, of any stranger that is among the children of Israel:" (Ezekiel xliv, 9.) Scott, in his notes, in his Commentary, upon this subject, remarks: "There was no law to exclude unregenerate persons, who were circumcised and ritually clean, from the ordinances of the temple, so that this must denote a different constitution."

4th. "The temple and its out-buildings are here stated to be built on a square, at least, of very nearly an English mile on each side, or four miles in circuit. This is far greater than either Solomon's temple, or that after the captivity, ever was; or, indeed, than the mountain of the temple was capable of containing, according to the description of the Jewish writers. This shows that the vision cannot be explained of any temple that has hitherto been built; or, indeed, of any literal temple —but figuratively and mystically."*

5th. "By this measure, the city would be near forty miles in circuit, or ten miles on each side of the square, which was vastly larger than Jerusalem ever was. Doubtless, the large dimensions, of the city and land, were intended to intimate the great increase of religion, and the propagation of the gospel in the times predicted. . . . . . The land here divided, is never called Canaan, nor the city measured, Jerusalem; probably because they were figurative of spiritual blessings to the

---

* Scott's Commentary: Notes on Ezekiel xlii, 15-20.

church, and to Israel, but 'the Lord is there;' or, 'Jehovah-Shammah,' (marg.) is the name given to this holy city."—*Scott*. (Ezekiel xlviii, 30–35.) Other reasons might be assigned for our belief, that by the temple described by Ezekiel, Christianity, in its advanced stages, is to be understood; such as repeated reference to "tables," signifying, probably, the "table of the Lord," from which the Lord's supper, in after-times, was to be administered.

After this long digression, we proceed to notice Ezekiel xliv, 21, 23, 24. We believe that it contains,

1st. A republication of the law against alcoholic wine, originally recorded, Leviticus x, 8–11, with additional sanctions addressed to those who, under the Christian dispensation, are denominated "a holy and royal priesthood," (I Peter ii, 5–9,) **and, as** proving **the** perpetual obligation thereof upon them.

2d. A prediction of the benefits to be derived from universal obedience to this law, during the millennium.

1st. *A republication of the law against alcoholic wine, originally recorded, (Leviticus* x, *8–11,) with additional sanctions addressed to those who, under the Christian dispensation, are denominated " a holy and royal priesthood," (I Peter ii, 5–9,) and, as proving the perpetual obligation thereof upon them.*

**If we** could, for a moment, be elevated (as the apostles were, in the mount of transfiguration,) into a region of supernal blessedness and glory—breathing the pure atmosphere of heaven—drinking of the clear "water," and eating of the soul-satisfying fruit of the "Tree of Life"—gazing upon the Lamb of God, in all His majesty, sublimity and beauty— absorbed in Divine contemplations of ineffable sweetness and loveliness—forgetful of everything "that defileth, or worketh abomination, or maketh a lie,"—it would be impossible for us to conceive how any brother, in the church militant upon earth, could contend, earnestly, for the use of alcoholic liquors in the house of God, or in any place, however remotely connected with His worship or service! There is, in our belief, the greatest antagonism between being *spiritually* and *spirituously-*minded. "To be carnally-minded, is death; but to be spiritually-minded, is life and peace."

It would almost seem as if members, not a few, of Christian churches, in modern times, had mistaken *spiritually* for spirituously, in the reading of this passage, and, by this slight change in the termination of the word *spirit*, made a startling alteration in the meaning of the expression, and the character of the Gospel. For, to be **spirituously-minded is one of the worst and most common forms of carnal-mindedness, and is signally** destructive of the "life and peace" which are exclusively the purchase of the Redeemer's blood, and the gifts of the Holy Ghost!

Let us now examine this law and its objects, clause by clause, with profound attention, earnestly praying for the Holy Spirit, that He would lead us into all truth respecting it.

"Neither shall any priest drink wine, when they enter into the inner court." **By any priest,** here, we are to understand, any Christian; by "enter into the inner court," the supernatural change wrought in the sinner, by the Holy Spirit, when he is born again, **and made a new creature by faith in Christ Jesus. By the whole we are to understand, that no "*king and priest*** unto God," from the moment of his conversion, or entrance into the kingdom of God, by faith, is to drink of any intoxicating alcoholic liquor, in his normal state of health, according to the views already presented in former letters. Comparing this passage, "Neither shall any priest drink wine," with the corresponding one in Leviticus x, 9, where the words, addressed to Aaron and his sons, are: "Do not drink wine nor strong drink, thou nor thy sons with thee," &c., it is evident that reference is made, in the former, to a more extended line of priesthood, than the latter: even that line which consists of all the members of Christ's mystical body, "chosen in Him before the foundation of the world, that they should be holy and without blame before Him, in love:" (Ephesians i, 4.)

That this is the meaning, will be made plain by consulting the 7th and 9th verses of the same chapter, Ezekiel xliv. "In that ye have brought strangers, uncircumcised in heart, and uncircumcised in flesh, to be in my sanctuary, to pollute it." "Thus saith the Lord God: *No stranger uncircumcised in heart, nor uncircumcised in flesh, shall enter into my sanctuary.*" Compare Romans ii, 28, 29: "For he is not a Jew, which is one outwardly; neither is that circumcision, which is outward in the flesh: But he is a Jew, which is one inwardly; and circumcision is that of the heart, in the spirit, and not in the letter; whose praise is not of men, but of God."

The allusion would seem to be, more especially, to the millennial period, (as has been noticed above,) when the fulness of the Gentiles shall be come in and so all Israel shall be saved—the out**ward** and inward circumcision, referring to the former, and the inward, the circumcision made without hands, (Coloss. ii, 11–13,) to the latter ; or rather, both having reference to purification of heart, and corresponding holiness of walk and conversation, ".clean hands and a pure heart," in Jew as well as Gentile, at the blessed epoch, when "there shall be one fold, and one shepherd," (John x, 16,) and "they shall not hurt nor destroy **in** all my holy mountain, saith the Lord:" (Isaiah lxv, **25.**) If any should demur to this interpretation of the passage, **and** say that by entering into the inner court, is only to be understood *literally*, entering into christian places of worship, **to hear** the gospel preached, pray and sing praises to God, &c.; to such we would reply, that if the views we have enunciated before, respecting the superior character of the spiritual dispensation under which we live, be correct, and also our views respecting the correlative passage in Leviticus, concerning the Aaronic priesthood, we do not see how the correctness of these additional views can be justly impugned; **for, if under "the law,"—"the ministration of death,"**—the Aaronic priests were absolutely required, by Divine authority, to abstain from wine and strong drink, (alcoholic liquors,) at all times, to fit them for the right performance of **their** sacred duties, (as, we trust, has been proved,) how **much more** shall the holy royal priesthood, **"the kings and priests unto** God,"—under "the gospel," "**the ministration of the Spirit**," which is "much more glorious,"—be required **to abstain from** wine and strong drink, at all times, to fit them for the right performance of their sacred duties ! **If we were right in the one instance,** in our interpretation, we do **not see** how we can be wrong in the other. But to proceed: "**And they shall teach my** people the *difference* between **the holy and the profane, and** cause them to discern between the unclean **and the clean.**" We have passed over the 22d verse, as more remotely connected with our present subject. (That it does bear some relation to it, however, might, without difficulty, be shown, if we were to look into the vast importance of *Christian* men having **Chris-***tian* wives, (II Cor. vi, 14,) so that their children might be brought up by *Christian* mothers, "**in the nurture and admoni-**tion of the Lord," and that they **might** early be initiated into the principles and practice of *pure* temperance, **such as is** taught by the apostle Paul, in his **epistle to** Titus, ii, **3, 4,** hereafter to be considered.)

Taking the Scriptural **view of the subject** which **we do,** we cannot avoid interpreting this paragraph as referring to moral and religious duties, (not ceremonial,) or, **at least,** only so far as regards christian ordinances, such as the Lord's supper. We are to understand by it, then, that all Christians are to teach God's people (probably those afterwards to be converted,) "according to the election of grace"—to distinguish between those principles and acts which are holy, just and good, or according to this law; and those principles and acts which are

8

unholy, unjust and wicked, or contrary to its letter and spirit: It is implied here, also, and expressed in Leviticus x, at the first promulgation of the law, (in regard to the Jewish priesthood,) that Christians are to distinguish between holy and profane, &c., themselves, and practise what they preach before they teach others: Rom. ii, 21:) and, in order that they may be qualified **to** obey this law, as thus explained, they are to abstain from **the** use of intoxicating drinks, as noticed in the preceding paragraph. A wide range of duty is included in this injunction, to which we can merely advert. But let us ponder well, the importance which "the Spirit of truth" attaches to this law of abstinence from intoxicating liquors, by Christians, both as regards personal and relative duties—duties to God, self, and mankind. Conscience is God's vicegerent within the soul of man. It is its office to distinguish between good and evil. One of its greatest enemies, if not the greatest, is alcohol. A man, in any degree, under the influence of that poison, although he may not **be** incapable of distinguishing between extreme acts of savage cruelty and God-like benevolence, or the feelings leading to them, may **yet have his** conscience so blunted as to remain unaffected by those delicate touches of the convincing Spirit which require corresponding sensitiveness to discern them, and by which, in the region of thought, reformation is to begin. It is this insensibility of the eye of conscience, (to change the figure,) to the fainter and more ethereal tints of guilt; an insensibility occasioned by the habitual action of, at first, small, but gradually increasing portions of alcohol, upon the brain, which is so much to be dreaded and deprecated, just because it is its nature not to excite alarm, but on the contrary, to creep on stealthily—serpent-like, and progressively—till it lands its miserable victim in a state of hopeless bondage.

Other sinners, upon occasions, have their memories exercised, and **their** imaginations employed, in spreading out before them their past evil deeds, in dread array, in all their portentous gloom and hideous ugliness. But the slave of strong drink **has his memory** so soaked and saturated with alcohol, that all its reminiscences smack thereof, and are jaundiced thereby.* He lives in an enchanted region, peopled by the phantoms of a crazy, bewildered, besotted imagination, which clothes everything in its own deceitful livery; "calls evil good, and good evil; puts darkness for light, and light for darkness; puts bitter for sweet, and sweet for bitter!" Alcohol is everything everywhere, to the poor, miserable, infatuated wretch. He not only drinks alcohol, but he thinks alcohol, **breathes** alcohol, speaks alcohol. He sees alcohol in every shifting scene of creation. The dreadest, or the loveliest landscape has no sublimity or beauty apart from *it*. **He hears it in the music** of nature's most melodious songsters, as they chant their morning hymn, or evening requiem to God, their Creator. He tastes it in the most luscious fruits, he smells it in the most grateful odors. It envelopes his whole exterior, so that he can touch nothing else. It enters into the most secret recesses of his soul, and constitutes the *substratum* and *frame-work*, both of his mind and body.

It snaps the sinews of **natural affection** asunder, stupifies the conscience, stultifies the understanding, enervates the will, corrodes the heart, drags piety up by the roots, stifles the voice of prayer, insinuates itself into the house of God, and intrenches itself and nestles there, transforming it into "a den of thieves, and a cage of unclean and hateful birds;" and, not content with all this wickedness and sacrilege, it has even the barefacedness, effrontery, and presumption, to make itself *one* with the precious, spotless, sin-atoning blood of the Son of God! In *alcohol*, the worse than brutified,—the devil-possessed **man**, —lives and moves and has his being. It is himself, **his God**, his all and in all.

---

* For the primary idea here, I am indebted to Sir Wm. A'Beckett, Chief Justice of Victoria, in one of his speeches. I have somewhat enlarged upon it.

"And in controversy they shall stand in judgment, and they shall judge it according to my judgments;" i. e., Christian ministers and laymen, placed in judicial situations, shall abstain from alcoholic liquors, and thus shall so far be qualified to inquire in litigated matters brought before them, according to God's judgments or laws, and shall decide accordingly; that otherwise, if they should drink wine, or strong drink, they would be liable and likely to "stumble in judgment," is evidently implied: (Isaiah xxviii, 7 : lvi, 9–12.)

"And they shall keep my laws and my statutes, in all my assemblies; and they shall hallow my sabbaths;" i. e., observing the law, against alcoholic liquors, upon all occasions, Christians shall be so far in a fit state of mind and body, to observe and preserve order and decorum in all God's assemblies, (the meetings of His saints,) in accordance with His laws and statutes, and shall *do so;* and, shall also keep holy his sabbaths.

The converse of these propositions, is manifestly set forth in Ezekiel xxii, 26, compared with Isaiah xxv, 7 : lvi, 9–12, as referred to, when speaking of the law, addressed to Aaron and his sons, under the Jewish economy.

How much might be said, in illustration and confirmation of the truth implied under the last clause—that the use of alcoholic liquors, upon the Lord's day, by so-called Christians, is one of the chief causes of its awful profanation, of the terrific catalogue of crimes committed upon it, and of the insults which God receives during its sacred hours! But shortness of time, and mass of matter upon other topics we have to handle, prevents enlargement. Suffice it to refer to the criminal statistics of the sabbath, in all the large cities of Christendom, to show that the desecration of that day, is chiefly owing to the sale and consumption of alcoholic liquors, during its sacred hours.

What the effects will be, of the banishment of wine and strong drink from the house of God, as well as from the houses of Christians, is a problem to be answered in future times, which, if we were to judge only from the tenacity with which the churches, at present, cleave to the "cup of Devils," **would** seem to be far distant.

We are thus led to a very brief notice of the second head of this branch of our subject, viz: *a prediction of the benefits to be derived from universal obedience to this law, during the millennium.* May it not be confidently stated that, *as* have been the evils resulting from the general, nay, all but universal use of alcoholic liquors, contrary to **the** Divine law, *so* will be the benefits which shall result from the all but universal disuse of them, and, especially, from their complete dismissal from the house of God, and the table of our Lord and Saviour, Jesus Christ? If nine-tenths of the crime, three-fourths of the poverty, a vast proportion of the diseases, corporeal and mental; and of the curses, desecrations, desolations, abominations and woes, which have ground and afflicted, and still grind and afflict miserable, sin-stricken man, have sprung, and do spring, from the violation of God's law, which forbids the use of alcoholic, and by implication, of all *other intoxicants*, everywhere, **and at all times, by man** in his normal state of health—and, especially, at all sacred ordinances; is it not certain that the general observance of this Divine commandment, from sincere conviction and Christian principle, will be attended with a proportionate abatement of these enormous evils? But not only so;—Is it **not obvious**, also, that if Christians have enjoyed, in some degree, **(O how** wonderful the patience and forbearance **of God!) the light** of Jehovah's countenance, although **they may be** said to have cut off **one of** the wings of **the eagle-eyed,** true-hearted religion **of Jesus, even** *temperance*, **(by means of which,** when restored **on the one side,** with faith **on the** other, **love** and hope occupying **the** centre, she is destined **to** soar with single aim, straight and rapid flight, and unruffled pinion, to the **highest** heaven, and bask forever in the quenchless sunshine of Immanuel's glory!) they will have much more of the light of His gracious countenance upon earth, when they receive implicitly, and follow steadfastly, "the truth as it is in Jesus," respecting wine and strong drink, so plainly revealed in Scripture, "that he may run that readeth it,"—although, hitherto, alas, it has been buried in a heap of superstitious garbage, and made of none effect by the tradition of the elders? We may rationally and scripturally expect, that much of the blessedness and prosperity of the millennial age will be connected with the universal observance of the law which we have been considering, and which has, hitherto, been treated as a nonentity by the christian world!

"If thou turn away thy foot from the sabbath, from doing thy pleasure on my holy day; and call the sabbath a delight, **the** holy of the Lord, honorable; and shalt honor Him, not doing thine own ways, nor finding thine own pleasure, nor speaking thine own words: then shalt thou delight thyself in the Lord; and I will cause thee to ride upon the high places of the earth, and feed thee with the heritage of Jacob, thy father: for the mouth of the Lord **hath** spoken it:" (Isaiah lviii, 13, 14.)

I have yet to endeavor to re-echo the voice of the apostles, upon this subject, if God permit, but not in my present letter, which is, already, of unusual size.

Believe me,<br>
My dear brother in Jesus,<br>
Yours affectionately,<br>
JOHN MAIR.

## LETTER XII.

My Dear Sir,

The next question, to be considered, is:—Do the writings of the apostles confirm the doctrine of "Moses and the prophets," (as we have viewed it,) that it is unlawful for Christians—a "holy priesthood"—to drink of alcoholic liquors, in their normal state of health?—If so, then we may reckon it established. If not so, then it must follow that our rendering of the texts, which we have examined, must be erroneous; for it is impossible that the inspired writers can be at variance, on a moral problem, of such unspeakable importance, involving, not only the happiness of man, but the glory of Jehovah. Let us proceed, deliberately and prayerfully, to investigate this subject, in the following order:

I. The texts, in the Apostolic writings, which enjoin abstinence from wine, &c., upon Office-bearers of the church.

II. The texts, in the Apostolic writings, which enjoin abstinence from wine, &c., upon Christians generally.

1st. The texts, in the Apostolic writings, which enjoin abstinence from wine, &c., upon Office-bearers of the church.

There is an apostolic precept, (I Timothy iii, 2,) forbidding the use of wine to bishops, (presbyters, or pastors,) not only when engaged in the sacred ordinances of God's house, but at all times, if we are correct in our interpretation of it, in the original. It stands thus, in the authorized version: "A bishop must be vigilant:" "*Dei oun ton episcopon einai, . . . . nephaleon;*" the last word being thus translated, in a "Greek and English Lexicon of the New Testament, by Edward Robinson, D. D., &c., a new edition carefully revised, by S. T. Bloomfield, D. D.:" "*Nephalios, ia, on, (nepho,)* sober, temperate, *abstinent, especially in respect to wine.*" The word, in the authorized version, quoted above, is translated "vigilant;" for what reason, we do not know,—neither can we see any *good* reason, why it should not be translated "abstinent," in respect to wine, according to the authority above cited. By "*wine*," if this translation be adopted, we are to understand, of course, *intoxicating* wine, carrying out and enforcing the precept originally addressed to Aaron and his sons, by God Himself, after the appalling catastrophe of Nadab and Abihu, when they were destroyed by fire, from His presence : (Leviticus x, 1, 2.)

By "*paroinon*," in the 3d verse of the same chapter, we understand, "*not given* to (*unfermented*) *wine.*" We find the word "*nephaleous*," again in the 11th verse, translated, in the authorized version, "sober,"—applied to the wives of deacons. We do not see, why it may not be translated "abstinent from wine," here, as well as in the former instance of course, meaning intoxicating, or alcoholic wine. (It is repeated, Titus ii, 2, with reference to aged men, who, in like manner, are required to be abstinent from alcoholic wine.) Thus, we find that bishops, and the wives of deacons, according to this view, are forbidden the use of alcoholic wine. But, some will probably ask : what of the deacons themselves ? Are they permitted the use of intoxicating wine ? Assuredly not. They are required, in the 8th verse, to be "not given to much wine ;" by which we are to understand, that they are not to be given to much *un*intoxicating wine,—for see, what fearful errors we should be led into, if we were to conceive, that they were allowed, by Him, "in whose sight the heavens are not clean," "and who chargeth His angels with folly," to drink of *in*toxicating wine, "the wine, wherein is excess,"—to excess—(asotia, insalvability,) as would be implied by *much*, if referred to such wine. This supposition, if valid, would be fatal to all the well-ascertained facts and principles, which we have endeavored to enunciate in former letters. It would inflict a death wound upon the cause of temperance throughout the world, and clothe weeping humanity in her most sable attire. It would produce, if possible, lamentation in heaven, and exultation in hell. It would confound the everlasting distinctions between right and wrong, truth and error. It would shake the throne of the Eternal!

But these are impossibilities, the very thought of which, were it to lay hold of the mind, would extinguish the light of reason, and extort, from the hardest heart, a wail of insufferable anguish! We should, at once, cast it from us with righteous indignation, and abhorrence, as altogether impious and atheistical, were it not that, with all its baseness, it numbers amongst its friends and advocates, **men of high note, in the** Christian world, whose arguments we must endeavor to dispose of, and whose prejudices we must endeavor **to overcome.**

1st. What is to be understood by the phrase, "not given to wine," as applied to bishops, supposing it to refer to intoxicating wine, or, as we are authorized to call it, "poisonous wine?" It would seem to have this meaning : that bishops are not to be in the habit of drinking intoxicating, or poisonous wine, in such quantities as to injure them in soul, or body, or both. How much this would be, in any, or every instance, is **not** stated ; neither is it stated, what number of **times would be** necessary to constitute a habit of drinking. All **this is left to** be decided by each individual bishop, according **to his** knowledge and inclination. But the question at once **occurs** here, how can **the** habit referred to, **and** prohibited, be injurious to the soul or body of any bishop, if each single act be not injurious ; for it is *intoxicating*, or *poisonous* drink, which is used, and what does *poisonous* mean, if not *injurious* to soul, or body, or both soul and body ? And, if each single act **must be** more or less injurious, (the nature of the thing, and **of the** man continuing the same,) how can the habit be **forbidden** without each specific act, constituting **a** part of it, being forbidden, also ? Let our opponents **give** a satisfactory answer to these questions, if they can. **We do** not see how **they can** be satisfactorily answered, according to their hypothesis, that *alcoholic* wine was intended, by the apostle Paul, in the passage quoted. If they had **taken** the pains to think, for a moment, what was the nature of **the** wine, for which they were so great sticklers, common sense would have told them, that its qualities did not, all of a sudden change their nature, by some magical power, **so** that what was not, in the least, injurious when first used, could, in an instant, become hurtful to man, (his nature remaining unchanged, also,) they would have abandoned their notions as untenable. But let us take another view of the matter:— It has been well said by the writer's grandfather, Professor John Stewart, author of a Commentary on Sir Isaac Newton's "Quadrature of Curves," and the bosom friend of Dr. Reid, the eminent Metaphysician, in an unpublished MS., that "every grand or capital precept of the moral law, necessarily supposes and includes under it, the prohibition of everything that has a **tendency to** the breach of it; and the requisition of all those things that have an evident and natural tendency, and fitness, to bring **about** the accomplishment and performance of it. Since all such things must be considered either as parts or branches of that capital precept, or as means and helps to the performance and obedience of it. This is as certainly true, as that the whole includes all the parts; and that he who would desire and accomplish any end, must desire and use the means **for** attaining that end."

Now, bearing this great truth in mind, even if the former remonstrance should be slighted, can it **be** believed, by our adversaries, that the Apostle, inspired by the Holy Spirit of truth, could have had intoxicating wine in his mind's eye, when he said: "A bishop must not be given to wine;" meaning, must not be in the habit of drinking such wine, but may take of it occasionally, when he could not have been ignorant (and they must admit,) that the use of it, in the smallest quantity, must, at least, have a tendency to intoxicate—poison—or injure the mental, or bodily faculties, or both, of him who uses it, in violation of the law of God, contained in the 6th commandment, as explained by our Saviour, in his Sermon on the mount, the immutable foundation of all true **morality.**

If the preceding reasoning, with the data upon which it is founded, be incapable of being refuted, it will apply, *a fortiori,* to the case of the deacons, next to be considered.

2d. What is to be understood by the phrase, "Not given to much wine," as applied to deacons, supposing it to refer to intoxicating wine? It would seem to have this meaning: That deacons are not to be in the habit of drinking *much* intoxicating wine, so as to be *very* injurious to them. It is evident, **that** the turn of the expression demands an interpretation consistent with license to deacons to drink a larger quantity of intoxicating, or poisonous wine, than bishops; for the phraseology in the one case, is: "Not given to wine,"—in the other: "Not given to *much* wine." But, the question at once arises here: How is it possible that God, who is "no respecter of persons," could, consistently with His infinite justice and holiness, have granted permission to one class of persons, to drink a smaller, and to another, equally dear **to Him, a larger quantity of** poisonous wine? We leave this, with the many other equally posing questions which could easily be proposed, to the solution of our adversaries; satisfying ourselves now, with saying that, **by** this interpretation of the passage, under consideration, deacons would seem to be at liberty to drink *much* intoxicating wine, at longer or shorter intervals, no matter if each separate drinking bout should be very injurious, provided it could not be said of them, they themselves, being judges, that they were habitual drinkers of intoxicating wine. We may be pardoned for noticing here, once again, in his own words, the principle so luminously and forcibly expounded by Professor Youmans; that nothing short of prohibition will prevent the evils of alcoholic intemperance,—a principle equally applicable to the

Supreme Government of Heaven, as to the subordinate governments of earth; and which, could not be binding upon the latter, if it had not emanated from, and been acted upon by, the former:

"It is in vain to urge, that Government lends its sanction only to the *moderate* employment of alcoholic beverages, and reprobates their excessive use. This is impossible. Government cannot fix the magic line, up to which, indulgence is safe and commendable, and beyond which, it is dangerous, and to be prohibited. Government must either consent to the habit, through all its imperceptible degrees of growth, or it must interdict it entirely. In this case, the beginning is everything. Put out your shoot in the soil, and the forces of nature will take care that it becomes a tree. Start your drinking habit, and the laws of nature will see to it, that it shall grow, and bear fruit after its kind. It is preposterous to attempt a defence of Government, by saying that, it only justifies a commencement of drinking practices. As well might the culprit, on trial for arson, plead innocence, on the ground that he did not burn the dwelling, but only fired a train of combustibles that led to it."

Under the present head, and, as illustrative of these views, it may be mentioned, that Timothy, himself a distinguished bishop, seems to have been, what might be called, an *ultra*-abstainer from wine, and that St. Paul seems to have deemed it right, to impress on him the necessity of using "a little wine for his stomach's sake, and his often infirmities:" (I Timothy v, 23:) or medicinally. It is, indeed, difficult to say, whether he may not have carried his principles of abstinence so far, as to deny himself the innocent gratification of drinking moderately of unfermented wine; or rather, it appears highly probable that he did so, or that he abstained from "the fruit of the vine" (Nazarite like,) altogether, except at the Lord's table. If this be a correct view, it will easily account for the seeming anomaly of the Apostle granting permission to the bishops to drink wine in small quantities; meaning, of course, unintoxicating wine, or "fruit of the vine," as implied in the expression, "*me paroinon:*" "not given to wine:" (I Timothy iii, 3;) and to deacons—subordinate officers—to drink the same, with less restraint, as implied in the phrase, "*me pollo oino prosechontas:*" "not given to much wine:" (I Timothy iii, 8.) What more natural than that the profoundly learned Apostle, when laying down rules for the guidance of bishops in the Christian church, should have his mind turned to the priests, who held a corresponding rank in the Jewish church, and the law imposed upon them, concerning wine and strong drink; a law, which in words, at least, did not extend to their assistants, the Levites? What more natural, again, than that he should carry out the injunction, laid upon the priests of the Jewish Church, to the fullest extent, in regard to the bishops of the Christian church, not in letter only, but in spirit also; and, that he should, therefore, absolutely interdict *their* use of intoxicating wine, upon all occasions?

And, finally, what more natural, than that the disinterested, noble-hearted, far-seeing Apostle of the Gentiles, after dealing with the pastors, should go on to their assistants, the deacons, and (remembering no special law under the Jewish dispensation, debarring the class corresponding to them, the Levites, from the use of intoxicating wine,) should speak to them, with reference to the unfermented "fruit of the vine," *only*, and grant them permission to use it, or *un*alcoholic, *un*intoxicating wine,—the only lawful wine of Scripture,—with somewhat greater liberty, than was conceded to the bishops, but still, under the limitation of strict temperance, as implied in the expression, "not given to much wine,"—a similar license being granted to aged women in his epistle to Titus: (Titus ii, 3.) It is hardly necessary to add, that this license is, in the nature of the case, perfectly inconsistent with the supposition, that they could have been granted liberty to drink of intoxicating wine, in the smallest quantity, by the Apostle. Reference to the epistle of Paul to Titus, another eminent minister of the Gospel, intrusted with the superintendence of the church at Crete, (Titus i, 7,) will tend to confirm the views expressed above; for there we find the very same word, "*paroinon*:" "not given to wine," made use of, in relation to bishops, which was used in the 1st epistle to Timothy; (I Timothy iii, 3;) and we see no reason why it should not be taken in the same sense, viz: "Not given to (*un*fermented) wine."

It is true, that we do not find the word "*nephaleon*," here; but, we find "*osion*," and "*egkrate*:" the one "holy," and the other "temperate;" (v. 8,)—which words, would well convey the same meaning of abstinence from intoxicating wine. We conclude, then, from the premises, that alcoholic wine is forbidden to bishops and deacons of the Christian Church.

I am, my dear brother,
Yours affectionately,
JOHN MAIR.

### LETTER XIII.

MY DEAR SIR,

Having endeavored to show, that the apostles, in their writings, extend to the office-bearers, of the Christian Church, the anti-alcoholic doctrines primarily applied to the Aaronic priesthood, in the Old Testament; we now, believing in the "analogy of faith," proceed to examine particular texts, which go to prove that the same doctrines are extended, by them, to Christians generally. The subject of this letter has been partly anticipated. Some attention has, already, been given to several texts, in former letters, (Numbers 8 and 9,) under the head of "The teachings of Science and of the Bible, respecting drunkenness, or its equivalent poisoning, in relation to the brain, and mind of man."

We shall endeavor, as far as the nature of the theme, perspicuity and precision will admit, to be brief, and avoid repetition,—but reference to certain points, before treated of, seems necessary in this place. We found, in our investigation into the nature of *drunkenness*, (No. 9,) or, the adjective corresponding to it, "*drunk*," that the **term** was not sufficiently precise, in the ordinary sense attached to it, to convey, accurately, the true meaning of Scripture, viz: That any degree of disorder, or perversion of the mental or bodily faculties, which should interfere with self-government,—hinder "**nice and accurate** distinctions between delicate shades of good and evil, **and** corresponding actions,"—"just judgment **in any** difficult **point** at issue,"—"devout sentiments,"—"**capability of** engaging in prayer to God, with faith, fear and fervor;"—or, "the faithful observance of religious ordinances,"—was a stage of "drunkenness," or its synonyme, "poisoning;" and, therefore, was interdicted in those passages of Scripture which forbid that sin; such as "Be not drunk (poisoned,) with wine, wherein is excess:" (Ephesians v, 18.) It had, also, been attempted to be **shown, by a train of** hypothetical **reasoning, (No. 7,) that one or other of the following** suppositions, **must be admitted to** be true, **viz:**

1st. That the drinking of alcoholic liquors, in **any quantity**, is injurious to man in his normal state of health.

2d. That there is a line, up to which the drinking of alcoholic liquors is not injurious to man,—but, beyond which, it is injurious,—which has not been discovered.

3d. That the line has been discovered, up to which the drinking of alcoholic liquors is **not** injurious to man, but beyond which, it is injurious.

The two first of these suppositions bear, upon their **face**, the necessity for total abstinence, in order to prevent the accession of the first stage of intoxication, or poisoning; and, the last, although according to **it, the** desiderated line has been found, would, practically, demand the same thing; for it were an utter impossibility, that every man, when drinking, could have his own physician by his side, to warn him when to stop—the **moment** the perilous point was reached—and the question could **not be** safely trusted to his own decision. But, not only have **these** difficulties to be surmounted, **before we can** fall in with the current doctrine, that it is lawful to use alcoholic liquors, in any measure, in man's normal state of health; we have, moreover, the positive testimony of Carpenter, McCulloch, Youmans, Gregory, Reid, (No. 7,) and a host of other celebrated names, in the Old and New World, to sustain us in the conclusion above arrived at, that abstinence, from alcoholic liquors, is necessary to prevent intoxication in all its stages.

The analogy of Scripture, (as far as it has been explored by us, including the interdict, of wine and strong drink, to the priests of Aaron,) of reason, science, and experience, respecting drunkenness, leads **us**, therefore, to expect, that if there *are* any apostolic precepts, concerning the use of alcoholic liquors, by Christians **in general, to** be found in the New Testament, they will be precepts of total abstinence from such drinks, in man's normal state of health.

We believe that there are such apostolic precepts, or declarations equivalent thereto, to be found in different parts of the New Testament. To certain passages bearing this interpretation, we have already referred; and, we have endeavored, by the literal translation of the words "*nepho,*" and "*nephalios,*" to draw attention **to** the fact, that apostolic testimony, in this behalf, seems to be stronger than has usually been imagined. What more proper than that the Apostle Peter, in his first epistle to the strangers, scattered throughout Pontus, Galatia, &c., suffering persecution for the cross of Christ, (I Peter i, 1–7,) after holding out to them, as incentives to resolution, and perseverance, and consolations under trials,—their high and holy destiny, and the sources of it;—"elect, according to the foreknowledge of **God**, the Father, through sanctification **of the** Spirit unto obedience and sprinkling of the blood of Jesus Christ;"—their being "begotten again unto a lively hope by the resurrection of Jesus Christ, from the dead, to an inheritance incorruptible, and undefiled, reserved in heaven for them;"—their security in Him, "kept by the power **of God,** through faith unto salvation," &c.: What more proper, we say, than that the Apostle should follow up the announcement, of these heart-stirring motives, by this spirited and pointed exhortation: "Wherefore gird up the loins of your mind, be sober, (temperate, including **abstinent from** wine, wherein is excess,) **and** hope to the end for the grace that is to be brought unto **you** at the revelation **of Jesus Christ ?"**

And so, in **like manner, what** method could have been adopted by the same Apostle, more necessary, or better suited, to secure the end he had in view, of keeping them in "the narrow way," and preserving them from relapsing into "excess of wine, revellings, banquetings," &c., after presenting to their minds, such motives as the sufferings of Christ for them, and the near approach of the **day of judgment; than that he should sum up** the whole pathetic appeal with these emphatic words: "**Be ye therefore sober, and watch unto prayer:**" (I Peter iv, 1-8:) or, as we prefer, and as we seem justified in rendering the passage, according to Barnes, (Notes **I Peter** iv, 7; and Robinson's Lexicon—*Sophronizo*:) "Be ye therefore *thoughtful*, including under it, the idea of watchful, (*sophronesate*,) and *temperate*, including under it the idea of abstinence from intoxicating wine, (*nepsate*,) **in** order to prayer. Again, what more natural, than that the same ardent Apostle, who had suffered so much from the impetuosity of his temper, **and** unwatchfulness, should enjoin upon all, to whom he addressed his first epistle, whether office-bearers, or private members of the church, along with submission, one to another, and humility, and confidence in God, (I Peter v, 5-8,) the duty of vigilance, and temperance, in these memorable words: "Be sober, be vigilant; because your adversary the Devil, as a roaring lion, walketh about, seeking whom he may devour: whom resist stedfast in the faith;" or, as we would rather see the passage translated: "Be temperate, including the idea of *not* swallowing intoxicating wine, ("*nepsate*,") be vigilant; ("*gregoresate*;") because your adversary the Devil, as a roaring lion, walketh about, seeking whom he may *swallow down*, ("*katapie*.") This rendering of the passage, we think, brings out more forcibly and fully, than that of the authorized version, what appears to be the mind of the Spirit, who would thus, by the most energetic and alarming language, draw the special attention of Christians, in every age, to the necessity of abstaining from alcoholic liquors, by arousing their fears of the tremendous consequences to be apprehended from their use, even in the smallest **quantity**. It seems highly probable that St. Peter, when he penned it, had the 7th verse of the 28th chapter of Isaiah, vividly before his mind; the figure of speech employed by him, as applicable to the Devil, being precisely the same which occurs in it, in reference to wine, thus: "But they also have erred through wine, and through strong drink are out of the way; the priest and the prophet have erred through strong drink, they are *swallowed up* of wine, they are out of the way through strong drink," &c. The day of judgment alone, will be able to reveal what havoc of human souls shall have been perpe**trated** by alcohol! Can the churches—will the churches of **Christ** make no effort, to dry up this unintermitting fountain of temporal misery and everlasting woe,—heedless of the wails of the lost millions of souls, swept, by its pestilential streams, and surging billows, into "the lake which burneth with fire and brimstone, which is the second death!" Will they still cleave to their own empirical nostrums for the cure of this monstrous malady, and persist in rejecting the sovereign remedy which God has graciously provided and revealed, for that purpose?

We subjoin a tabular view of the apostolic texts we have had under notice, in relation to this subject, as they appear in the authorized version; and, as we have ventured to render them, arranged in parallel columns, to enable the reader, at one view, to institute a comparison between them, and to judge which translation is more in harmony with "the analogy of faith," and more clearly conveys the apostolic meaning.

    I am, my dear friend,
      Yours most affectionately,
         JOHN MAIR.

## Table of Apostolic Texts on the Temperance of Christians in general.

| Precepts according to the authorized version. | Precepts according to another rendering, with remarks. | Motives to obedience. |
| --- | --- | --- |
| **ST. PAUL.** "Be not drunk with wine, wherein is excess; but be filled with the spirit." (Ephes. v. 18.) | **ST. PAUL.** Be not drunk with wine, wherein is insalubility (asotia,) (reference is here made to alcohol, the poisonous principle of wine) but be filled with the spirit. | "For ye were sometimes darkness, but now are ye light in the Lord; walk as children of light." (Ephes. v. 8.) *Therefore*, as the children of God, "abstain from wine wherein is excess." |
| "Ye are all the children of light, and the children of the day; we are not of the night, nor of darkness. Therefore let us not sleep as do others; but let us watch and be *sober*. For they that sleep sleep in the night; and they that be drunken are drunken in the night. But let us who are of the day be sober." (1 Thess. v. 5-8.) | Ye are all the children of light and the children of the day; we are not of the night, nor of darkness. Therefore let us not sleep as do others; but let us watch, and be *temperate* (including abstinent from "wine wherein is excess," *nephomes*.) For they that sleep sleep in the night, etc. But let us, who are of the day, be *temperate*, including abstinent from wine, wherein is alcohol, etc.) | For yourselves know perfectly that the day of the Lord so cometh as a thief in the night; for when they shall say peace and safety, then sudden destruction cometh upon them, as travail upon a woman with child, and they shall not escape. (1 Thess. v. 2, 3.) *Therefore*, as a "peculiar people," *abstain* from "wine wherein is excess." |
| **ST. PETER.** "Wherefore gird up the loins of your mind, be sober, and hope to the end," etc. (1 Peter, i. 13.) | **ST. PETER.** Wherefore gird up the loins of your mind (including abstinent from wine etc., "*nephontes*,") and hope to the end. Probably the analogy between the race which the Greeks ran for an earthly fading crown, and that which Christians run for a heavenly unfading crown, may have struck the Apostle, and hence the thought may have occurred to | "Elect according to the foreknowledge of God, the Father, unto obedience;" "begotten again unto a lively hope;" "to an inheritance incorruptible and undefiled;" "kept by the power of God through faith unto salvation;" "that the trial of your faith being much more precious than of gold |

# BIBLICAL TEMPERANCE. 105

him that, as loose, trailing garments would have hindered a competitor from winning the race, and receiving a corruptible crown at any of the Grecian games; and they were, therefore, ordered to be braced up, so intoxicating wine, if not refrained from, would probably prevent a Christian from winning the "race set before him," and obtaining a crown of life; and it is, therefore, interdicted by the law of God.

that perisheth, though it be tried with fire, might be found unto praise, and honor, and glory, at the appearing of Jesus Christ, whom, having not seen, ye love; in whom, though now ye see him not, yet believing, ye rejoice with joy unspeakable and full of glory." (I Peter i, 2–5, 7, 8.) *Therefore*, as redeemed with the precious blood of Christ, "*abstain* from wine wherein is excess."

But the end of all things is at hand, therefore, thoughtful (including watchful, according to Barnes, "sophronesate,") and *temperate*, (including *abstinent* from wine, etc., "nepsate,") in order to prayer.

"Forasmuch as Christ hath suffered for us in the flesh, the time past of our life may suffice us to have wrought the will of the Gentiles, when we walked in lasciviousness, lusts, excess of wine, revellings, banquetings," &c. "The end of all things is at hand." *Therefore*, as "washed, justified, sanctified" persons, abstain from "wine wherein is excess." (I Peter iv, 1–7.)

Be temperate, (including not *swallowing* "wine wherein is excess," "nepsate,") be vigilant, because your adversary, the devil, as a roaring lion, walketh about, seeking whom he may *swallow up*, or *gulp down* ("katapie.") The resemblance between this passage and Isa. xxviii, 7, is very striking. "But they also have erred through wine, and through strong drink are out of the way; the priest and

*Abstain* from "wine wherein is excess," ye elders, *because* it is your duty to "feed the flock which is among you, taking the oversight," &c.; and *because* when "the chief shepherd shall appear ye shall receive a crown of glory that fadeth not away." *Abstain* ye younger, also, whose duty it is to "submit to the elder," and to be "clothed with humil-

---

* "But the end of all things is at hand, be ye therefore sober and watch unto prayer." (I Peter, iv. 7. Comp. Luke xxi, 36.)

* "Be sober, be vigilant, because your adversary, the devil, as a roaring lion, walketh about, seeking whom he may devour." (I Peter, v. 8.)

---

* Let it be remembered that the term "sober," in modern acceptation, may include an early stage of alcoholic poisoning, (as pointed out in Letter IX) and, therefore, ought to be excluded from researches having any claim to precision.

## Table of Apostolic Texts—(Continued.)

| Precepts according to the authorized version. | Precepts according to another rendering, with remarks. | Motives to obedience. |
|---|---|---|
| | **ST. PETER.**<br><br>the prophet have erred through strong drink; they are *swallowed up* of wine; they are out of the way through strong drink; they err in vision; they stumble in judgment," and indicates Peter's familiar acquaintance with the prophecies respecting alcoholic liquors, as does his reference in the 16th verse of 1 Peter i. ("Be ye holy for I am holy,") to Lev. xi. 44, his intimate knowledge of the *Divine* prohibitory law, addressed by Jehovah to Aaron and his sons, in the 10th chapter of the same book (Lev. x. 8–11;) and it is well worthy of particular notice, that the Apostle, in the 1st verse of the chapter we have been considering, thus speaks to the elders: "The elders which are among you, I exhort, who am also an elder;" and afterwards joins the private members of the Church, as expressed in these words "Yea, all of you," (5th verse) along with them, making the injunction to abstain from wine binding upon all Christians. Comp. Lev. x. 8, 11; Ezek. xxii, 26; xliv, 21–24; Isaiah lvi, 9–12. | ity," "Yea, all of *you*," both young and old, officers of the Church, and private members, "a royal priesthood," with one accord, guard against *swallowing* down "wine wherein is excess," (asotia)—alcohol—that fearful brainpoison) "because your adversary, the devil, as a roaring lion, walketh about seeking whom he may *swallow up*, whom resist steadfast in the faith." (1 Peter v. 1–9.) |

## LETTER XIV.

My Dear Sir,

We have only one other injunction to consider under this head. It relates to Kings. The words are these: "It is not for kings to drink wine, O Lemuel, nor for princes strong drink:" (Prov. xxxi, 4.) That this prohibition may be applied to all Christians, seems evident, upon similar grounds to those already dwelt upon, in relation to priests; for all Christians are both kings and priests unto God, "and as such, the highest style of man;" and are bound to preserve their minds, at all times, capable of exercising the noble functions with which God has endowed them, in the best manner possible, (which the dietetic * use of alcoholic wine, places beyond their power,) according to His infinitely wise and holy law.

III. The alarming and opprobrious epithets given to wine and strong drink, in the Bible.

There are many alarming and opprobrious epithets given to wine and strong drink in the Bible; and, we are disposed to think, that they have the force of literal precepts against the use of these liquors, by man in his normal state of health. A man, to whom is justly attached the name of liar, or thief,—and who is commonly known under that nickname,—needs no detailed history of his departures from truth, or honesty, to warn people against him, or to make them shun his society. Hence the point of the vulgar proverb, "Give a dog a bad name, and hang him" It is enough to deter persons, who have an ordinary regard for self preservation, from venturing beyond the bounds of an enclosure, if they see inscribed on a board, in large letters, the words: "Spring Guns," or "Man Traps," set here. The practice of labelling substances as "poisons,"

---

* By dietetic use of alcoholic wine, we mean all ingestion of wine, by man, which is not medicinal.

which are deleterious to man in health,—although in sickness they may be beneficial,—is universal, where the safety of human beings is duly cared for by the State, or by individuals, where sales **of these** things are made. In these and many **other** cases, which might be mentioned, infamous, opprobrious, menacing, or alarming epithets, are deemed sufficient to prevent the evils which would otherwise be likely to occur,—and save a multitude of words. **How** admirably has this method been had recourse to, in the Bible, **in** the case of intoxicating wine, for holding **out** to mankind, **a** salutary warning of the danger they incur, by at all intermeddling with a thing so destructive of human happiness, except when sickness converts the poison into a remedy; or, to speak more correctly, the condition of the organism, and of the vital powers, so modifies its action, as **to** produce beneficial, instead of hurtful effects, upon the constitution.

Take the following, as specimens of these terrific epithets, and judge **if** they have not, or if they ought not to have, all the force of prohibitory injunctions; and to deter all persons, of sound mind, from taking liberties with that arch-poison, alcohol? "Their wine (that of the heathen,) is the poison of dragons, and the cruel venom of asps:" (Deut. xxxii, 33:) contrasted with the wine of God's ancient people, mentioned in the 14th verse of the same chapter, under the inviting appellation of the "pure blood **of** the grape." Here alcoholic wine is properly named "the cruel venom of asps;" for while *it* is so subtle and fatal as to cause death of the body in three hours,—and this kind of serpent cannot be charmed by musical sounds, as, it is said, others can: (Psalm lviii, 4, 5:)—alcohol is an evil spirit, which mounts, with wonderful rapidity, to the brain,— the seat of man's intellect,—intrenches itself there, dethrones reason and conscience, seizes the reins of government, and throws the whole microscosm into a state of disruption and misrule. Having thus usurped the government, it hurries on its wretched victim to self-destruction, or to the commission of some horrid crime, to be atoned for at the gallows; or, it causes him to rot upon the face of the earth, a lump of physical, moral, and social carrion,—loathsome, corrupting, and debasing to all around him.

We have already offered some remarks (No. 8,) upon the other phrase, in this connexion, "the poison of dragons," illustrative of the end to be served, by the association of alcoholic wine with its mighty patron, "the great dragon,—that old serpent, the devil!" The next epithet to be noticed, is "the cup of devils," or of demons,—the wine which is sacrificed to them, and which they delight in, as their life's blood,—*that*, by means of which Satan and his hosts revel in human gore, luxuriate in the profanation of God's holy name, His holy day, and other sacred institutions; whereby they stir **up and prepare** their emissaries for the perpetration **of crimes of the** greatest enormity; sapping the foundations of self-respect, blasting reputation, curdling "the milk of human kindness," converting it into poison; rendering the husband's heart cold, callous, and insensible to the piteous cries, the convulsive sobs, and passionate appeals of the wife of his bosom, and the children she has borne to him; depriving the mother of the tenderness and gentleness natural to her, and substituting, for these dove-like qualities, the ferocity of a tigress robbed of her whelps. towards her helpless offspring! "Fire Water" is the name given by the North American Indians to ardent spirits; and Robert Hall is understood to have called them, (properly plural, as signifying legion,) "double distilled d———n;" but, to us, it seems that these names, appropriately terrific though they be, **and** savoring of **the** "bottomless pit," are far less expressive of their intrinsic vileness and destructiveness, than the soul-harrowing epithets applied to them in Holy Writ, referred to above; and we are of this opinion, because these Scriptural epithets represent the Devil *himself*, and bring him, with his confederate spirits, palpably before the imagination, as the very concentration and essence of all evil; while those of man are abstract terms, denoting the qualities of a substance—terms comparatively powerless, in exciting trepidation and abhorrence! Besides, they are not binding upon conscience, as the others are, and therefore they may be disregarded with impunity, while the Divine statutes are universally obligatory.

"Wine is a mocker, strong **drink** is raging; and whosoever is deceived thereby, is not wise:" (Prov. xx, 1.)

"To mock," according to Johnson, is "to deride, to laugh at, to ridicule." "Mocker," according to the same eminent lexicographer: 1st. "One who mocks, a scorner, a scoffer:" 2d. "A deceiver, an illusory impostor." Wine, in this portion of the revealed Word of God, is personified, and described as a mocker, or as one (an evil spirit,) who laughs at, or ridicules **certain persons** or things; or scorns, or scoffs at them, as may best suit his purpose. And does not alcoholic wine answer, most accurately, to this description? Where will you find a creature so thoroughly conversant in all the arts of fraud and imposture as this creature? (the perversion of the fruit of the vine, as the Devil and other apostate spirits are of the angelic nature,) and yet, alas! grave divines, and sage moralists, are not wanting, who, afraid of a *transcendental* morality, above that of the Gospel, call it "a good creature of God." Why do they not form themselves, then, upon the model of this good creature? Why do they not adopt his system of trickery? **Why** do they not, as he does, scoff at things sacred and divine? Why do they not, as he does, bar the door of God's sanctuary, and shut their families and servants out **of** it upon the Lord's day?\* Why do they not constitute themselves the patrons and encouragers of every form of vice, crime, profligacy, and sensuality? Why do they not act consistently, and turn a deaf ear

---

\* Surely distilleries, breweries, taverns, saloons, &c., **the** Devil's and alcohol's **work-shops do** this to a monstrous extent.

to the cries of haggard, naked, squalid, beggared children, their favorite alcohol's victims? In naming it "a good creature of God," they prove that they have been "deceived by it," and therefore "are not wise;" for there is not a single unambiguous passage, which they can quote, in the whole Bible, which warrants its receiving this commendation, while it abounds with expressions of opposition and hatred to it, as an evil thing.*

The next epithet to be noticed, is, "raging," as applied to strong drink. "Strong drink is raging." By "strong drink," here, is to be understood, all other kinds of intoxicating drinks, except wine, as far as they were known to the Jews; and alcohol, being the chief poisonous principle in them all, the term is applicable now, to every species of alcoholic beverage. In Johnson's Dictionary, "to rage," is "to be in a fury, to be heated with excessive anger." Of course, it is not meant that strong drink is heated with excessive anger, (under the present phase of the subject,)—a child would know this; but that the person, using it, is on the verge of that state of mind, or has actually fallen into the vortex, where the reason is unseated, and the bestial and malignant appetites and passions dominate, like a devouring conflagration, sweeping everything before them in one tremendous mass of ruin. What must the state of that man be, who exposes himself to the impulses of unbridled passion, with all its dreadful consequences, by the use of strong drink, when this solemn warning of the Lord, is so expressly against it: "Ye have heard that it was said by them of old time, thou shalt not kill; and whosoever shall kill, shall be in danger of the judgment: But I say unto you, that whosoever shall say

---

*Another view may be taken of this passage: Instead of wine being personified as "a mocker," its victims may be considered as mockers—wine standing for wine-drinker. This is the view taken by Scott, and other commentators, and this is the light in which we shall offer a few remarks upon the following context.

unto his brother, Raca, shall be in danger of the council: but whosoever shall say, thou fool, shall be in danger of hell fire:" (Matt. v, 21, 22.)

If drinking strong drink can be a justifying cause of anger, or other evil passions, then may all the robberies and assassinations, and deeds of darkness, which have been committed by men, under the influence of intoxicating drink, be justified; and then the black list, which has been kept, of these deeds, in the book of God's remembrance, since the reign of alcohol began, will prove a dead letter, and all the executions of such criminals will have been judicial murders. But we would not have the traffickers in strong drink, or those who directly, or indirectly, encourage its use, to lay this flattering unction to their souls. He, who, in a state of intoxication, deprives a brother man of life, is, in the sight of God, we apprehend, and, according to human law, doubly guilty; first, of the crime of drunkenness, and then, of the crime of murder; nor do we see how the accessaries, to crimes of this description, whether churches, governments, distillers, brewers, or other promoters of them, can escape punishment, unless they repent, and find pardon through the merits of the Lord Jesus Christ.

For the want of some better preventive, we could wish (alas! that such a wish should be necessary,) that the rulers in Christian countries, would, under heavy penalties for omission, require every man (and he must be a member of a Christian church, in full communion,) who proposes to sell alcoholic drinks, to have erected, in a conspicuous place over his shop, or house door, a sign-board, having the following inscribed upon it, in flaming characters: "Sold here, in defiance of the Word of God, 'wine and strong drink:'" "Wine is a mocker, strong drink is raging; and whosoever is deceived thereby, is not wise:" (Prov. xx. **1**,)

"Look not thou upon the wine when it is red, when it giveth his color in the cup, when it moveth itself aright; at the last it biteth like a serpent, and stingeth like an adder:" (Prov. xxiii, 31, 32.)

"Woe unto him who giveth **his neighbor drink, that puttest** thy bottle to him, and makest him drunken also," &c.: (Hab. ii, 15.)

"Ye cannot drink the cup of the Lord, and the cup of devils:" (I Cor. x, 21.)

Each vender should, also, be required to have engraved upon every bottle, decanter, measure, or utensil, in his establishment, the following words, along with his Christian and sur-name, and the name of the church to which he belongs, viz: *Our* "wine is the poison of **dragons, and the cruel venom of asps:**" (Deut. xxxii, 33.)

"Be not among wine-bibbers," &c.: (Prov. xxiii, 20.)

"The drunkard shall come to poverty:" (Prov. xxiii, 21.)

"Be not deceived: neither fornicators, nor idolaters, . . nor drunkards, shall inherit the kingdom of God:" (I Cor. vi, 9, 10.)

I am, my dear brother,
Most affectionately yours,
JOHN MAIR.

## LETTER XV.

My Dear Sir,

The most express and comprehensive of all the statutes, against the use of intoxicating wine, remains to be considered. We refer to that contained in Prov. xxii, 31, 32: "Look not thou upon wine **when** it is red, when it giveth its color in the cup, when it moveth itself aright; at the last it biteth like a serpent, and stingeth like an adder." This precept, though primarily addressed to Solomon's son, evidently applies to all mankind, according to the word: "All Scripture is given by inspiration of God, and is profitable for doctrine, for reproof, for correction, for instruction in righteousness: that the man of God may be perfect, thoroughly furnished unto all good works:" (II Tim. iii, 16, 17.)

No one, who has observed the process of the vinous fermentation, can doubt that, in this passage, Solomon gives an accurate and beautiful description of it. It is the sole process by which the poison, *alcohol*, is generated.* The meaning of the passage, plainly is: That all persons are enjoined to keep at the greatest distance from the temptation of drinking wine, in their normal state of health; but, if it applies to all men, it must include the blind as well as those who have the use of their eyes; the meaning, therefore, must not be restricted to not looking with the organs of vision upon, or. turning them away, from "the wine when it is red;" but must apply, also, to not looking with desire of the mind upon, or turning with aversion from it, as a forbidden object; and, that this is the true sense of the passage, will be more evident, when it is remembered that the eye is the feature of the face most expressive of desire—that when its function can be exercised, it is naturally turned towards the desired object; and, that by a beautiful figure of speech, the look is put for the desire, in the instance before us.

---

*It is said, under the article Fermentation, in Rees' Cyclopedia, that the product of alcohol seems to be one of the last effects in the completion of the process of fermentation; for if the liquor is distilled while yet in a state of high fermentation, *it will not* yield a drop of alcohol. Through the kindness of Mr. Delavan, the question, as to the time when alcohol is generated, has been submitted to Professor Chandler, who, in his letter to him, of 22d September, thus writes: "The results of all my enquiries and experiments, on the subject of Fermentation, coincide with the views which I have already expressed. Alcohol is found the moment the process of fermentation begins, and the quantity continues to increase till the fermentation ceases. I have had a long conversation, **on the subject,** with Dr. Goessman, late assistant to Professor Wöhler, of Gottingen, who **has** devoted himself to organic chemistry. His views, on the subject, coincide, perfectly, with my own."

[Since the above was written, Professor Chandler has submitted the question to a series of most interesting experiments, the details and results of which are annexed at end of this Letter.]

We can hardly conceive it possible, that language could have been **made use** of, by the inspired Monarch, which could have expressed, with more aptness, or precision, his design to produce, on his reader's mind, settled aversion to alcoholic wine, (the type of all intoxicating liquors,) than that employed by him, in the text under consideration. For, 1st. He strikes, by it, a decisive blow at the *subject*, the appetitive principle in man, by the emphatic words: " Look not thou upon ;" (by this, signifying: " Do not desire, or do anything having the least tendency to enkindle desire, or to increase it.")  2d. He strikes a no less decisive blow, at the interdicted article, or object, (the moment it becomes *objectionable*, that is, as soon as alcohol has begun to generate in it,) in the graphic and pictorial words: " the wine when it is red, when it giveth his color in the cup, when it moveth itself aright;"—concluding the passage with the reasons, why he *so* objects to it,—" at the last it biteth like a serpent, and stingeth like an adder," &c.* We can conceive a philosophic and benevolent mind,—viewing drunkenness, or the effects of using intoxicating drink, as a great evil, and desirous of discovering a remedy for it,—reasoning in this manner : " I find that the **use of wine, beyond a certain limit, is injurious** to man, and ought not to be indulged in. I will restrict myself to so much daily, and I will advise all, **over whom I have** any influence, to act in a similar manner ;"—**or**, he might go a step farther, and say: " I will drink no more wine, the strength of which exceeds, so much of alcohol ;" or, " I will only drink the weakest wine ;" or, " I will not drink wine at all, which has any *superfluous* spirit in it," (that **is**, upon the almost universal supposition of Christendom, that there is *no* wine without *some*

---

* Uniting the two members of the sentence, according to the authorized version, the reading is: " Look not thou upon the wine when it is red, when it giveth his color in the cup," &c. According to the proposed paraphrase: " Do not desire, or do anything, having a tendency to enkindle, or increase desire for the wine, when it **is red**."

spirit.) This would seem to be the *ne plus ultra* of human prudence, and self-denial, in this matter. But, does not this opinion clash with the fact, that teetotalers have, for years past, gone beyond this fancied ultimatum, and abstained from intoxicating wine, and all intoxicating drinks? It seems to do so, certainly; but, we apprehend, that if the truth were known, it **might** be found, after all, that what has been claimed as a human discovery, may, unwittingly, have been derived from the sacred records; and that, somehow or other, such passages as this we are now considering, or others, referred to in former letters, may, in reading the Scriptures, have made impressions upon the minds of the early projectors of the temperance reformation, in their young days, the truths being retained long after the primary impressions were made, but the sources, whence they were obtained, being forgotten by them; and thus, not only the Bible have been deprived of its due, but the Divine sanction, which alone can give power and permanence to the doctrine of total abstinence, been kept out of sight, and out of mind, as a thing not existing. As to Mahomet, who can doubt that he, Prometheus-like, must have stolen from the heavenly records, his law against wine,—from those writings which contain more powerful testimony against its use, in one emphatic interdict, such as this memorable one, of the wisest of men, Solomon, or that other one of his (not to mention a tithe of those, to be found, elsewhere in the Bible, which frowns upon alcoholic liquors of all kinds:) " Wine is a mocker, strong drink is raging; and whosoever is deceived thereby, is not wise."

In corroboration **of** this idea, we may notice that, we have examined the Koran, **and** find only the two following passages, which have any relation to " wine," in that book: " They (the infidels,) will ask **thee, also,** concerning wine **and lots;** Answer **in** both there is **great sin, and some things of use unto men,** but their sinfulness is greater than their use."* Again, "O true believers, surely wine, and lots, and images, and divining arrows, are an abomination of the work of Satan; therefore, avoid them, that ye may prosper. Satan seeketh to sow dissension and hatred among you, by means of wine and lots, and to divert you from remembering God and your prayers. Will you not, therefore, abstain from them?"†

Who, after this information and acquaintance with the scriptures, which have been quoted in previous letters, (if at all unprejudiced,) would not return his verdict for the Bible, against the Koran, as the more formidable antagonist of alcohol, even upon the groundless supposition, that the one, as well as the other, was of Divine authority? But who, knowing the one to be a tissue of falsehoods, with a thread, here and there, of truth, spun into it, and the other, a fabric of Divine truth, without the least interweaving of error, will hesitate to declare his conviction, after prayerful and careful examination of the evidence which has been adduced in these letters, from the Bible, in favor of the Christian and universal duty of total abstinence from alcoholic liquors in man's normal state of health, except the man who is prepared to prove that the followers of Mahomet are, and have been, intellectually incapable of knowing what is a prohibition, and, therefore, have been deceived, when they imagined that their prophet prohibited *their* use of wine; or, that the testimonies of Scripture are not so strong against it, as those of the Koran; or, that much stronger arguments must be used, than those of the Bible, superadded to those of the Koran, to substantiate the doctrine of total abstinence. For our own part, we apprehend that the radical remedy applied by Solomon,—"not to look upon the wine when it is red,"—when the process of fermentation is going on in it, and alcohol is being formed; or, as we have endeavored

---

* Al Koran, (Tegg., London, 1830,) p. 29.   † Id. pp. 93, 94.

to explain the passage, (according to the spiritual character of God's law,) *not* to desire it, or do anything tending to excite, or increase the desire of *it* ;—is beyond the discovery of man's reason, unenlightened by revelation, because of the peculiarly deceitful and enticing qualities of the contained poison. Upon **what** other supposition can the repeated interdicts of alcoholic **wine,** and other alcoholic liquors, in Scripture, be accounted for, when, as far as we know, alcohol is the only material poison which is interdicted, (except by implication,) in the revealed Word of God? If **the** necessity for total abstinence **from it,** and its consequences, could have been discovered, and the duty enforced by reason, observation, experiment, or human law; would God have deviated so far from His wonted course, as to have issued so many special interdicts against it,—when He has left man to **his** own instincts, perceptive reasoning, and moral powers, aided by the light of Scripture shed upon this arch-poison, to **discover, and** when discovered, to avoid other poisonous substances? But, it is not only the duty to abstain from this *seductive*, ***poisonous thing***, which, we apprehend, could not have **been** discovered by man's natural efforts; even if that duty could have been discovered **and** performed, **the farther** *spiritual* duty, not to have a desire after anything, **with the** remotest tendency to the violation of that law, (an exemplification of the perfect system of Christian **morality,) could not have** been discovered, or if discovered, could not have been complied with, apart from the Divine authority, the evangelical motives, and awful, eternal sanctions of vital Christianity. How fitting**, then, that Solomon, in** his regal capacity, so eminent a type of the Prince of Peace, should have been the honored instrument in God's hands, first to communicate this wondrous precept in all its fulness, so fraught with blessings, to mankind ! It must ever be viewed as a splendid monument to the wisdom of this most illustrious man, proving, beyond a doubt, that his penetration into the most hidden recesses of the human heart, was of the highest order, and rendering it probable that, of **all who preceded the Redeemer, he was the one who approached nearest to the perfect standard of his master's unerring skill, in making known to the human race, the extent and spirituality of God's law,**—although, **alas! in the** practice of pure morality, he fell so infinitely short of **his Divine antitype.**

Let us look once more, "*not* upon the **wine**," which, "at the last biteth like a serpent, and stingeth like **an** adder," but upon the statute, proclaimed by Solomon **for** its destruction, and see if it is not the very summit of spiritual jurisprudence! How could he have gone farther this **way, than to interdict** looking upon**, or lusting after the wine when it assumes its red color,** (indicative of the **presence of alcohol dissolving the** coloring matter **of** the grape,) and develops **its air globules,** in the process of fermentation? seeing that, previous to this process, it is lawful and right, not only to look upon it, but to drink it, as a "good creature of God, not to be refused, if it be received with thanksgiving: For it is sanctified by the word of God and prayer:" (I Tim. iv, 4, 5.)

I am, my dear brother,

Yours most affectionately,

JOHN MAIR.

---

*Prof. Chandler's opinion on the formation of Alcohol during fermentation.*

EDWARD C. DELAVAN:

Dear sir: Perhaps you recollect that, just previous to your departure for Europe last Autumn, I reported my opinion on the formation of alcohol during fermentation. At that time I made some experiments with a view to decide the period during the fermentation, at which alcohol makes its appearance. A mixture of strawberry juice, sugar and water, was allowed to ferment, and as soon as it showed signs of fermentation was tested periodically for alcohol. I found that, as soon as fermentation was fairly set in, alcohol could be detected, the proportion of which increased daily, as long as fermentation continued.

I have arranged the results of the experiment in the form of a curved line. They sustain the opinion which I first gave, i. e., that alcohol is the direct result of the decomposition of the grape sugar. The cane sugar is first converted into **grape sugar**, by combining with water, and the grape is then dissolved, **by contact with** the decomposing ferment of the juice, into alcohol and carbonic acid.

5th day 0.03 per cent alcohol by vol.
6th day 0.15    do    do    do
**7th** day 0.50    do    do    do
**8th** day 0.85    do    do    do
12th day 1.50    do    do    do
15th day 1.84    do    do    do
18th day 2.66    do    do    do
21st day 3.00    do    do    do

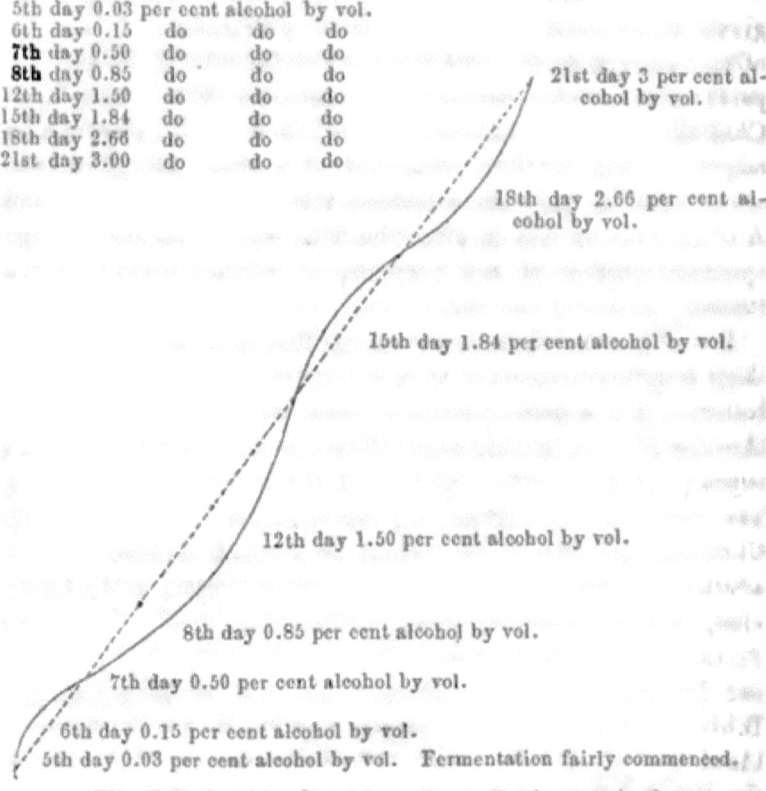

21st day 3 per cent alcohol by vol.

18th day 2.66 per cent alcohol by vol.

15th day 1.84 per cent alcohol by vol.

12th day 1.50 per cent alcohol by vol.

8th day 0.85 per cent alcohol by vol.

7th day 0.50 per cent alcohol by vol.

6th day 0.15 per cent alcohol by vol.

5th day 0.03 per cent alcohol by vol. Fermentation fairly commenced.

1st day.

The slight deviation from a constant regular increase in the percentage of alcohol is probably due to the variation of the atmospheric temperature—heat facilitating and cold retarding fermentation. You will observe the curve varies but slightly from the dotted line drawn from 5th day to the 21st day. These results are in direct opposition to the extract from Rees' Cyclopedia "Fermentation:" 'If a liquid be distilled while yet in a high state of fermentation, it will not yield a drop of alcohol.'"

Respectfully yours,
C. F. CHANDLER.

## LETTER XVI.

My Dear Sir,

The **Lord's supper** is an ordinance which has given rise to keen and envenomed controversy. It has too often been made the Shibboleth of ecclesiastical or political party spirit, or the test of qualification for office, under most Christian Governments. These and other gross errors, which might be mentioned in connexion with this ordinance, have arisen from a palpable misconception of the design of its Author, or a perverse and irrational interpretation of the perspicuous language in which He expressed Himself, at its institution.

But, it is not our intention to say anything more respecting these manifest departures from the truth of the Gospel, in these letters. We purpose to direct attention to a deviation from the rule of Scripture, in another matter, relative to the Lord's supper, which we deem of the highest importance, but which has been entirely ignored by ministers of the Gospel, and Christians generally. We allude to the use of alcoholic, or adulterated wine, instead of "the (unfermented) fruit of the vine," to represent the pure, sin-cleansing blood of the Lord Jesus Christ, at His supper. We hope to be able to prove, by and by, that the only substance which is authorized in the Bible to be used, as the proper emblem of the Redeemer's blood at "the Lord's supper," is "the (unfermented) fruit of the vine." But, previous to entering upon this investigation, it may not be amiss to say a few words in regard to the vile compounds dispensed at that sacred ordinance, and their compounders. And here we cannot do better than quote from your "Series of Letters to Professing Christians," published in 1841; and, your "Letter to the Bishops of the Episcopal Church, on the Adulteration of Liquors, &c.," 1859.

In the former you **say**: "**The** adulterations are of three kinds: that **which** is made on the spot in wine regions, and when fermented wine is both strengthened by the addition of ardent spirits, and adulterated by foreign admixtures. This kind of adulteration has a close connexion with the communion question; for, in fact, the wine considered the purest and purchased as the purest, is indebted to ardent spirit, run from the distillery, for its principal strength. As evidence of this I will state a fact, received from the lips of a large dealer and importer of wine. His conscience was aroused on the subject of Communion wine. Knowing the general imposition practiced upon the churches, he resolved to import the pure, fermented wine, free from any admixture whatever; he accordingly wrote to his agent at Madeira, giving strict orders that not a drop of ardent spirit should be added. The wine came, but, to all appearance, *undiminished in strength*. Surprised at this he determined to ascertain the cause, and wrote to his agent for a positive answer to the question: 'Was my order strictly complied with?' The reply was: 'We complied with the letter, but not the spirit of your order. We put *no* brandy into the wine, but we put the wine into the brandy, and the reason was, had we not made this addition, it would have spoiled before reaching you.' . . . . There is another kind of adulteration, far more extensive than the last. It is the pure, fermented wine, rendered more intoxicating by poisonous drugs, because the drugs used are cheaper than alcohol. Even when wine is only worth a penny a bottle, such is the cupidity of the dealer, that he will practice this kind of art to increase his gains. Is this the kind of wine proper for the Lord's table?

"But, by far, the most extensive and alarming adulterations, are the liquors sold as wine, *in which there is n.t a drop of the fruit of the vine.* This trade is one of the secrets which the day of Judgment can alone unfold. . . . . An aged divine related to me what actually took place under his own knowledge. He was called to the death-bed of a manufacturer and dealer in liquor, *called wine*. In the course of his conversation with the dying man, he put the question: 'Are the statements made in the temperance papers, respecting the adulterations of wine, true?' 'Yes,' said he, 'they are all true, and I am now suffering the deepest pangs of remorse for what I have done in this matter.' In connexion with this fact, the druggist of the town admitted, publicly, that while this trade was in its greatest state of prosperity, the sale of *sugar* of *lead* was in the greatest demand. I wonder what this dying man would have said, if he had been asked: 'Is the wine you have been making and selling, a proper substance to commemorate the dying love of that Saviour, before whom you are shortly to appear?' . . . . A gentleman of New York, of high standing, informed me, not long since, that he purchased a bottle of champagne, said to be pure as imported, and had it analyzed, and found it to contain one quarter of *an ounce* of sugar of lead; and this is the wine the higher classes are now drinking in large quantities, especially the young.[*]

"*Receipt for making good Port Wine.*—Take of good cider, four gallons; of red beets, two quarts; logwood, four ounces; rhatany root, bruised, half a pound. First infuse the logwood and rhatany root in brandy and a gallon of cider, for one week; then strain off the liquor and mix the ingredients; keep it in a cask for a month, and it will be fit to bottle.[†]

"Another dealer came to the Temperance office, while the pledge only extended to ardent spirits, and said to me: 'You are doing more good than any man in America. I do not sell one cask of ardent spirits where I used to sell twenty,—here is a hundred dollars to help you on.' I was a little surprised that this man should hand me money to destroy his business; but, on enquiry, I found he had become an extensive wine fabrica-

---

[*] The Enquirer: Vol. I, No. 1, p. 10.
[†] Letter on Adulteration of Liquors, by E. C. Delavan, p. 19.

tor—turning his ardent spirits into an article *he called wine*—and was realizing, at least, forty thousand dollars a year by this change of business.

"I once called into an establishment where the keeper was dealing out liquor to some young men; after the youths had left, I asked him if he was not aware that what he had dealt out to them, was a fabricated, drugged liquor. 'Yes,' was his immediate reply, 'I know all this—nothing would tempt me to **drink** the poisonous stuff; but they will have it, and if I do not sell it, others will.'.* Medical men, advanced in life, have assured me that the effect of using intoxicating liquors *now*, is much more fatal to health and life, than thirty years ago. Then, liquors were comparatively pure. The alcohol in them was usually the only ingredient they had to contend with; and then a habitual drinker, if he lived so long, did not become a known drunkard under twenty years; but now it frequently occurs, that the same amount of habitual drinking produces disease and intemperance in three years. This change, these medical gentlemen attribute to the presence of other poisons than the poison of alcohol, in the intoxicating liquors used by the people in such quantity. I could fill a volume with facts going to show, that as to wine, it is next to impossible to find any in this country, pure; I mean pure, fermented, unenforced wine, and I believe the same in regard to distilled spirits.† The use of strychnine, in the manufacture of whiskey, is henceforth to be punished as a felony, in Ohio. By means of this drug, used in connection with tobacco, distillers were making five gallons of whiskey from one bushel of grain; whereas the quantity obtained by the former old process, was but half as much.‡

"Hitherto, the adulterations have been gross and clumsy; logwood for coloring matter, a mild percentage of alcohol, gooseberry wine for champagne—and resin-water for every-

---

\* Letter on the Adulteration of Liquors, &c., p. 8.
† Delavan on Adulterations, **p. 16.** ‡ Id. p. 16.

thing, being the basis of the English wine market. But now more subtle chemical agents are brought into play; and, until Science **has organized a detective police** in proportion to her evil doers, we, the poor wine-bibbing public will be in a sad plight; drugged and poisoned by every wine-bottle in our bins; duped and cheated by our merchant, and his house in Bordeaux; the unresisting prey of the doctor and manufacturing chemist, melancholy spectacle of the potency of **a name, and the** ignorance of the uninitiated!

"Henceforth, **let no one** boast **of his** fruity port, of **his** tawny, or of **his** full-bodied. Those small, strong-smelling bottles, on **the dusty shelves of an** analytical chemist's laboratory, will rise **up in judgment** against him; butyric ether, **acetic** acid, and that deadly cognac oil, will **stand** out against them, accusing witnesses of **his** simplicity and ignorance. Henceforth, the mystery of wine-making **is** at an end; but wine itself is a myth, a shadow, a very Eurydice of life. There is no such thing, we verily believe, as honest grape-juice now remaining— nothing but a compound of vile, poisonous drugs, and impurely obtained alcohol; all our beautiful Anacreontics **are fables** like the rest, for wine hath died out "**from the** world, and *the laboratory is now the vineyard!*"\* Owing to **a** mysterious **disease,** called the Fideum, whose ravages destroy the **vine, the** vintage in Maderia is nearly annihilated. **From the** year 1847 to 1850, **the** annual produce of the island averaged 16,915 pipes; in 1855, the whole produce **was** 29 pipes. From 1846 to 1852, the annual produce of the upper Douro in Portugal, was 91,533 pipes; the vintage of 1856 produced, with the addition of water, only 4,000 pipes of a liquid fit only for the merest purposes of local consumption." [Talk on change.]

"Awake ye drunkards, and weep and howl, **all ye** drinkers of wine, because of the new wine, for it is **cut off** from your mouth:" (Joel i, 5.)

---

\* Dickens' Household Words.

"Yea, ten acres of vineyard shall yield one bath:" (a Jewish measure for **liquids**, containing about seven gallons and a half:) (Isaiah **v**, 10.)

A **few** remarks may now be proper, regarding the proportion of alcohol contained in the *fermented* wines of the Jews, during the sojourn of our Saviour and his apostles on earth. The Rev. Walter Henry Medhurst, in a sermon preached by him at John street chapel, Bedford Row, London, January 30th, 1838, from the text: "Add to your faith—temperance:" (II Peter i, 5, 6:) has this passage: " It will readily be granted, that the wines of Judea were far less intoxicating than the wines in common use in this country; that they were about the strength of Frontenac, or *vin de grave*, containing only 12 or 13 per cent of spirit, and this could be drunk in larger quantities, and with less injurious effects, than our brandied wines in England. Yet that they were fermented wines, and contained a certain proportion of latent alcohol, is, we think, as clear as the noon-day sun." Admitting the proportion of alcohol, above mentioned, to be correct, in regard to **the** beverages of intoxicating liquor drinkers; (but denying the accuracy of the author's conclusions as to the use of such wine, by the Jews at their passover;) let us compare *it* with the proportion of alcohol contained in the Port wine of the present day, according to the table of the distinguished chemist, Brande,* or that given by Barnes, in his Commentary.† The former estimates the proportion of alcohol in Port wine, at 22.96; the latter, highest kind, at 25.83; **lowest,** 21.40 per cent. Take the medium at 22 per cent of modern Port wine, and compare it with the medium of ancient Jewish wine, at 11 per cent, and explain the fact that each devout Jew, at the Paschal supper, was requested to drink five cups of such wine, equal to about two pints and a half of liquid, or half a pint of brandy, (brandy containing about five times the proportion of alcohol which the wine supposed

---

* Dictionary of Arts—Article Wine.   † Notes **on** John, ii, 11.

to have been used by the Jews upon that occasion did;) without bringing the gravest charge of intemperance against the parties concerned, even according to the lax views on that subject, held by moderate drinkers of the present day. Pardon this mode of appeal. We know that you spurn such an idea from you with righteous indignation, as unjust, ungenerous, and false. The preceding remarks are founded on data derived from the article "Passover," in Dr. Kitto's Cyclopædia of Biblical Literature, where it is stated, that one of the ordinances of the *Hilchoth Chametz*, (whereby are typified the four blessings expressed in Exodus vi, 6, 7,) is that all persons, whether men or women, are bound on this night to drink four cups of wine, and this number is not to be diminished. Besides these four cups, wine was also drunk during the supper. " Such a quantity of wine of the modern kind," says the writer of this article, ("about two and a half pints English,) exclusive of water, drunk by each person present, would have transformed this sacred meal into a sad scene of revelry and drunkenness, which, considering the grave and temperate habits of the ancient Jews, we are not warranted to make."

We leave these judicious and pertinent observations to speak for themselves. May they tend to open the eyes of Christian lovers of modern wines, to the impiety imbodied in their use of them at the Lord's table, for thus they act, as if it were possible that the Lord Jesus Christ, the wisest and the most benevolent of beings, could have said to His Apostles, the night in which He was betrayed, "Drink ye all of *it*;" meaning not the *corrupted* fruit of the vine *only*, but far more—the intensely deceitful, polluted, and impoisoned cup, *now* habitually and almost universally dispensed at His table, as the symbol of His precious blood!

Trusting in Divine wisdom, grace and strength, we purpose, in future letters, to treat of the Communion question, as it has been called, in the following order:

PART I. Christian duty, relative to the symbol of Christ's sin-atoning blood, to be used at "the Lord's supper."

§ 1. The Divine Rule relative to the use of "the (unfermented) fruit of the vine," at the Lord's supper, as the sole symbol of Christ's sin-atoning blood, *definite* and *unalterable*.

§ 2. The Divine Rule relative to the quantity of "the (unfermented) fruit of the vine" to be used at the Lord's supper, as the sole symbol of Christ's sin-atoning blood, *indefinite* and *discretionary*.

§ 3. When, and how often, should the Lord's supper be administered?—Questions not positively resolved by Apostolic precept, but aid afforded in answering them by Apostolic usage.

PART II. Reasons suggested for the preference given to "the (unfermented) fruit of the vine," above all other things, as the Divinely appointed symbol of the sin-atoning blood of the Lord Jesus Christ, at His supper.

§ 1. The natural fitness of "the fruit of the vine," to be the Divinely appointed *symbol* of Christ's sin-atoning blood, to be used at His supper.

§ 2. The natural fitness of "the fruit of the vine," to be the Divinely appointed *antidote* of alcoholic intemperance.

§ 3. The moral power of "the fruit of the vine," to be the *antidote* of alcoholic intemperance, from the man-perceived, Heaven-revealed relation of that fruit to, and association with, the sin-atoning blood of Immanuel; His preference to it, and appointment of it to be the sole symbol of that blood, to be used at His supper in remembrance of Him.

§ 4. The grand ultimate objects to be subserved by the preceding adaptations, "Glory to God in the highest, on earth peace, good will toward men."

I remain, my dear brother,
Yours affectionately,
JOHN MAIR.

## LETTER XVII.

My Dear Sir,

Is not the forbidden, *corrupted* "fruit of the vine," which flourishes now in the courts of the Lord's house, the counterpart presentment of the forbidden, corrupting fruit, that erst grew in the midst of the garden of Eden along with the Tree of Life? "And out of the ground made the Lord God to grow every tree that is pleasant to the sight, and good for food; the Tree of Life also in the midst of the garden, and the tree of the knowledge of good and evil:" (Gen. ii, 9.)

"And the Lord God commanded the man, saying, Of every tree of the garden thou mayest freely eat: But of the tree of the knowledge of good and evil, thou shalt not eat of it: for in the day that thou eatest thereof, thou shalt surely die:" (Gen. ii, 16, 17.)

Has it not been shown in former letters, by incontrovertible facts and arguments, that God has forbidden man to drink of the corrupted, or fermented fruit of the vine; and have not allusions been made to the dreadful punishments which have been inflicted by Him, even in this life, on the transgressors of this benign and salutary law?

On the other hand, is not the Divinely enjoined and eulogized *un*corrupted, or *un*fermented "fruit of the vine," which has been banished from the courts of the Lord's house, the counterpart presentment of the incorruptible fruit of the "Tree of Life," that erst grew in the midst of the Garden of Eden along with the tree of the knowledge of good and evil? What material thing in the world, has been so productive of evil to man, as the corrupting fruit of the forbidden tree *eaten* of by our first parents? What material thing in the world, next to the corrupting fruit of the forbidden tree, has been so productive of evil to man, as the *corrupted* and *corrupting* fruit of the forbidden tree—alcohol—*drunk of* by their progeny?

Is the Tree of Life anywhere else mentioned in the Bible, besides Genesis? **Yes,** and in such **a** way as clearly to show, that by it we **are** to understand the symbolical, or sacramental representation of the Saviour of mankind.

It is spoken of, as existing in the paradise *above*, in evident relation to the "Tree of Life"—in the paradise *beneath;* thus, "In the midst of the street of it, and on either side of the river, was there the Tree **of Life,** which bare twelve (manner of) fruits, and yielded her **fruit every month: and** the leaves of the Tree, were for the healing of the **nations**:" (Rev. xxii, 2.)

But is there anything in the Bible, to lead us to the discovery of what the Tree of Life really was? for we believe it to have been an actual fruit-bearing tree. What saith the Scripture? It is written: "I (Jesus,) am the true vine:" (John **xv, i**:) **and,** "Drink ye all of *it*." . . . . . "But I say **unto you,** I will **not** drink henceforth of **this** fruit of the vine, **until** that day when I drink it *new* with you in my Father's Kingdom;" **or, in Heaven,** according to Hammond, Bishop Hall, and others: thus, "It is not long that I shall abide with you, nor shall I again **celebrate** this or any the like feast among you, till we meet in *heaven*, and partake of those joys which are wont to be figuratively expressed by new wine."—*Hammond.*

"I will no more in this *mortal state* drink henceforth of *this fruit of the vine*, but I shall reserve myself for a more comfortable draught, sweeter than all the new wine earth can afford, which I shall enjoy in my Father's Kingdom, whereof ye shall be blessed partakers with me."—*Bishop Hall.*

**But how is** fruit of **the** vine to be **obtained** in heaven as often as it may be desired, fresh, and of superior quality to that of earth, at all seasons? The answer to this question has been already given from the Apocalypse, but that the words may be indelibly impressed upon the heart's memory, let them be repeated:

"And he shewed me a pure river of water of life, clear as

crystal, proceeding out of the throne of God and of the Lamb. In the midst of the street of it, and on either side of the river, was there the Tree of Life, which bare twelve (manner of) **fruits, and yielded her fruit every month : and the leaves of the tree were** for the healing of the nations :" (Rev. xxii, 2.)

Thus, fresh fruit would be within reach every month ; **and as** no other tree is mentioned in heaven, *but* **this one only; and as** " things which are revealed, belong unto us and to our children ;" and as Jesus pledged Himself to "drink of the fruit of the vine *new*," with His Apostles in the paradise above, the only inference which can **be drawn** from these premises is, that " the Tree **of Life** " must be the tree which will produce the fruit of the vine, to be drunk by Him and His Apostles in the regions of everlasting happiness ; or, in other words, must be the vine in its highest state of perfection. No doubt these conclusions apply, in a figurative sense, to the fruit of the vine in heaven, signifying the spiritual delights thereof; but, if it be true that the enjoyments of heaven are represented by drinking of the fruit of the vine, which is the Tree of Life, *then* it will follow, that while the vine is the Tree of Life, metaphorically in Heaven, it must, to **preserve consistency,** have been the Tree of Life *literally*, **in the garden of Eden,** before the fall of our first **parents.**

Milton, in his Paradise Lost, will throw some light upon this interesting subject. He puts the following language into the mouth of the Hierarch Raphael, giving an account of the sublime transactions connected with the apostacy of the fallen angels :

> . . . . "And what surmounts the reach
> Of human sense, I shall delineate so,
> By likening spiritual to corporal forms,
> As may express them best; tho' what if Earth
> *Be but the shadow of Heaven and things therein,*
> *Each* to other like, more than on Earth is thought?"

An evening meal in heaven, the arch-angel thus describes :

Could the Lord's supper have been in the poet's mind, when he gave utterance to these words?

> . . . . "Evening now approached—
> (For we have also our evening, and our morn
> We ours for change delectable, not need;)
> Forthwith from dance to sweet repast they turn
> Desirous; all in circles as they stood,
> Tables are set, and on a sudden pil'd
> With angel's food, and rubied nectar flows
> **In pearl, in diamond,** and in massy gold:
> *Fruit of delicious vines—the growth of Heaven.*
> On flow'rs repos'd, and with fresh flowrets crown'd,
> They eat, they drink, and in communion sweet,
> *Quaff immortality* and joy, secure
> Of surfeit, where full measure only bounds
> Excess, before the all-bounteous King who show'r'd,
> With copious hand, rejoicing in their joy."

Here, it may be remarked, how closely this most sublime of **earth's bards adheres** to Scriptural truth, in his account of the nectar of heaven, describing it as "Fruit of delicious vines— the growth of Heaven," in drinking of which, "Angels quaff immortality and joy." Is it not possible, that if our first parents had eaten of the Tree of Life prior to eating of the forbidden fruit, they too might have secured to themselves immortality? That tree being the sacramental sign and seal of life and felicity, partaking of it *in faith*, might have been instrumental in perpetuating these blessings, as partaking of **the** Lord's supper *in faith*, according to the Divine rule, would **be** in preventing apostasy, by creating a deadly hate to "the poison of dragons,"—"the wine wherein is excess,"—"the cup of Devils,"—the love of which has brought so much dishonor upon the **church of** Christ, disgraced and removed so many of **His** ambassadors from the sacred office, and annually, (according to the Rev. W. Reid,) degraded or expelled from the ranks of **His** army, 30,000 soldiers in Great Britain alone!

How different the views of Milton from those of the majority of Christians in the present day, who would make intoxicating wine the emblem of celestial delights, so that "an innumerable company of angels, and the spirits of just men made perfect," instead of "quaffing immortality and joy," pure, and unsullied, "the fruit of delicious vines—the growth of Heaven," in the paradise above, would be quaffing misery and death, and turning heaven into hell, as they drank "of the wine of the wrath of God, which is poured out without mixture into the cup of His indignation:" (Rev. xiv. 10.)

Mark how the prince of poets **judges of** the forbidden **fruit**, the counterpart of intoxicating **wine, the** darling of modern churches, which, if the use of it be persevered in at the celebration of the most precious of ordinances, bids fair to bring on a second deluge, not of *water*, (the everlasting covenant of God forbids that,) but far worse, of *fire-water!*

. . . "Sky lowr'd and muttering thunder, some sad drops
Wept at completing of the mortal sin
Original; while Adam took no thought,
Eating his fill, nor Eve to iterate
Her former trespass, fear'd the more to soothe
Him with her lov'd society, that now
As with *new wine intoxicated* both
They swim in mirth, and fancy that they feel
Divinity within them breeding wings
Wherewith to scorn the earth: *but that false fruit*
Far other operation first display'd,
Carnal desire inflaming, he on Eve
Began to cast lascivious eyes; she him
As wantonly repaid; in lust they *burn*."

Milton thus inimitably describes their melancholy state:

. . . "Soon as the force of the fallacious fruit
That with exhilarating vapor bland
About their spirits had play'd and inmost powers
*Made* err, was now exhal'd and grosser sleep,
Bred of unkindly fumes, with conscious dreams,
Encumber'd, now had left them;—up they rose
As from unrest, and each other viewing
Soon found their eyes how open'd, and their minds

12

> How darken'd; innocence, that as a vail
> Had shadow'd them from knowing ill, was gone,
> Just confidence, and native righteousness,
> And honor from about them, naked left
> To guilty shame; he cover'd, but his robe
> Uncover'd more."

A few remarks may here be offered upon this master-piece of Satanic invention, the mystery of alcohol. In the temptation practised by the Devil in Paradise, his object was to draw man into sin. By **this** temptation in regard to the fermented fruit of the vine, his object was to keep him in it, to bind him, in more adamantine chains irrecoverably to himself. He did not at first seek to deceive our first parents, by flatly telling them that the Tree of the knowledge of good and evil was the Tree of Life. He felt that he could not have been able to convince them **of a** thing **so** palpably false, as no doubt the one tree was very different in appearance from the other. Instead of that, he insinuated into the mind of the mother of the human race, a **doubt as to** the benevolence of God, and thus struck at the very **root of** all truth and virtue. Having made Adam and Eve, and with them the whole human family, the victims of his malevolence, by initiating them into the mystery of sin, he never devised a more perfect plan for rivetting its chains upon mankind, than that by which he seduced them into the belief that the seed of the woman, the Lord Jesus Christ, had appointed the *fermented* fruit **of the vine to be the** symbol of his sin-atoning blood.

Satan knew full well, that the juice **of** the grape could be changed into an intoxicating drink **by** fermentation, (for he must have remembered what was the cause of the drunkenness of Noah, **Lot, and** others,) and he resolved to watch for his opportunity to foist upon man fermented grape-juice, instead of the pure fruit of the vine, as the proper symbol of the blood of his invincible enemy.

This opportunity would offer itself when the love of Chris

tians began to wax cold—then he would find it no difficult matter to convince them, that the Saviour must have intended the "fruit of the vine," when it became elevating and exhilarating, and not till then to represent His blood; because it was so prone to fermentation, and during that process, acquired excellent and almost superhuman medicinal qualities not before possessed by it, which rendered it a most suitable emblem of that sovereign and infallible remedy for all the spiritual maladies of mankind, "the blood of the Lamb!"

Whether Satan, by this or some other ingenious artifice, succeeded in blinding the eyes of Christians to the evil nature and destructive effects of alcoholic liquors, plainly set forth in so many portions of Scripture, and keeping them in ignorance of the Divine statutes prohibiting their use, (so many of which occur in the Bible,) it is certain that they have been greatly deceived in this matter, and there can hardly be a doubt of the old Serpent having been the prime agent in the first allurement, or of his having used unabated efforts ever since to keep them in profound ignorance of the true nature of Bible temperance, by all sorts of stratagems, misrepresentations, and temptations.

All our inquiries hitherto, have led to the conclusion that the use of alcoholic liquors, by man in his normal state of health, is condemned by the word of God, and the remarks just made (if sound,) are corroborative of the same doctrine.

If we had lived before the Christian era, and possessed the same amount of knowledge upon this subject that we now do, we should have been prepared confidently to affirm, that if the Messiah, after His advent, should choose the fruit of the vine to be the symbol of His blood, it would be the *pure, unfermented* "fruit of the vine,"—not the *fermented* or *corrupted*,—which he would choose for that purpose.

In the nineteenth century after the humiliation upon earth, and exaltation into heaven of our blessed Lord, we are more confident than we could have been at any previous period, that we shall find, after rigid and impartial investigation, a perfect harmony existing between the Mosaic and Prophetical records, respecting wine of every kind, and our Divine Redeemer's choice of it in its pure state, to be the appropriate and significant symbol of His blood.

The duty of all Christians to drink only of what He used and enjoined the use of at His supper, will appear more imperatively binding as we proceed.

I remain, my dear brother,
Yours affectionately,
JOHN MAIR.

## LETTER XVIII.

My Dear Sir,

That the Divine Rule, relative to the use of "the **unfermented** fruit of the vine" at the Lord's supper, as the **sole symbol** of Christ's sin-atoning blood, is definite and unalterable, may be shown under the following heads:

### IN A CEREMONIAL POINT OF VIEW.

I. The Ceremonial Law prohibiting the existence of ferment, or any fermented article in the house of a Jew, or the use of such in a solid or liquid form (bread or wine,) at the Passover Feast, and during the seven days of unleavened *bread;* and the obligation of Jesus to obey it.

II. The *Language* used by the Evangelists, implying strict adherence to the Ceremonial Law in the use of unfermented **things** only, (bread and fruit of the vine,) at the Passover, of which our blessed Redeemer partook the night in which he was betrayed—the *Fact* that the same unfermented fruit of the vine was used by our Saviour, at the institution of His supper, as at the immediately preceding Passover supper—and the *Law* explicitly laid down by Him, strictly requiring of all Christians the use of the unfermented fruit of the vine as the symbol of His blood at His supper till His second coming.

## IN A MORAL POINT OF VIEW.

I. The Moral Law, prohibiting man in his normal state of health, from using fermented **wine, or other** alcoholic liquor, because of its signal tendency to impair and pervert the *bodily* and *mental* faculties, and prevent him from performing his duties to God, himself, or his neighbor—solemnly ratified by our Lord Jesus Christ, choosing "the unfermented fruit of the vine" to be the sole symbol of His sin-atoning blood at His supper, through all generations, till His second coming.

## IN A CEREMONIAL POINT OF VIEW.

I. *The Ceremonial* **Law** *prohibiting the existence of ferment, or any kind of fermented article in the house of a Jew, or the use of such in a solid or liquid form (bread or wine,) at the Passover Feast, or during the seven days of unleavened bread; and the obligation of Jesus to obey it.*

This Law is to be found recorded Exodus xii, 15, 19 20: xiii, 3, 6, 7: "Seven days shall ye eat unleavened bread; even the first day ye shall put away leaven out of your houses: for whosoever eateth leavened bread from the first day until the seventh, that soul shall be cut off from Israel." "There shall no leavened bread be eaten—Unleavened bread shall be eaten seven days; and there shall no leavened bread be seen with thee, neither shall there be leaven seen with thee in all thy quarters."

Dr. Lees, in the article "Leaven," Cyclopædia of Biblical Literature, remarks: "All fermented substances were prohibited in the Paschal Feast of the Jews; (Ex. xii, 15, 19, 20,) also, during the succeeding seven days, usually called the Feast of Unleavened Bread, though *bread* is not in the original."

God forbade either ferment or honey to be offered to Him, in His temple, (i. e., in the symbolical rites,) while they were permitted in offerings designed to be consumed as food;" (Num. xv, 20, 21.) And thus writes Prof. Moses Stuart: "The command, in Ex. xii, 15: xiii, 3, 7, is not expressed by *bread*, but by declaring that they should not eat *anything fermented*. Now as the word translated *eating*, is in cases without number, employed to include a partaking of all refreshments at a meal, that is of the drinks as well as of the food, the Rabbins, it would seem, interpreted the command just quoted, as extending to the *wine* as well as to the bread of the Passover. The Rabbins, therefore, in order to exclude every kind of fermentation from the Passover, taught the Jews to make a wine from raisins or dried grapes, expressly for that occasion, and this was to be drunk before it had time to ferment. . . . . . . I cannot doubt that *ferment*, in its widest sense, **was** excluded from the Jewish Passover, when the Lord's supper was first instituted; for I am not able to find evidence to make me doubt that the custom among the Jews, of excluding *fermented wine* as well as *bread*, is older than the Christian era." \*

**To the same** effect are the following quotations: "The Passover Law, in the prohibition of all fermented things, furnishes another example of symbolic teaching. Ferment was rightly viewed by the ancients **as** *corrupted* matter, and hence excluded from the purest offerings, both among the Jews and Gentiles." "The frame of mind in which we are to celebrate the Christian Passover," says Jones, "is described to us in terms borrowed from the Jewish; this feast we are to keep with the unleavened bread of sincerity and truth, free from all impure mixture of worldly affections, pharisaical **pride,** hypocrisy and false doctrine. Here we perceive, an **evil or** corrupted thing is the type of moral corruption, and could not, **therefore,** also be the appropriate type of 'the bread of life.' Bread, simply as bread in its generic sense, may be used as the symbol of pure truth; but the fermented bread, as such, cannot. Thus water, simply as water, **or** specifically clean or pure water, appropriately symbolizes the water **of** life; but tainted or bitter water cannot. Is it not evident then, from such examples, that the physical

---

\* Dr. Robinson's Bibliotheca Sacra. New York, 1843: p. 507.

qualities of such things must determine their symbolic or figurative expression." \*

In a letter, as late as 1844, from a Jew, who, previous to his conversion, was for many years a Hebrew teacher among his people, and residing in Manchester, England, there are the following passages: "All the Jews then, with whom I have ever been acquainted, are in the habit of using *unintoxicating wine* at the Passover; a wine made in this country expressly for the occasion, and generally by themselves." "In short, the Jews, as far as I know, use a perfectly *unintoxicating wine* at this delightful feast; **the reason why they do so being, that the use of the common fermented wine would be a contravention of the Law of the Passover."** †

These quotations may suffice to show, that it is the right interpretation of the language made use of by Moses, in the estimation of men versant in the literature of the Hebrews, and competent judges of the matter. But we would by no means adhere to the voice of authority, however celebrated, if opposed to common sense; and we are clearly of opinion, that the views adopted by these writers are in accordance with the dicta of this sound arbiter. What is the principle upon which the law, forbidding the use of leaven or ferment, seems to have been based? Is it not the principle of corruption? Did not the Almighty Lawgiver, prior to the promulgation of this law, by the hand of His servant Moses, clearly discern the end from the beginning? Did He not perceive that the law in its development would exert a powerful influence upon the physical, moral, and religious destinies of man? Was there in His sight an essential difference between solids and fluids, so that He should have appointed a law debarring His creature man

---

\* A Lecture on the Harmony of Teetotalism with the Divine Word, abridged from the works of Dr. Lees, p. 5.

† An earnest Appeal in behalf of Total Abstinence, addressed to Ministers of the Gospel, &c. By G. Marshall, Esq., of Nova Scotia: p. 67.

from the use of *corrupted* food under special circumstances, while under the **same** circumstances He should have deemed it unnecessary to forbid him the use of *corrupted* drink?

Does not every person of sound understanding, see how very easily a law of this sort could be evaded by converting a solid **into** a fluid substance for the occasion, as for example, bread into gruel, &c. It were perfect foolery, and worse than foolery —it were gross impiety—to **entertain** such degrading thoughts of the All-wise Ruler of **the** Universe, and of His laws which are characterized by infinite skill, and perfect adaptation to the wants of man. The natural interpretation of this **law,** is obviously this: That no corrupted thing, solid or fluid, should be in the house of a Jew, or used by him during the seven days of the Passover, because the ordinance of the Passover was **typical** or symbolical of Him who could not see corruption.

**We** proceed now to show, that it behoved our blessed **Redeemer** to adhere strictly to the requisitions of the Ceremonial **Law,** in His ordinance of the Passover Feast. Our Lord was an Israelite, or **Jew,** of the seed of Abraham, according to the flesh, (Rom. ix, 5,) and as such, the eighth day He underwent the initiatory rite of circumcision; (Lev. xii, 3: Luke ii, 21.) that rite forming an essential part of the national covenant. He was also baptized by John, (Matt. iii, 15,) for thus said He, "it becometh us to fulfil all righteousness;" and presented before the Lord at Jerusalem, (Ex. xiii, 2: Luke ii, 22.) These instances of His strict obedience to the Ceremonial Law are given, as illustrations of the truth, that being circumcised He "was a debtor to do the whole law," ceremonial as well as moral:" (Gal. v. 3.)

There can be no doubt, therefore, that He would strictly observe the Passover law, with regard to unfermented things. Indeed, His own emphatic language is conclusive upon this subject: "Think not that I am come to destroy the law, or the prophets: I am not come to destroy, but to fulfil: For verily

I say unto you, till heaven and earth pass, one jot or one tittle shall in no wise pass from the law, till all be fulfilled:" (Matt. v, 17, 18.)

II. *The Language used by the Evangelists, implying strict adherence to the Ceremonial **Law in** the use of unfermented things only (bread, and fruit of the vine,) at the Passover, of which our blessed Lord partook the night in which He was betrayed.*

It is well worthy of notice, that at the commencement of the account of the Passover supper, given by each of the Evangelists, Matthew, Mark and Luke, the nature of that supper as a meal, consisting of unfermented things, is distinctly pointed out, thus: Τῇ δὲ πρώτῃ τῶν ἀζύμων (*Te de prote ton azumon,*) in the authorized version. "Now **the first day of** the feast of unleavened bread;" literally, Now the first (day) of unleavened, or unfermented things: (Matt. xxvi, 17,) Ἤγγιζε δὲ ἡ ἑορτὴ τῶν ἀζύμων (*Eggize de e eorte ton azumon,*) in the authorized version. "Now the feast of unleavened bread drew nigh;" literally, Now the feast of unleavened, or unfermented things drew nigh: (Luke xxii, i.) And again: Ἦλθε δὲ ἡ ἡμέρα τῶν ἀζύμων (*Elthe de e hemera ton azumon,*) in the authorized version. "Then came the day of unleavened bread;" literally, Then came the day of unleavened, or unfermented things: (Luke xxii, 7.) That the rendering, we have ventured to give of these passages, is correct, will be demonstrated by attention to the following remarks, explanatory of Mark xiv, **1**: Ἦν δὲ τὸ πάσχα καὶ τὰ ἄζυμα μετὰ δύο ἡμέρας (*En de to pascha kai ta azuma meta duo hemeras,*) according to the authorized version. "After two days **was** *the feast of* the Passover, and of unleavened bread;" literally, **After two** days was the Passover and the unleavened, or unfermented things—omitting the words in italics, "*the feast of*," and using the nominative instead of the genitive case. In the twelfth verse of the same chapter: Καὶ τῇ πρώτῃ ἡμέρα τῶν αξύμων (*Kai te prote hemera ton azumon;*)

the literal rendering of the words, "And the first day of unleavened bread," is: And the first day of unleavened, or unfermented things. Our rendering of the first verse of this chapter is the only rendering which can be received, so as not to bid defiance to the most common rule of grammar—that an adjective must agree with its substantive in gender, number, and case—for *azuma* is the neuter gender, plural number, and nominative case of the **adjective** *azumos*, and if translated bread, (as it has been in **the** authorized version,) it will not agree with *artoi*, the plural number of the masculine noun "*artos*," which is the word used in the same chapter to signify bread, and in all the other Gospels; while the word "*lagana*" (supposed to be understood,) is nowhere to be found in the New Testament, if we are to receive Dr. Robinson's Lexicon, edited by Dr. Bloomfield, as competent authority upon this subject. On the other hand, the translation proposed above, viz: "unfermented things," meets all the requirements of the case, and is perfectly in accordance with the established grammatical rule in similar instances—as illustrated by the following examples—where an adjective in the neuter gender, plural number, is associated with things, (*erga*, a neuter noun plural being understood.) "Thou in thy lifetime receivedst thy good things, (*ta agatha sou*,) and likewise Lazarus evil things:" (*ta kaka*;) (Luke xvi, 25.) "If I have told you earthly things, (*ta epigeia*,) and ye believed not, how shall ye believe, if I tell **you** of heavenly things:" (*ta epourania*:) (John iii, 12.) What has been said under this head will, we trust, plainly prove that the language of the Evangelists, Matthew, Mark, and Luke, in regard to the Passover, **must** apply, not to *unfermented* bread only, but to unfermented things, (bread, and fruit of the vine.) That unfermented fruit of the vine was actually used at this Passover by our blessed Redeemer, will appear an incontrovertible fact to any one, who, with an attentive and unprejudiced mind, reads continuously from the 7th to the 18th verse of the 22d chapter of Luke's Gospel, adopting the literal translation of the 7th verse, Then came the day of unfermented things,—instead of "Then came the day of unleavened "bread, when the Passover must be killed,"—concluding with the words: "For I say unto you, I will not drink of the fruit of the vine, until the Kingdom of God shall come;" at which the account of that sacred feast ends. The contrary supposition, that the liquid used at that feast was *fermented*, would involve the impious and blasphemous assumption, that the Divine Redeemer violated the law, which He Himself had enacted; an assumption, which every Christian must repudiate **and shrink** from, with abhorrence and detestation! setting at defiance the analogy of faith, and offering cruel violence to the language of the inspired Evangelists.

*The Fact that the same unfermented fruit of the vine was used by our Saviour at the institution of His supper, as at the immediately preceding Passover supper; and the Law explicitly laid down by Him, strictly requiring of all Christians the use of the unfermented fruit of the vine, as the symbol of His blood at His supper, till His second coming.*

As it has been established, we trust, upon a foundation beyond the power of ingenuity or malevolence to shake, that unfermented bread, and fruit of the vine, were used at the last Passover, and must have been used by our Divine Master on that occasion, in accordance with His own Law; we shall hold it to be established, also, **upon** immovable foundations, that the same unfermented bread, and fruit of the vine, were used at the Lord's supper immediately following, unless the determined contenders for the use of alcoholic intoxicating wine thereat, shall bring some feasible argument to show that fermented bread and wine were substituted for unfermented, at the **end of** the one and the beginning of the other supper, not to honor and symbolize the Redeemer and His blood, but to oppose and stigmatize them. We merely ask of any honest, right-feeling, right-thinking man, to read carefully the narratives of Matthew, Mark, and Luke, upon this subject, assured that he will arrive at the same conclusion which we have arrived at, that unfermented bread and fruit of the vine, were the articles used by our Lord at the Passover supper, and at His own supper.

As to the law, explicitly laid down by Him, (our Saviour,) strictly requiring of all Christians the use of "the unfermented fruit of the vine," at His supper, much need not be said. To those who would sneer at the proposed use of unfermented fruit of the vine, and reject it, upon the ground of the ordinance of the Lord's supper being a ceremonial, or ritual appointment, and its having been the universal custom of the churches **of** Christ to dispense alcoholic, or drugged wine, from time immemorial, at the Lord's supper, as the emblem of the Redeemer's blood, we would observe: True, it is a ceremonial appointment, **(in one** sense,) as circumcision and the Passover, under the Jewish dispensation were; but as it was the duty of the Jews to perform the rite of circumcision in the prescribed manner, and to present *only* clean animals without blemish, at the Passover, and as burnt offerings, were offered up according to the ceremonial law, as typical of the one great sacrifice to be offered up in the fulness of time for "the sin of the world;" so it is the duty of all Christians, to use *only* uncorrupted fruit of the vine, as the emblem of the pure blood of the Lamb of God— the Lord Jesus Christ, who has atoned for sin on the accursed tree. We hold this doctrine to be true, and must maintain it, until all that we have written upon the subject can be proved to be erroneous; and until those who differ from us, can make it plain that there is no essential difference in the sight of God, as revealed by Him in His Word—between a drink which contains the poison, alcohol, and one which does not.

Scott, the eminent commentator, would seem to be of the same mind as to the general principle. Whether, if he were living, he would assent to our application of it, we cannot tell.

His words are these: "Indeed, ritual precepts are for the time, equally obligatory; except when they come in competition with moral duties, and then the Lord will have mercy and not sacrifice." (Exodus, Notes chap. xx, **1**.)

Upon this subject, Bishop Butler expresses himself with great energy to the same effect, in the following words: "As it is one of the peculiar weaknesses of human nature, when upon a comparison of two things, one is found to be of greater importance than the other, to consider this of scarce any importance at all; it is highly necessary that we remind ourselves, how great presumption it is, to make light of *any* institutions of Divine appointment; that our obligations to obey *all* God's commands whatever, are absolute and indispensable; and that commands *merely* positive, admitted to be from *Him*, lay us under a moral obligation to obey *them*; an obligation *moral*, in the strictest and most proper sense." *

As to a long habit of sin, affording a plea for continuing to break any, the least of God's commandments, no one who knows the exceeding sinfulness of sin, and admits the truth of St. James' position,—" Whosoever shall keep the whole law, and yet offend in one point, he is guilty of all:" (James ii, 10,)—can hold such a doctrine for a moment. We maintain, then, that it is the duty of all Christians, (in this point of view,) at the present time—and it will be the duty of all Christians, till Christ's second coming—to use unfermented fruit of the vine *only*, as the symbol of His blood at His supper, because their Lord and Master used it at the institution thereof; if it be granted that it is their duty to observe this ordinance *at all*, for we cannot conceive that He would have used *it* under such solemn circumstances, if He had not intended that all His followers should do the same upon all occasions.

---

\* The Analogy of Religion, Natural and Revealed, to the Constitution and Course of Nature. By Joseph Butler, D. C. L., late Lord Bishop of Durham. Part II, Chap. 1.

But we have other, and stronger arguments to advance. Hear the language which our blessed Lord addressed to the disciples, the night in which He was betrayed, respecting the cup which He presented to them, and its contents, and say if it is not plain, precise, and *commanding;* and if, when viewed in connexion with *that* subsequently addressed by St. Paul, primarily to the church at Corinth, and secondarily to all Christians, there can be a question as to the duty of obeying that command in relation to unfermented fruit of the vine, without evasion or prevarication?

It is necessary to remember that the *title* or *index* to the chapters in the Gospels of Matthew, Mark, and Luke, where the Lord's supper is treated of, is the unfermented things, or "the day of the unfermented things;" so that with the perfectly allowable and even required prefix—"*unfermented,*" in every instance where the cup, or "fruit of the vine," is mentioned—there can be no doubt as to the true meaning of the inspired writer. Let us examine the passages, relative to this subject, in the Gospel of Matthew, and introduce the term "unfermented fruit of the vine," where it is referred to: "And He took the cup, ('unfermented fruit of the vine,') and gave (it) to them saying, Drink ye all of it; ('unfermented fruit of the vine;') For this ('unfermented fruit of the vine,') is my blood, which is shed for many for the remission of sins. But I say unto you, I will not drink henceforth of this ('unfermented fruit of the vine,') until that day, when I drink it ('the unfermented fruit of the vine,') new with you in my Father's Kingdom:" (Matt. xxvi, 27–29.)

In these three verses, "the unfermented fruit of the vine," is five times explicitly and emphatically referred to, either with the definite article or demonstrative pronoun. We have gone over the corresponding passages in the Gospels according to Mark and Luke, in the same manner, and find that in the former there are six, and in the latter three similar references to "the fruit of the vine,"—in all, (if we have not erred,) **fourteen in number**, in six verses,—and in the 11th chapter of I Corinthians, from the 25th to the 29th verse, where St. Paul treats of the Lord's supper, six additional references—total twenty. After this can it be said, that any ritual command in the Bible is more distinctly or repeatedly laid down, or more emphatically (within so small a compass,) than that which enjoins the use of "the unfermented fruit of the vine," **as the symbol** of the Saviour's sin-atoning blood, at His supper; and if so laid down, can it be disregarded without sin?

### IN A MORAL POINT OF VIEW.

*The Moral Law prohibiting* **man, in** *his normal state of health, from* **using** *fermented* **alcoholic wine,** *or other alcoholic liquor, because of its signal tendency to impair and pervert the bodily and mental faculties, and prevent him from performing his duties to God, himself, and his neighbor —solemnly ratified by our Lord Jesus Christ, choosing the unfermented fruit of the vine to be the symbol of His sin-atoning blood, at His supper, till His second coming.*

We trust it has been made abundantly plain, in the course of this investigation, by copious references to the Divine Word, that God's moral law is specifically directed against the use of fermented, alcoholic wine, and other alcoholic liquors **by** man in his normal state of health; and *this* on account of its signal tendency to impair and pervert the bodily and mental faculties, and prevent him from performing his duties to God, himself, or his neighbor.

Scott, to whose Commentary we have so often referred, has the following judicious remarks, which, with others **quoted from** Jonathan Edwards, **in** a former letter, seem fully to justify us in the course we have pursued, in receiving the testimony of God, in whatever form communicated, as tantamount to a law against alcoholic liquors, if His disapprobation of their use has been evidently implied in that testimony. In speaking of the ten commandments, **Scott says:** " We are authorized by the example of Christ, to interpret **every** one of these commandments in **the** strictest, most spiritual, and extensive sense of which it is capable. Even repentance, and faith in a Mediator, **and** all evangelical graces and duties, are exercises of this entire love of God, and **are** required of sinners placed under **a** dispensation of mercy; though originally **the law had** no direct connexion with redemption, **but lay at the foundation** of another covenant. We **may,** therefore, **waive** the controversy concerning the *rule of duty*, whether this **be the ten** commandments, or the whole word of God; for the one, properly understood, will be found as broad as the other, seeing we cannot love God, *with all our hearts*, unless we love every discovery **which He is** pleased to make of His glory, believe every testi**mony, and** embrace every promise which He gives; seek His **favor in** the use of **all** the **means** which He appoints, and employ ourselves in diffusing **the** knowledge of His glorious excellencies and wonderful works, according to our ability and opportunity, and the **station which we** occupy in society." *

That the law against the use of alcoholic liquors, by man in his normal state of health, is part of the Divine law of love, appears to be perfectly undeniable. The law of alcohol, however, is not one-sided, and we should take an imperfect view of it, **if** we were to keep out of sight that counterpart of it, **which** concerns the medicinal use of alcoholic liquors, which **more** properly **and** strictly falls within **the** province **of** the physician. Reference has been made **to the** employment of alcohol **as** an agent in the cure of disease, **in** a former letter, where it has been shown by appeal to Professor Miller's work, "Alcohol, its Place and Power," that great watchfulness is required in its medical application. Nevertheless, it ought not

---

* The Holy Bible, containing the Old and New Testament, with explanatory notes, &c. *Notes,* Exodus **ch. xx, v.** 1.

to be forgotten that it is, at times, a useful medicine. But even in this department it must candidly be admitted, that it has often been most indiscreetly and improperly used, and no small debt of gratitude is due to Dr. Mussey, for the light which he has thrown upon the subject, in his Prize Essay on Ardent Spirits. It would almost seem as if the universal impression upon men's minds throughout Christendom had been, that not only were alcoholic drinks absolutely necessary for the preservation of health, but also that alcohol was a universal remedy for "all the ills that flesh is heir to," mental and bodily; for where, until of late years, was the liquid prescription of a physician to be met with, which had not some alcoholic ingredient?—and where was there an occasion, joyful or mournful, public or private, social or domestic, at which wine or strong drink was not introduced as indispensable? There is something amazingly absurd, as well as sinful, in the very thought that such opposite ends, as have been alluded to above, could have been accomplished by the very same heaven-appointed means.

Who, having any head at all, would dream of clothing himself with the same thick woolen clothing in the dog-days, as in the depth of winter? Who, but a madman, would propose such a thing as having the grates or stoves of his bedroom, or sitting-room, full of intensely ignited fuel, when the thermometer was at blood heat, and a few half-extinguished embers there, with the thermometer at 20° below zero? Who, in the name of common sense, would prescribe mutton-chops or plum-pudding, as diet for a patient in a high state of inflammatory fever? But all such absurdities, great as they would be, seem to have met their parallel, and more than parallel, in the presumptuous application of alcoholic liquors in the most antagonistic states of the mind and body of man; and *this* too, in the teeth of the plainest and most powerful appeals of Scripture against such a course, and in breach of laws *positive and moral*, more explicit or precise than which, never did any adorn any statute book!

We shall next endeavor to show, that the *moral law against the use of alcoholic liquors, in man's normal state of health, and by implication (if not positive statute,) for their use when necessary in disease, has been solemnly ratified (as well as carried out,) by our Lord Jesus Christ choosing the "unfermented fruit of the vine"* **to be the sole** *symbol of His sin-atoning blood at His supper, through all generations, till His second coming.*

It is well known that very generally, professing Christians have maintained the doctrine, that alcoholic wine was used by the Lord Jesus Christ at the institution of His supper, and that the same wine was commanded by Him to be used by His disci**ples,** at the future celebrations of that ordinance.

**In** recent times, a controversy has arisen upon this subject, and although a majority of professing Christians still adhere to **the** opinion, that *fermented, intoxicating* wine was the liquid which was dispensed **at the first** communion held in "the upper room," at Jerusalem, the **night** in which Jesus was betrayed; yet there are not wanting, those who feel convinced that this is a gross and unfounded error, and are assured that *unfermented, unintoxicating* "fruit of the vine" (as, we trust, has been satisfactorily proved,) was the liquid which was dispensed upon that occasion, and which, according to the command of the Lord Jesus Christ, ought always to have been dispensed at that holy meal.

Immanuel, before whose All-seeing eye, time past, present, and future, **has always** been disclosed, was perfectly aware, from all eternity, of the errors which would creep into the church, in regard to wine; and, therefore, He guarded this precious ordinance with peculiar care against misconception, and false interpretation. But that even essential truth may long remain in hopeless darkness, is well known to all who have read the history of the church, and remember the gloomy ages which preceded the dawn of the Reformation. It need not excite surprise then, that *that* which, although highly important, cannot be deemed absolutely indispensable to salvation, was permitted for a long season to be hidden from the church of Christ, and that a prominent error occupied its place, or in other words, that intoxicating wine, has for many ages supplanted "the unfermented fruit of the vine," in the belief and usage of almost, if not all Christian churches. One opposed to the doctrine we advocate, might say, because Jesus used and commanded intoxicating wine to be used at His supper, it is right for His followers to do the same. We admit the conclusion if the premises can be proved ; but, as it cannot be proved that He used intoxicating wine, and has been proved that He used and commanded to be used, "*unfermented fruit of the vine*," *at His supper*, we are entitled to take the words out of our opponent's mouth, and say, because our Saviour used unfermented, unintoxicating wine at His supper, therefore we ought to do the same. But, as he goes farther and argues that, because Jesus used intoxicating wine at His sacred meal, therefore he and his party may lawfully use it at their meals ; we, on the other hand, have an equal right to argue that, as Jesus has been proved to have used unfermented, unintoxicating wine at the institution of His supper, therefore we may lawfully use it at our ordinary meals. But, moreover, if by this affirmative command, to use *unintoxicating* wine, we are to understand by implication, a negative command also, (according to the canon of interpretation : "Negatives include affirmatives, and affirmatives include negatives,") not to use intoxicating wine at his supper, which cannot be contradicted, (bearing in mind the many instances pointed out, of the Scriptural prohibition of such wine,) will it not appear obvious that the Saviour's appointment of unfermented fruit of the vine (or wine,) to symbolize His blood, is to be taken as a solemn ratification and enforcement of the moral law against the use of intoxicating wine in every instance, in man's normal state of health? When this great truth **shall** be universally received, as no doubt it will, we believe that the recognition of this Divine appointment of "the unfermented fruit of the vine" to be the symbol of our Redeemer's blood, will be followed by the blessed consequences **to** be traced to such **a ratification. And, as** "every good and **every** perfect gift cometh **down from** the Father of lights, with whom is no variableness, **neither shadow of** turning," we can see no just reason why these **blessed** consequences should **not** be traced up to Jesus as their source, and therefore why the honor should not be given to Him, of purposing that these effects should follow, in the manner mentioned above.

**If** our opponent could show, by irrefragable arguments and indubitable facts, (such **as we** have used concerning alcoholic wine,) **that** non-alcoholic, non-intoxicating wine is specially forbidden, **in** different parts of Scripture, as an article not fit for man's use, in **any** quantity, in his normal state of health, (in addition **to proving that** alcoholic wine is commanded to be used by the **Lord, as the** symbol of His blood, at His supper,) we should certainly allow him **the** benefit of these truths to the fullest extent, in establishing and endorsing all that had been written upon the subjects of fermented and unfermented wine in the Bible, previous to the solemn hour **when** Jesus appointed (by assumption,) the fermented **wine to be the** perpetual symbol of His blood,—because **of that being the** last great public testifying act of the Redeemer, prior to the crucifixion,—intended to commemorate it forever! We *only* claim the same privilege. The Devil has not been slow to avail himself of the advantages to be derived from this argument. Although utterly false, that our Great High Priest made use of intoxicating wine as the symbol of His pure blood, or that in any of His laws, unfermented wine is prohibited; yet Satan has seduced Christians without number, into the belief of these things, as if they were truths established by the revealed word of God; and he has filled their mouths with arguments, based upon the false foundation, that alcoholic, intoxicating wine was appointed by their Lord to be the symbol of His blood, in favor of the use of the same kind of wine for the dietetic *use* of man. We do not find fault with their reasonings, but with the falsity of their premises, and therefore we do not see how they should censure our reasonings, or deny the justice of our conclusions, if they cannot annul our facts. This we give them an opportunity of doing, if they can. When the belief, that the Lord Jesus Christ instituted His sacred supper with alcoholic wine, has taken firm hold upon the mind as an established religious principle, (to gainsay which, a few years ago, would have subjected one to the charge of infidelity,) impressed upon the tender hearts of children by their parents and teachers, associated with the most important and sublime of all events, the death of the Son of God—sacramental occasions of high, spiritual enjoyment, and inspiring records of martyr heroism; we need not wonder that it should be found difficult to dislodge such a welcome guest. But, although much may be said in extenuation of the guilt of some who were inveigled in this sin in times of ignorance, yet no such palliation can be pleaded in behalf of others, who, in these days of wide-spread, accurate, scientific, and statistical knowledge, and increased Scriptural information upon this subject, will not come to the light "lest their deeds should be reproved."

Indeed, this vice (the use of intoxicating wine as the symbol of the Saviour's blood,) under the mask of virtue, although it may seem, or rather because it does seem venerable from hoary age, and honorable and sacred from intimate alliance with the atoning sacrifice of Christ, is all the more to be repented of and deprecated, seeing it has usurped a pre-eminence and power in the hearts, homes, and sanctuaries of Christians, the consequences of which are daily becoming more and more appalling, disastrous, and heaven-daring! Thus, truth is vilified, and error exalted. Thus evil is called good, and good evil; darkness put for light, and light for darkness.

According to this view, we can explain such gross perversions of texts of Scripture as the following: "Wine is a mocker, strong drink is raging:" (Prov. xx, i:) turned into, "*Excess* of wine is a mocker,—*Excess* of wine is raging." \* "It is not for kings, O Lemuel, it is not for kings to drink wine, lest they drink and forget the law:" (Prov. xxxi, 4, 5:) thus paraphrased by that excellent, but in this instance, mistaken divine, Matthew Henry: "It is not for Christians to drink *to excess*, and to allow themselves in those riotings and revellings which even the sober heathen condemned and abhorred." † What is this but to add to, and take away from the Scriptures of Divine truth, and will not St. John's awful denunciation (Rev. xxii, 19,) apply to such an **act** performed in the present day?

**So** much for the sin of adopting a glaring falsehood as an article of religious belief; and yet these instances are only atoms in the mass of evils which, if we had time, we could trace up to this origin. Thus, it has been attempted to be shown, that the rejecters of the true doctrine respecting "the unfermented fruit of the vine," and the believers in the false doctrine, that Jesus instituted His supper with alcoholic, intoxicating wine, espouse the cause of Satan's error against God's truth, and *what* is far more terrible and lamentable, put lying words (*ignorantly*, we hope—innocently, we dare not say,) into the sinless lips of Him who came to destroy the works of the Devil! Are they not (in this respect,) "the children of **the** night, and of darkness:" (I Thess. v, 5.) "They grope in the dark, without light, and he maketh them to stagger like a drunken man:" (Job xii, 25.) Do they not

---

\* A Lecture on the Harmony of Teetotalism. (Abridged.) By Dr. Lees: p. 10, &c.

† The Communicant's Companion. By Rev. Matthew Henry: p. 293.

substitute, for the steady, serene light of heaven,—capable of leading them into all truth,—the flickering glimmer produced by sparks of their own kindling, which **only serve to draw them** farther into the whirlpool of **error.**

How different the case of those who believe that Jesus instituted His sacred supper with "the unfermented fruit of the vine," as has (we trust,) been proved above, by ample Scripture testimony. They "stand up for Jesus" and His truth, in regard to temperance, against the Devil and his lies. Their eye (at least in this respect,) is single, and their whole body full of light. "They are the children of light, and the children of the day:" (I Thess. v, 5.) Their firm belief of **this one precious** guiding truth, like a pole-star, **leads them safely into a** wide, luminous region of kindred truths, before undiscovered by them, and indiscoverable by those who have no such steady, propitious light, to point their way to unexplored treasures. They are the children of wisdom, and protest against the devilish calumny, that the Lord Jesus Christ was, in the remotest sense, "a wine bibber;" meaning a drinker, or encourager of those who drink alcoholic wine, while they witness to the truth that He was the **uncompromising** enemy thereof, as a beverage for man, having at His last supper, by His choice of "the pure blood of the grape," to be the symbol of His sin-atoning blood, given His Almighty "Fiat" to every interdict of "wine and strong drink," contained in the sacred volume.

O that the churches of Christ may soon be aroused from their lethargy, and lay hold of the truth as it is in Jesus, respecting temperance!

    I am, my dear brother,
      Yours affectionately,
        JOHN MAIR.

## LETTER XIX.

My Dear Sir,

Our Creator would have us, we apprehend, to use every good creature **of** His, which He has provided for nourishment or refreshment, not beyond the point where the natural desire ceases, (although at liberty to desist sooner.) This rule applies to the drinking of "the unfermented fruit of the vine," at the Lord's supper. **Even** the wholesome, nutritious juice of the grape, which has not undergone the process of the vinous fermentation, is not to be indulged in to excess at that ordinance. But while this is true, it is no less true, that no rigid, ascetic rule is laid down in Scripture, preventing the communicant at the Lord's table from doing more than slightly tasting or sipping of "the cup of blessing," as if it were possible that our generous Benefactor, who loved us, and gave Himself for us, could have laid any undue restraint upon us, in the **use of** that which He has set apart to be not only the symbol of His own precious blood, but also the lively emblem of the enjoyments of heaven.

There is a vast difference between drinking to excess of a liquid good for man, and drinking without fear, of the same liquid. The devout communicant, at the Lord's supper, ought to be able to drink of the good wine, provided by the Master of the feast, without apprehension, that by taking a mouthful, more or less, he may do himself serious injury. But who can do this, who sits down at the communion table of almost any of the churches of the present day? The first time the writer of these letters made up his mind that he could no longer drink of the noxious liquor dispensed at the Lord's supper, he felt an acrid, burning sensation in his throat, while the so-called wine was descending into his stomach, a similar feeling to which, he doubts not, has been experienced by others under similar circumstances. A short time since, when he was discoursing with a dear friend, a highly esteemed clergyman, that humble disciple candidly owned, that he felt giddy after partaking of **the** sacramental wine at the communion **of** Christ's body and blood. Most probably he did not **swallow** more than a single mouthful. But if a mouthful would make him *vertiginous*, how much would it have required to make him *drunk*, in the common acceptation of that term? Be it remembered he is a teetotaler, and as such he would not offer a drop of intoxicating wine to any one, except at the most solemn ordinance of the **religion of** Jesus, of which he is one of the stewards; but at *that*, he has no particular **scruples hindering** him from administering it, **in** token of love to his Saviour! We do verily believe that *that* mouthful, small and insignificant as it might seem to a downright toper, was a mouthful *too much*. In other words, that **it** was a violation of the law of nature and of revelation, which would have good Christians never to venture upon such a draught, or hand the intoxicating cup one to another at the Lord's supper.

If this person had been previously a confirmed drunkard, and only recently reformed, is it not highly probable that *this mouthful* would have set him all agog, as soon as he left the sacred precincts, to obtain a larger **quantity of the fiery potation**? We cannot doubt that it would; **and, if this be true,** do we not thence derive an irrefragable argument against the use of alcoholic, and otherwise drugged wine, at the Lord's supper? For it is to be feared, there are individuals in almost every congregation who have so keen an appetite for alcoholic liquors, as only to require to have it set on edge by the communion cup, and who, from their participation of it, may **have** to date their relapse into a desperate career of "rioting **and** drunkenness!"

You spake so forcibly and pointedly upon this subject, many years ago, that we cannot refrain from introducing here, your admirable remarks. Would that they had been attended to by all Christian ministers and congregations: "It may be said by some, if these men be Christians, they will not fall before so slight a temptation." If I understand this objection, it is the **same that** might be urged against all exhortation. Paul, I think, viewed the question in a different light: "Through thy knowledge shall the weak brother perish, for whom Christ died?" This objection assumes another, and more general form, when it is said, a man who has not resolution enough to stand such a temptation, is not to be relied upon; let us ask what kind of resolution the reformed inebriate is expected to have? Moral, of course; but is this sufficient to reach the cruel and insatiate antagonist he has to contend against? His enemy is a physical evil, which has produced a moral debility,—so that upon the supposition that his moral resolution is as firm as any man's **who sits** down at the table with him, his physical nature is not equal to the same encounter; and, till this defect in his bodily frame is removed, neither his spiritual nor mortal nature has strength **to resist.** *His case is exactly like those who are predisposed to certain diseases—moral resolution is not sufficient to prevent them. It may avail before going into the region of infection, but once there he must yield to their influence.*

"The drunkard's disease slumbers within him; the moment he comes within the influence of the cause which originated it, his **longings** begin, and in too many cases, his moral resolution fails. Drunkenness is, therefore, not like some other moral evils, which **have** the seed in the thoughts, it exists immediately in the *flesh*, and through its influence holds the mind in subjection; therefore to discipline the sensual nature by entire abstinence from all that **would in** the least degree provoke the return of the disease, is not only consistent with true religion, but sound philosophy. . . . . My attention was forcibly called to this important subject, while I had charge of the Temperance

Press at Albany, on the old ardent spirit pledge. A single year brought in reports of 5,000 drunkards reformed on that pledge, in the State of New York alone ; the next year **full half of them were reported from the same sources, as having gone back to their *old habits* of intemperance, *without breaking* their pledge;on *fermented drinks*, so that on that pledge we ceased to report the reformation of drunkards.**

"Many had joined churches, and went *immediately from the alcoholic cup, received from the hands of the minister, to the grog-shop, and abandoned themselves to drunkenness, and became lost to their families, to themselves, and I fear, to heaven.*\* Though the reformation on the wide scale we **now** see it, be new, the change for which we plead, and for the same reason, has been urged for **a long time ; but then it was to** meet a single case here, and there, scattered over the country, but now their numbers can be counted by thousands. The church did not see any necessity for preparation to receive accession to her ranks from this class ; but they have come, *and she is not ready to receive them.* They have come without her aid, and certainly with but slight invitation, if any. They have come by thousands, and may come by tens of thousands. They have left the temple of Satan—the grog-shops—have **fled from** alcohol, **as from the face of the** serpent ; **and many of** them are running to the church of the living God for refuge ; and some of them are so much in earnest, that they are clinging to the horns of the altar ; but let not the infidel hear it,— they meet even there, *on the sacred altar of God, their terrible foe.*

. . . . "In examining both sides of the question, so pregnant with consequences to the reformed, converted drunkard, who can question what stand the church should take ? Now that the reformed drunkards are knocking at our church doors for admission, shall they be refused, unless they partake within its sacred precincts, **the** very substance that all their experience tells them will send them again back to drunkenness. No, I cannot believe it. The church will, without delay, inquire into the question, and will, I have no doubt, offer not only to communicants generally, but to the converted drunkard, the fruit of the vine in which there is nothing to **mock**. Some suppose the agitation of this question will re-act disastrously upon the **general** cause of temperance; to my mind, the reverse will be the result. Now the religious mind of the country is beginning to understand the question, and cannot be deceived as to the real point at issue.

"*This great and last principle*, yet to be settled in the Temperance Reform, belongs legitimately to the church, not **to** temperance societies to settle; and, should they unitedly resolve to use the 'fruit of the vine,' free from alcohol, they will set the key-stone in the arch of temperance, and by this simple act, do more for this great cause of benevolence, than all the efforts yet made. *Let her expand her doors, and proclaim to the world, that the drink of the drunkard is no longer tolerated within her walls; and the reformation will, in my judgment, then rush on to final triumph, with a rapidity that will astonish the world!*"—The Enquirer: Letter viii.

You wrote these prophetic words, which I have italicised, some eighteen years ago, and they are still prophetic. The church has not responded as you anticipated ere now, to your earnest expostulation. But the time no doubt will come, when **she will** be roused to her depths—when a movement from without if not from within, will cause her to banish alcohol forever from her sacred altars.

For this long digression, we ought to apologize to you, but we are convinced that no apology will be required by the candid reader, for introducing words of so much weight, and arguments so invincible.

As the wine used at the Lord's supper, when first instituted by our Divine Redeemer, was unfermented and *salutary*, having been made **(we** trust,) abundantly plain in previous letters, we may safely conclude that **He never** intended to impose any needless restraint upon the partakers of it. His language accordingly was: "Drink ye all of *it*:" (without stated limitation:) (Matt. xxvi, 27.)

"After the same manner also He took the cup, when He had supped, saying, This cup is the New Testament in my blood: this do ye, as oft as ye drink *it* in remembrance of me: For as often as ye eat this bread, **and drink this cup, ye do shew the Lord's death till He come**:" (I Cor. **xi, 25, 26.**)

The last passage is considered **generally, we believe, as an** encouragement to frequent communion. But if **it had** been intoxicating wine which was enjoined, it would have been unsafe to use of it frequently, even in small quantities. How much more unsafe to drink of it freely and frequently. This is a corroborative evidence of the truth of our main position, that only unfermented wine can be lawfully used to commemorate the Lord's death.

The language of Solomon may aptly be applied to those who drink with joyous liberty, of the pure blood of the grape, and might safely be put into the lips of Christ's ambassadors, at the communion of His body and blood: "Eat O friends, drink, yea drink abundantly, O beloved." **Not so with** regard to the vile, poisonous stuff which the communicant must force himself to drink, at that most sacred feast, (will he, nill he) or painful alternative, cease to be recognized as a member of Christ's visible church, and submit to be treated as "a heathen man, and a publican."

"Nevertheless the foundation of God standeth sure, having this seal, The Lord knoweth them that are His; and, let every one that nameth the name of Christ depart from iniquity:" (II Tim. ii, **19.**)

"Whether it be right in the sight of God to hearken unto you more than unto God, judge ye:" (The Acts iv, 19.)

"We ought to obey God rather than men:" (The Acts v, 29.)

We conclude, then, that the Divine Rule, relative to the quantity of "the unfermented fruit of the vine" to be used at the Lord's supper, as the symbol of Christ's sin-atoning blood, is indefinite and discretionary; or, in other words, that it is lawful for any Christian, who partakes of the Lord's supper, to drink without painful restraint, of that good creature of God, "the fruit of the vine," with thanksgiving up to the point *enough*, but not beyond it; as he would drink of milk, **or** any other wholesome beverage, provided for his use by the all-wise and bountiful Creator, and gracious, self-sacrificing Redeemer.

§ 3. When and how often, should the Lord's supper be administered? Questions not positively resolved by apostolic precept, but aid afforded in answering them by apostolic example.

**May not** the Lord's supper be justly considered as a most important part of the Lord's day? Are they not both the sacred institutions **of** King Jesus, "the sinner's friend, though sin's eternal foe?" **Are** they not intended to show forth His praise, and to glorify the Triune Jehovah, by holy, heaven-appointed means? Is it possible, that the Lord's day can be duly observed while the Lord's supper is neglected or desecrated? Does not the Lord's supper stand in the same relation to the Lord's day, as the principal meal (in the East, called supper,) does to ordinary days? The common day would be incomplete without its chief meal. The body would become enfeebled for want of sufficient nourishment; and so must the Lord's day **be** incomplete, and the soul of the Christian languish and wax faint, if it be not accompanied with the Lord's supper? If we neglect to break bread, and drink the cup of blessing every returning Lord's day, in remembrance of His death, how can we suitably and with full effect meditate upon His resurrection?

"This cup is the New Testament in my blood; this do in remembrance of me, For as often as ye eat *this* bread, and drink *this* cup, ye do shew (or, shew ye) the Lord's death till He come:" (I Cor. xi, 25, 26.)

Can these emphatic, delightful words, mean less than that we should commemorate the Lord's death as often as we commemorate His resurrection, that is, every Lord's day? But how can we do *this* with "the wine wherein is excess," (the principle of moral and physical ruin—the enemy of God and man?) That the Lord's supper was observed every Lord's day, in apostolic times, seems hardly to admit of doubt. Thus it is said: "Upon the first day of the week, when the disciples came together to break bread, Paul preached unto them:" (Acts xx, 7.)

This language would seem to convey the meaning that, "to break bread" was the chief object of the disciples in meeting together upon the Lord's day, and that the preaching was an adjunct to the ordinance, and not indispensable to its administration.

"Breaking of bread," says Scott, "or commemorating the death of Christ in the Eucharist, was one chief end of their assembling. This ordinance seems constantly to have been observed every Lord's day, and probably no professed Christians absented themselves after they had been admitted into the church, unless they lay under some censure, or had some real hindrance."

"Specially should this day (the Christian Sabbath,) be given to the commemorative feast. It was of old called 'the day of bread.'

"Unworthy is our regard to it, low is our state of devotion, if its weekly repetition could pall. It is unimaginable that the early churches ever assembled, and this was not the act of their highest transport—that Christian strangers when they met, found not in this their familiar home feast, and endeared banquet—that martyrs ever took their last embrace of each other, without being fortified by the holy signs. They died in a profession of which they were not ashamed. . . . . It was the nucleus of all worship and instruction. It gave significance and weight to all. The table of the Lord was ever spread. There the saints discerned the Lord's body, and had communion **of His** flesh and of His blood. It was the feast of charity. Blessed scenes! Why past **ye so soon** away? Why do not our hearts burn within us? Why is not this the never-failing staff of our pilgrimage? Why is not this the characteristic haunt of our discipleship? It cannot return too frequently. 'As often as ye do it.' Do we not mock that word?—remember Christ Jesus. 'This is to be done in remembrance of Him;' 'Ye do shew the Lord's death till He come.' 'Before our eyes He is evidently set forth crucified among us.'

"The practice of the first churches should be revived; the Spirit who sat on them, might then visit us with their pentecost." \*

**What** could be conceived more befitting the character and profession of the disciples of the Saviour of sinners, than when they had met together upon the Lord's day, that they should be occupied in commemorating that one sacrifice, in virtue of which, they were delivered from the guilt and bondage of sin, and made free with the liberty wherewith Christ maketh His people free. It is difficult for us to conceive how St. Paul, and **his** colleagues—all men of eminent piety—could have allowed **a** single Lord's day to pass over their heads, without commemorating Christ's dying love to their immortal souls, when we remember the persecutions which attended them; their ardent love to their once despised and crucified, but now risen and glorified Redeemer; their need of the use of every legitimate means for fanning the flame of devotion, upon the altar of their hearts; the recent institution of this holy meal; the duty of

---

\* The Christian Sabbath. By R. W. Hamilton, LL.D., D. D.

confessing their Lord and Master before men; the distinctive character of this precious ordinance, and its admirable adaptation to subserve all these purposes!

Perhaps, then, we shall not greatly err, if we look upon this solemn rite as a test of **genuine** discipleship, no less than a bond of Christian union, not delivered to us by our gracious and merciful High Priest with rigid rules, defining with strictness the exact number of times when it **shall** be observed by us, as if we needed to be coerced into the performance of a duty so sweet and attractive; but, bestowed upon us as a precious boon from heaven, which we shall be eager to partake of, **as often as** our hearts glow with fervent gratitude to Him "**who** loved us **with an** everlasting love, and gave Himself for **us,**" when we meet together to worship Him, upon His holy day.

**In accordance** with these sentiments, it would seem that the Lord's supper was administered in the church at Troas, customarily upon the Lord's day; and if so *there*, why not in all the assemblies of the saints, while yet their first love glowed with intense ardor in their hallowed bosoms?

The language used by the sacred historian Luke, **who, himself** was present upon **the occasion** referred to, **conveys the** meaning that such was the case at least at Troas, for the adverb *when,* seems to include the preceding six days, upon which the people were engaged in their secular **labors, and to** contrast them with the first day of the week, **set** apart to the special service of God; as much as to say, during the six days of lawful worldly occupation, there was **no** administration of the Lord's supper, or preaching of the word, to the whole body of the disciples taken in the aggregate, (although some of the affluent, **or** those laid aside by sickness, may have enjoyed the privilege,) but that on the sacred day of rest, "the first day **of** the week," on which Christ arose from the dead, all the Christians, without distinction of age, rank, or sex, should have the right and privilege of meeting together as "*One in Him;*" of having the Gospel preached ; and receiving the expressive memorials of Christ's body broken, and blood shed for them. The punctuality then, with which the sacred supper is administered according to the Lord's appointment, upon His day, may very properly be viewed as a test of the spiritual-mindedness and love to Christ existing in a congregation; and, *cæteris paribus*, that may be considered the most prosperous church, which most frequently commemorates the Saviour's dying love, *as* He has commanded. How could this ordinance have been administered, or be administered with highly intoxicating liquor weekly, without extreme danger to reformed drunkards, (not to speak of others,) some of whom, it is to be presumed, are to be found in almost every congregation.

What a libel it is upon Christianity and the purity of her institutions that, according to your statement, (Letter No. 15, Enquirer,) "The calculation is, that our churches consume about 80,000 gallons at the sacrament, yearly ;" (about 20,000 of pure alcohol.) "So long as the maker and vender can point to the church as a customer on so large a scale, they will throw back with contempt, the charge that they are engaged in an immoral trade."

Let Christians hold down their heads with shame, and blush at the perusal of the following melancholy narratives from the eloquent pens of distinguished ministers of the Gospel ; but **let** not *this* content them—let them be stirred up to righteous indignation, and determined, heroic, persevering action against the arch-enemy of man, and the cruel, soul-and-body-destroying poison, which has so long defiled the table of the Lord, as the root of most, if not all the evils which these writers so pathetically bemoan.

"We are a reproach amongst the nations for our drunkenness ! Drink, the demon drink has carried its ravages to the East, and many of its victims, during the last three years, have been found floating in the Golden Horn, or killed in crowds.

"Nine-tenths of the people I have seen drunk, have been *Englishmen*, and in the space of two hours, I have seen thirty swaggering and swearing in the most crowded thoroughfares of Constantinople. Often have men of other nations cast it in my teeth seeking to commend **the truth, and** painfully I had to confess to the fact.

"The influence upon others is ruinous, and **it is a fact that** probably within the last two years, one-third, yea more, of the cafés have been turned into drinking shops. Step by step the Gospel meets this dread foe, as the bitterest enemy to its triumph, and seeking to roll back the tide, is baffled **in every** effort. I appeal to every missionary **in the East wherever I have** been, **if I state not the truth, and if it is not true, that** through drink in the assemblies **of worship scarcely an Eng**-lishman is seen. If you demand facts, I can give you them from all quarters, and yet at home gentle songs are sung in favor of it. The church is silent,—Christians—many Christians are asleep—Oh! my country, my country, when shalt thou awake? Thou nursest a viper in thy bosom **which has** blighted the joy of many a household,—which has made many a mother's heart lonely, **and many a father sad,**—which has filled the prisons,—which has spread **ruin all around, and which,** like a blasting curse, has gone with thy sons to other lands, **to** hinder the truth, and make the name of Christian abhorred."— *British Messenger, April,* 1857.

Under the head of the "Doings of Drink," Dr. Guthrie, in a recent work, entitled "The City—its Sins and Sorrows," thus strongly writes about **strong** drink: "Not scared by the sanctity of the temple, it has defiled the pulpit. In all these particulars, **I speak what I know.** I have seen it **cover with a** cloud, or expose to deposition from the office **and honors of the** ministry no fewer than *ten clergymen, with some of whom I have sat down at the table of the Lord,* and all of whom I remember in the rank of acquaintances and friends." He thus delineates, "A minister at the Bar," with the pencil of a master: "Once a year, indeed, when church courts meet, our city may present a spectacle which fools may regard with indifference, but wise men with compassion and fear. A pale and haggard man, bearing the title of Reverend, stands at the bar of his church—not daring to look up, he stands there with his head buried in his hands, blushes on his face, his lips quivering, and a hell raging, burning within him, as he thinks of home—a broken-hearted wife, and the little ones so soon to leave their dear, sweet home, to shelter their innocent heads, where best, all haggard and disgraced, they may. Oh! my brother there, and oh! my brother here, learn to watch and pray that ye enter not into temptation."

Take along with these, a few scorching thoughts from the fervid breast of a brother divine, Mr. Arnot: "There is more in the public houses of Glasgow to stir the spirit of a minister, than all that Paul saw at Athens. In my ministry I meet the horrid fruits of these whiskey shops. I see men and women perishing in their pit-falls. The number of the victims is so great, that it overwhelms me. My brain is burning—my heart is breaking. The church is asleep, and the world too, and they are hugging each other. I am weary with holding in, I must cry. I would rather be counted singular in the sight of men, than be unfaithful in the judgment of God."

These are no common words, and of no common import. In characters of flame, they represent (at least to our mind,) the heart-rending state of God's church—nursing a viper in her bosom, "herself asleep, and the world too, hugging each other!" But have these excellent men, who uttered them, seen clearly what the viper is, which they have been nursing—or rather, have they realized *its presence in the communion cup?* Is it merely to the indifference of many of the watchmen on Zion's walls, and members of the church, to the astounding disclosures daily made in the public prints, of the diabolical acts of drunkards; and the desolations and the miseries, and broken hearts occasioned by them; and the tardiness of Government in applying some adequate remedy to the monster iniquity of Britain,—that they advert, in those soul-harrowing lamentations; or, have they not a strange, undefined, corroding anxiety about something in the heart's core of the Church, to which they cannot give utterance, which is marring her usefulness, and making her the butt of profane jest to her enemies? We need not repeat what *that is*,—we trust we have made it sufficiently plain in the preceding pages.

We wonder at the excesses of heathen nations—their **bestialities**—their self immolations—the destruction of their **widows and infants.** We may cease to wonder; their atrocious acts are part and parcel of their religion; and may not **the love of strong drink** be justly said to **be part** and parcel of ours, as it has been perverted by injudicious, short-sighted, prejudiced friends, or cruel and invidious enemies—not as it *is* in the Bible, or as it proceeded pure, from its infinitely wise and holy Author.

I am, my dear brother,<br>
Most affectionately yours,<br>
JOHN MAIR.

### LETTER XX.

My Dear Sir,

The reasons to be suggested for the Divine preference given to "the unfermented fruit of the vine," above all other things, as the heaven-appointed symbol of the sin-atoning blood of the Lord Jesus Christ, at His supper, may be classified under the following heads:

I. The *natural* fitness of "the fruit of the vine," to be the Divinely-appointed *symbol* of Christ's sin-atoning blood, to be used at His Supper.

II. The *natural* fitness of "the fruit of the vine," to be the Divinely-appointed *antidote* of alcoholic intemperance.

III. The *moral* power of "the fruit of the vine," to be the *antidote* of alcoholic intemperance, from the man-perceived, heaven-revealed relation of that fruit to, and association with, the sin-atoning blood of Immanuel—His preference to it, and appointment of it, to be the sole symbol of that blood, to be partaken of at His supper, in remembrance of Him.

IV. The grand ultimate objects, to be subserved by the preceding adaptations—"Glory to God in the highest, on earth peace, good will toward men."

1st. The natural fitness of "the fruit of the vine" to be the Divinely-appointed *symbol* of Christ's sin-atoning blood, to be used at His supper.

When Moses asked the Lord to show him His glory, the Lord said: "I will make all my goodness pass before thee, and I will proclaim the name of the Lord before thee, and I will be gracious to whom I will be gracious, and will shew mercy on whom I will shew mercy. And He said, thou canst not see my face: for there shall no man see me and live:" (Ex. xxxiii, 19, 20.) "No man hath seen God at any time; the only begotten Son which is in the bosom of the Father, He hath declared Him:" (John i, 18.)

All the teaching of the Bible is, by verbal or symbolic representation. We see the glory of God, *not* as it is essentially, but as it is reflected more or less vividly and distinctly in His word and works. It has been said by an author, whose name we do not recollect, that "The Gospel, together with the sacraments, is the only lawful, and the only lively picture of our Saviour." There is, then, a resemblance between the chief emblem or sign employed in the Lord's supper—"the fruit of the vine" and the blood which it represents—and the blessings which that blood has purchased; and the more perfectly the good qualities of the sign are investigated and understood, the more aid will be afforded in apprehending and appreciating the excellencies of Immanuel. "An idea of a spiritual or immaterial object, is not a thing to be learned at once, or grasped in a moment; it must enter the mind in parts and pieces, and **these parts or pieces** make good their passage into the mind, under cover of some material fact, or what we call emblem. This fact is a thing already understood; we keep it constantly before us; we fix especially upon its prominent and characteristic points; we revolve these day by day,—in them there seems to be wrapt up a principle, an idea different from them, **yet** connected with them, and with which, by reason of this connexion, we become familiar. As we contemplate this **idea, it seems to disengage itself** from its material enclosure, **and rise upwards, and we** find that **in reality** it **forms part of a higher circle of truth, and** belongs to **that very region which we had deemed so entirely inaccessible. While we knew it only in connexion with the** lower order of material facts, **we had learned to think** of it, and speak of it, by some name or sign. **That name** or sign we still retain, **now** that we have discovered that **the** suggested idea belongs to a higher and immaterial **order of** truths. This formation of ideas—this extraction of the **spiritual from** the material, **is a process** continually going **on.** It is the **natural process in the** mind of a being **composed of soul and body, and surrounded** on every side **by the** immaterial **and material world.** . . . The process of disengaging **the spiritual from the** material element, the inaccessible **from the accessible,** the incomprehensible **from the comprehensible,** is nothing **else than the** way in which the mind advances **in its onward progress** from infancy. This is the **way in** which we learn and **know,** and expand in mind and soul. The spiritual is at first unintelligible to us; we learn it by **our** observations upon **the** natural. The points where they meet, and come **in** contact with each other, **the** common principles, the common laws—these carefully pondered, gradually remove the indefiniteness of the spiritual, give them shape and distinctness, till by degrees they become equally intelligible with their cognates, while at the same time nothing of their spirituality has been parted with. It is not that we have found a material element in the spiritual, but we have found a spiritual element in the material."*

Let us endeavor to apply these principles to the case before us.

**1st.** "**The pure blood** of the grape" nearly resembles the vivifying and nutritious **sap,** which is essential to the organization and growth of the **vine, and** may be viewed **as** standing in **a** similar relation **to** it, **that the** blood **does to the life of** man, or that the blood of Jesus, which **was shed for** "**the** sin of the world," did to Immanuel. In other words, **in** "**the** pure blood of the grape," **or** "fruit of the vine," viewed sacramentally, we have a vivid representation of the atonement of Christ, or "His obedience unto death in the legal room of sinners."

**2d.** As the expressed and unfermented juice of the grape **affords a delicious,** nutritious **and** salutary drink, when mixed **with water, (called** "Sherbet" in the East,) **so** the blood of the **Lamb of God (the** atonement of Christ,) is of all blessings, **the greatest possible, because** when believed **in,** it delivers from the guilt, power and pollution of **sin,** and procures admission for the blood-bought, blood-washed soul, into the kingdom of heaven, and a right to all its immunities and privileges. This cannot be truly said of fermented, alcoholic, intoxicating wine, which has been so long unlawfully used, instead of "the pure blood of the grape," at the Lord's supper.

**3d.** The shedding of the blood **of** Jesus or His sacrificial **death,** is aptly set forth by the pressure undergone by the grape, causing the juice to flow out, and His *immutability* and *incorruptibility*, by its being preserved (by Divine commandment,) free from corruption or fermentation. A very different train of thought would naturally be suggested, by the presence of fermented wine at the Lord's table, (if the nature of the symbol were at all regarded as it ought to be;) for what is ferment?

---

\* Prophetical Land Marks. By the Rev. Horatius Bonar Kelso: p. 237.

According to Turner, "ferment, or yeast, is a substance in a state of putrefaction, the atoms of which are in continual motion." And what would such a figure applied to the soul imply, but dissolution of the moral principle—departure from original righteousness—in short, moral putrescence, or depravity ? The presence, then, at the Lord's table, of any substance undergoing, or having undergone, such a change as that above described by a distinguished chemist, as a symbol of Christ's blood, could denote nothing less than the mutability and corruptibility, or in the language of Irving, the peccability of the Lord Jesus Christ, who is "the same yesterday, and to-day, and forever; holy, harmless, undefiled, separate from sinners;" a doctrine utterly subversive of Christianity ! Moreover, the selection of unfermented bread and wine, by our gracious and merciful High Priest, to be the symbols of His body broken, and blood shed for us, ought to excite in our minds, emotions of the warmest gratitude and love to Him, for giving us tokens of His love to us, so admirably fitted to convey correct views of His essential attributes, and for debarring us from the use of those counterfeit signs, which would, if at all attended to, produce the very opposite results, and cause us to harbor doubts of the perfect righteousness, immutability, and incorruptibility of His nature, and consequent misgivings as to His ability to save us from our sins—the amazing and glorious object He had in view in becoming " God manifest in the flesh."

4th. As the judicious use of pure fruit of the vine, and pure bread, contributes largely to the formation of pure vital fluid, the great source from which all the constituent parts of the human body are derived, and by which it grows, waxes strong, and is perfected, so by the intelligent reception of a whole Christ, "whose body is meat indeed, and whose blood is drink indeed,"—or by faith in Him, the soul of the sinner, is not only first justified, but subsequently sanctified, under the influence of His word and Spirit, and grows up to Him in all things, at length attaining by continual increments of grace "unto the measure of the stature of the fulness of Christ."

To have any approach to a satisfactory idea of the absolute purity of the blood of Jesus, and its blessed, celestial, soul-saving influences, "the pure blood of the grape," in its purest possible state, must be multiplied to infinity, and viewed spiritually. Should the impure, alcoholic wine, habitually used as the emblem of Christ's blood, at His supper, be similarly treated, of what would it convey **the** most vivid **idea, if** not of the most consummate torments of Hell?

II. The natural fitness of "fruit of the vine" **to be** the Divinely-appointed *antidote* of alcoholic intemperance.

Personal observation, and the experience of others, as recorded in the annals of art or science, give no indication of the existence of a principle in "the fruit of the vine," or unfermented grape-juice, which as vaccinia (cow pock,) prevents small pox, would exert a similar power in the prevention of drunkenness, and the thousands of ills proceeding from it. Many men have eaten abundantly of grapes, fresh and dried, but it has never been observed that they obtained immunity from drunkenness, as those who milked the cows, in Gloucestershire, affected with cow pock, and who were in consequence inoculated with its virus, did from small pox.

All that the natural history of the grape teaches us is, that exquisitely formed air-proof bottles have been provided by the **God** of Nature, and a perfect mechanism, by means of which **the** gluten of the grape is prevented from coming in contact **with the** saccharine matter, while its texture remains entire, and that, therefore, while that state of things continues, the vinous fermentation, which requires the commingling of the two, cannot occur.\* It has also been remarked, that the poison

---

\* Fabroni, to whose inquiries we owe the theory of vinification, stated that sugar and gluten existed in the grape separately, and occupying distinct organs, so that the spontaneous fermentation of this fruit is impossible; but alcohol, is never generated in living structures, animal or vegetable—whence, **in** conjunction with the fact that that poison is generated by the vinous fermentation, it might have been **inferred**, that it is the duty of man to use the fruit of the vine in its unfermented state only, **as** aliment or refreshment; but no human sagacity could ever have discovered any peculiar adaptation in the fruit of the vine, fitting it to be the preventive of alcoholic intemperance. This must have been left to God only to reveal.

Believe me, my dear brother,
Yours affectionately,
JOHN MAIR.

---

### LETTER XXI.

My Dear Sir,

We **now** solicit your attention to the *Moral Power* of "the fruit of the vine" to be the *antidote* of alcoholic intemperance, from the man-perceived, heaven-revealed relation of that fruit to, and association with, the sin-atoning blood of Immanuel—His preference to it, and appointment of

---

that as soon as by any solution of continuity they are mixed, fermentation must commence. Accordingly an alcoholic odor may be perceived **in** those grapes that have been lacerated. Berzelius thought that **the** opinion **of** Fabroni was disproved, by the fact of the necessity for the **presence of oxygen in** order to the production of fermentation, whence he concluded that the manifestation **of** this action is due to the influence **of the** oxygen, and not to the mixture of the fermentable substance in the lacerated grape. I would observe on this point, that the grape contains a sufficient quantity of atmospheric air in its texture, **to** render that which it might receive being torn unnecessary; **so that if the two** substances were mixed in its interior, it is certain that **they** would meet in all the conditions necessary to fermentation. The opinion **of** Fabroni must, therefore, be admitted. Moreover, it is completely **confirmed** by anatomico-chemical observations; for on subjecting the **pulp of the grape** to the action of sulphuric acid, under the microscope, **I** ascertained **that the** sugar is contained in the vessels which form the skeleton **and** its net-work, and that the acid, glutinous pulp does not contain a particle **of** it.—*Raspail's Organic Chemistry.*—[Translated by W. Henderson, M. **D.**: pp. 336-7.]

it, to be the sole symbol of *that* blood, to be partaken of at His supper in remembrance of Him.

Here we have 1st, *The theme*—the moral power of "the fruit of the vine" to be the *antidote* of alcholic intemperance; 2d, *The source* of that moral power—the man-perceived, heaven-revealed relation of the fruit of the vine to, and association with, the sin-atoning blood of Immanuel, &c.

1st. The moral power **of the fruit** of the vine **to** be the *antidote* of alcoholic intemperance. **It is moral power** in the highest sense as an attribute of God, **and exercised by** Him that governs the Universe. All physical **power is** secondary and subservient to moral power. The more willingly we yield obedience to the rule of the uncreated, self-existent, immutable, infinitely-wise and holy God, the more we become assimilated **in character to the** Lord Jesus Christ, "who is the brightness of God's glory, and the express image of His person."

But how can there be moral power in "the fruit of the vine," and how can **it be** the antidote of alcoholic intemperance, by means of that moral power claimed for it? The moral power which fits "the fruit of **the vine**" to be the *antidote* of alcoholic intemperance, may be said to consist of all those gracious facts, associations **and** influences, which the Holy Spirit can cause to bear upon Christians out of the Holy Scriptures, in connexion with "the fruit of the vine," as the Divinely-appointed symbol of Christ's blood,—to induce them to abstain **from** drinking alcoholic liquors in their normal state of health. **This** antidote, like the holy anointing oil, (Exodus xxx. 22–25,) may therefore be viewed as consisting of several precious ingredients, to all of which, when compounded into one spiritual remedy, may **be** applied the distinctive appellation of "the fruit of the vine," i. e., sacramentally the blood of the Lamb of God, "which **taketh** away the sin of the world,"—the great centre of holy attraction, around which they all coalesce, and from which they all derive their heavenly **qualities**.

All the commandments of God are "holy and just and good," and therefore equally binding upon man; but there are certain **Divine** precepts, which **from the** supreme dignity of the person with whom they are particularly identified, the transcendently important nature of the events with which they are associated, and the signally tender character of the emotions they are fitted to excite, seem to possess superior claims to the cordial submission of all the blood-bought children **of God.** This **is** the case with the precept we now refer to. **When Jesus** pronounced the emphatic words, "Drink ye **all of it,"** He reclined at the Passover table, **in the midst of His Apostles.** He was about to lay **down His life for** "**the sin of the world,"** and for their sins in particular, **with one** solitary exception, **that** of the traitor Judas. His love **was** stronger than death— "many waters could not quench **it,"**—nay all the combined powers of earth and hell could not make the slightest impression upon it. He knew who was about to betray him—that it was one of the twelve. He knew that He should have to endure the impious jests of the infuriated populace, thirsting for His blood—that the dreadful agony of Gethsemane awaited Him, when "His sweat **should be,"** as it were, "**great drops of blood,** falling down to the ground,"—that many bulls should compass Him—yea, that "**many bulls of** Bashan **should beset Him** round,"—that "He should **be poured** out **like water,** and all His bones **be out** of joint,"—"**His heart like wax be** melted in the midst **of** His bowels,"—"His **strength be dried** up like a potsherd—**His** tongue cleave to His jaws." Above all, He knew **that ere** the work **which His Father had** given Him to do, should be accomplished, (and after praying for His murderers,) **He** should exclaim, "**It is finished!"** The Father, "whose daily delight **He** was, from everlasting, **from the** beginning, or ever **the earth** was," who had said, "Let all the angels of God worship Him," would hide His face from **Him,** so that He should be constrained to **cry** from the depths of His mysterious humiliation, "My God, my God, why hast Thou forsaken Me?" and yet having all of these and ten thousand other sources of indescribable, incomprehensible anguish of soul clearly spread out before His mental vision, resulting from the accumulated burden of a world's apostacy, guilt and ruin laid upon Him, He winced not, He faltered not—He forgot Himself that He might furnish a table for the consolation and benefit of those for whom He was about to "pour out His soul unto death;" love unparalleled, Divine, past finding out! It was on the eve preceding the completion of these heart-rending agonies, so soon to be endured upon the accursed tree, by Immanuel for sinful men, that He, with Divine dignity, sublime composure, and superhuman tenderness, instituted that supper, which was to be the sacred memorial of His death, till His second coming, "without sin unto salvation." Is it possible to conceive of events and sufferings more fraught with mighty import, more big with immortal consequences, more majestic in their character, more spirit-stirring, more heart-rending than these? Where is the soul, then, that will not respond to the appeal from the Saviour's lips, "Drink ye all of it, for *this* is *my* blood of the New Testament, which is shed for many for the remission of sins?" It has been shown before, what "*my blood*" is, sacramentally, viz: "the unfermented fruit of the vine," in its fluid form. What marvel then, that to this sacred liquid which Jesus Himself has called "*my blood*," an interest should attach, far surpassing that **which** belongs to any other substance, in the estimation of His true followers? In it, all the diversified rays of stupendous love, infinite wisdom, and matchless condescension, are concentrated—mingled with all the temporal, spiritual and eternal blessings, purchased for His disciples by His sacrificial death: He being "the True Vine," *it* is the true blood of Himself "the true vine," and all alcoholic mixtures are base counterfeits. Where can such an ennobling association as this be found, which has forever existed, and forever will exist between "the fruit of the vine," and "the blood of the Lamb?" Ransack all the repositories of science; all the museums of art; all the cabinets of antiquaries and men of taste; search out all the splendid insignia of royalty, and all the badges of distinction which have been conferred upon men for their illustrious deeds, handed down from the remotest ages to the present time; and out of all the vast collection select one, the most admired object, around which cluster the most endearing and cherished associations of power, wisdom and virtue, and it will be a child's toy—a mere bauble—a tawdry, worthless gewgaw—when **compared** with the precious, peerless **fruit of the vine,** destined **of God the Father, from all** eternity, **to** enrich **"the Tree of Life"** in Eden, before the Fall, to be the sacred symbol indissolubly associated with the sin-atoning blood of His only begotten Son in this apostate world, where He died for our salvation, at length to be exalted forever to adorn the banks of "the River of Life," in the New Jerusalem, and afford delicious refreshment to the redeemed in glory! But some one may say, You are making too much of a mere material object, and run the risk of idolizing "the fruit of the vine." Not so; we only go as far as the Spirit of Holy Writ authorizes us, and the epithets made use **of there** imply, that it has been designed and fitted by infinite wisdom and goodness, to be the mute and involuntary servant **of God in** working out a great temperance reformation, particularly wanted at this present time, which, when accomplished, will bring in a rich revenue of glory "unto Him that sitteth upon the throne, and unto the Lamb forever and ever!" There is a most essential and never-to-be-forgotten difference between an image devised and executed by man to represent God, contrary to His express commandment, and a symbol, designed, prepared and commanded by Him, to be used as a sacred memorial of Him. This is the character, and these are a few of the claims which "the fruit of the vine" has upon all true-hearted

Christians, as the Divinely-planned, produced, and appointed emblem of Immanuel's blood: It is to be used as Jesus has commanded, at His supper, not that it may be honored or loved for its own sake, far less idolized, (as that arch-poison alcohol, which has usurped its place in the sanctuary, is so prone to be,) but that it may be highly esteemed for His sake who so signally distinguished it, by choosing it to be the symbol of His blood; and may aid His faithful followers in honoring, loving, and glorifying Him, the God-man, who made use of it first for that purpose, and next (as we hope to be able to show,) for the purpose of drying up the flood of alcoholic intemperance!

We assume that, if "the fruit of the vine" had retained its place as the sole symbol of our Redeemer's sin-atoning blood, at His table, it would have greatly abated, if not entirely prevented, the desolating flood of alcoholic intemperance which has deluged the Christian church, and through it, much of the heathen world, since it was supplanted in the sanctuary by the intoxicating cup. And this we do, because we believe that while the fruit of the vine was faithfully being dispensed at the sacred feast, according to the master's pious injunction, the eye of the church would be kept in a sound state, by Him, and thus enabled to behold His character accurately reflected in it, (a mirror adapted by Him to that end,) as the uncompromising enemy of all "fleshly lusts (including drunkenness, its causes and effects,) which war against the soul." The arguments hitherto adduced by us, in support of the doctrine of "the fruit of the vine" being the Divinely-appointed antidote of alcoholic intemperance, are such as would naturally occur to a believer in that doctrine, who had never transgressed the law which commands the use of unfermented wine at the Lord's supper. But it is evident that the members of the church of Christ, in the present day, with few exceptions, are very differently circumstanced—they have habitually broken that law, so explicitly laid down in the Gospels of Matthew, Mark and Luke, by making use of intoxicating, alcoholic, and often otherwise **impoisoned** wine, at the Lord's supper; and, therefore, ought to be addressed as persons, of whom is required Godly sorrow for *that* sin, and "true repentance unto salvation not to be repented of." Thus we are called to view our theme from a different stand-point, and as he who has been in the habit of yielding to any grievous, besetting sin, deeming it a light matter, when awakened to a sense of his guilt and danger, can no longer treat it as a little one, **but as an aggravated offence against God, and against mankind, so, we** hope, that **the sin of habitually using intoxicating wine at the Lord's supper may be brought home to many hearts and consciences,** "in demonstration of the Spirit," **and** "**in the power of God,**" so as to lead **not only to the abandonment of the** baleful potion at the feast **of peace** and love, but to such a reactionary hatred of it, as will cause it to be branded with infamy and driven from the haunts of civilization, except in cases where, like opium and other narcotic drugs, it may be legitimately used in salutary medicinal prescriptions. A few of the ingredients of this antidote may here be **touched upon,** beginning with the bitter **ones,** and the **first person singular** may be used, for the sake of greater point and vividness. "Godly sorrow" first presents itself, **for my having so long** prostituted the Lord's supper to base purposes; the dishonor of my Saviour's hallowed name; and the physical, intellectual and moral bane of those who looked to me for an example; by my use of a **vile,** filthy mixture of poisonous and disgusting matters to symbolize His most pure and precious blood, at the most sacred of all His ordinances. Next comes abhorrence of Satan, for tempting me to commit this grievous sin; and **of myself, for** so long listening to his false and blasphemous insinuations; and yielding to his seductive voice, in drinking of that soul-and-body-destroying, alcoholic poison; believing it possible, that

16

such could be the emblem chosen by my Saviour as the pledge and proof of His everlasting love! Gratitude to my Saviour—God—should be pre-eminently mine, for emancipating me by His word and Spirit, from the galling bondage in which I was so long enthralled, while I received at second hand such false representations of "the cup of the Lord," "the cup of salvation," and "of blessing;" and neglected, diligently and prayerfully to "search the Scriptures" for myself, to see "whether those things were so." And now, let me rejoice with all my heart, that God has been graciously pleased to bestow upon me, and other poor sinners, such a sweet and blessed cup, not only not corrupted and poisonous, (a thing indeed impossible, though so long believed,) but refreshing and nutritious to drink, in remembrance of Him; instead of alcoholic wine, which is "a mocker," or "strong drink," which "is raging," like their progenitor and patron, "the father of lies," and "murderer from the beginning!"

The arch enemy of mankind—the Devil—succeeded in tempting Adam and Eve by one kind of lie—in making them believe, that by eating of the fruit of the tree of knowledge of good and evil, their minds would be enlarged and enlightened; and, that it was unkind in God to keep it from them. Having added to his craftiness by experience, and failed in his attempts to ensnare the Saviour of the world—nourishing a bitter, rancorous hatred against Him, for befriending mankind—he determined to do his utmost to ruin them by a new device, and has succeeded so far, marvellously in the attempt, by inducing so many to believe that their blessed Lord bequeathed to them as a good thing, that intoxicating cup, which the foul fiend well knew, He, as the sin-hating God, had not only not enjoined, but in the most express terms, denounced and prohibited. The more I meditate on my Lord's goodness in identifying Himself with the vine and its fruit for my sake, and that of other hell-deserving sinners, the more may I adore and love Him. The fruit of the vine," which Jesus Himself calls "*my blood*," with all its sin-cleansing, heart-cheering, hope-inspiring associations, is a rallying point to which Christians may always resort; a strong-hold in which they may always find shelter and protection from the enemy; a watch-word by which they may always communicate and re-assure each other, when taunted or tempted by Satan; a characteristic, holy badge, by which the church militant ought ever to be conspicuously distinguished from the armies of the aliens; they finding their chief sensual gratification in quaffing "the wine wherein is excess," ($ἀσωτία$—destruction,) "the cup of **Devils;**" while the true disciples of the Lord drink with exquisite delight **and thankfulness** "of the fruit of the vine," "the cup of the Lord," "the cup of salvation!"

We have **only noted** a few of the emotions and reflections which might probably arise in the mind of a penitent communicant, at the Lord's table, upon first drinking of "the unfermented fruit of the vine," of the existence of which, and the duty of using it, he had so long remained in profound ignorance. It must be evident to every intelligent, serious person, that there may be a great variety of "compunctious visitings," hallowed thoughts, tender sentiments of **sacred love, bright anticipations** of glory, sincere purposes of **greater devotedness** to God, and usefulness **to man, springing up in the** breasts of devout partakers of the **Lord's supper,** according to their diversified circumstances. But all who love the Lord Jesus Christ in sincerity, will find abundant materials for pious meditation, and all the sheep and lambs of the flock luxuriant pasture to feed upon, in the sufferings of Christ for them, and the blessedness to be revealed when He shall come "the second time in His own glory, and in His Father's, and of the holy angels," in connexion with "the fruit of the vine," the exquisitely appropriate and beautiful emblem of His sin-cleansing blood. As it was *the* forbidden fruit, which was the instrument in the hands of Satan of tempting our first parents to shake off their allegiance to God, so it is *a* forbidden fruit—that of alcoholic fermentation—"the cup of Devils,"—which he has continued to palm upon their deluded offspring—still turning them away from "the Father of Lights," (how many, the day of judgment alone can reveal,) they all the while—poor, silly, infatuated souls—dreaming that they are drinking of the cup of blessing, because the old Serpent, the liar from the beginning, gives to it that sacred name; and not content with that, has even blasphemously dared to surname it by "a name which is above every name—that at the name **of** Jesus, every knee should bow, of things in heaven, and things in earth, and things under the earth; and every tongue confess that Jesus Christ is Lord, to the glory of God the Father." But the antidote of this deadly fruit is not confined to earth, (as has been repeatedly noticed,) it adorns also the paradise above, as it did aforetime the earthly paradise. "In the midst of the street of it, (the New Jerusalem,) and on either side of the river was the tree of life, which bare twelve fruit harvests, (Dr. M. Stuart,) yielding her fruit every month, and the leaves of the tree were **for the** healing of the nations." The leaves of the tree for the healing of the nations? Yes, the fruit of the earthly vine scarce to be compared with the leaves of the heavenly vine.

This fruit of the vine is like the hem of Christ's garment, **which** the woman touched **in** faith and had the issue of blood stanched, for which she had suffered many things of many physicians, **for** twelve long years, and spent all that she had, and **was nothing** bettered, but rather grew worse: (Mark v, 25–29.) In like manner, many since her day have fallen victims to a more cruel disease, even drunkenness, " wasted their substance with **riotous** living," "suffered many things of many physicians"—found all their prescriptions of no value—and grew no better, but rather worse, under them—who, if with like precious faith to hers, they had partaken of "the fruit of the vine," at the Lord's supper, might have had the soul-inspiring, heart-cheering words, originally addressed to the poor woman with the issue of blood, applied to them by the Holy Spirit: "Thy faith hath made thee whole; go in peace and be whole of thy plague:" (Mark v, 34.) Alas! alas! for centuries past, how few (if any,) have thus partaken in faith of "the fruit of the vine," at the table of the Lord; we mean that faith, which sees in that cup the heaven-appointed antidote of alcoholic intemperance, or keeps its possessors from the use of alcoholic liquors?

Take the following illustration of this most consolatory truth: By the precious stone, the amethyst, we are to understand from its derivation, (*a priv.:* and $\mu\varepsilon\theta\upsilon\omega$,) an antidote against drunkenness.* Where do we find it in the New Testament? In

---

* "Queen Elizabeth's Cup," adorned with amethysts and other precious stones, as described below, affords an interesting illustration of the virtues ascribed to the amethyst as the preventive of inebriety.

This costly example of olden taste was exhibited at a *Soirée* given by Lord Albert Conyngham, on Wednesday, at the family mansion, in Hamilton-place. There were present the leading members of the British Archæological Association, of which Lord Albert Conyngham is President.

The Cup is in the possession of Colonel Gwatkin, whose mother (a niece of Sir Joshua Reynolds,) obtained it from her sister, who married the Marquis of Thomond, in whose family it had been preserved for a long period of time. The cup is of silver gilt; the rim around the cover is engraved with an arabesque, and bears traces of colored enamels and stones which have decorated the leaves and flowers of which it consists. This is the only piece of engraved work upon the cup; for the cover, sides, and knobs are completely covered with precious stones, many hundreds in number, secured in separate cells, and ranged closely together, in rows, entirely round the vessel. These stones are amethysts of various tints, the interstices of the setting of each being filled with small turquoises, which are, in some instances, as minute as seed pearls, to allow of every part of the cup being incrusted with jewels. The knob on the top of the cover, and the three upon which it stands, are similarly covered with jewels. Those which form the feet unscrew; a hollow tube affixed to the bottom of the cup passes partially through each, and a screw, the head of which contains an amethyst, fits into this tube from beneath, and completely conceals the mode

one place *only*, **near** the end **of** Revelation. In the last chapter but one, the 20th **verse**, **it is** spoken of as the last precious stone which garnishes **the** twelfth foundation of the

QUEEN ELIZABETH'S CUP.

**of** securing them. **A false bottom of** thin silver is held on by these **screws**, and covers a cypher; the letters being "E. R.," conjoined in a scroll, **characteristic** of the reign of **the** Sovereign whose ownership has thus been carefully **stamped** upon it.

walls of the New Jerusalem; and with what does it seem to be connected there, if not with the tree of life, (the vine as already explained,) described in the 2d verse of the following, the last chapter of the same book, as if to show that the "fruit **of the tree** of life," or of the vine, was possessed of power to prevent drunkenness, or was the antidote thereof? Does not the amethyst's place, **last** of all the garnishings, also, seem to indicate, that the anti-alcoholic virtues of "the fruit of the vine" should not be discovered till far on in the history of the world; and is there not something which seems to favor this idea, in the fact that in the list of graces of the Christian, **the** fruit of the Spirit, "*temperance*" comes last (Gal. v, 23,) (in opposition to "drunkenness, revellings and such like,") (Gal. v, 21;) doubtless including under it, abstinence from alcoholic, intoxicating drinks, as has been shown in many parts of these letters by proof of Holy Writ—if we have not been deceiving ourselves, "beating the air," and spending our strength for naught. And here it may not be uninteresting to remark, that

---

The weight of the cup is considerable; it holds about half a pint. It exhibits more barbaric magnificence than real taste, yet is characteristic of the time in which it was made. In the reign of Elizabeth, a superstitious belief in the hidden virtues of precious stones was current, which gave them a value independent of their rarity or beauty. The amethyst in particular, was believed to possess the power of repelling intoxication, and it therefore became a fitting incrustation for the cup of a female sovereign; hence this gift was liberally decorated with so valued a stone.

The belief in the medical and magical virtues of precious stones was a doctrine much inculcated by the Arabian naturalists, who believed that the amethyst prevented inebriation, and the turquoise strengthened the eyes, and was a remedy against poison; and it was from the East that we obtained our belief in their hidden efficacy. During the time of Elizabeth, it is not likely that much faith was placed in such mysticism; but the affectation which characterized her court might have induced the maker of this cup to resort to the quaint conceits of an older faith, to render his work the more acceptable.

We have selected these interesting details from a paper by Mr. Fairholt, F. S.A., drawn up with his usual care, and printed in the number of the *Journal* just issued to the members **of the** British Archæological Association.

if our views be correct, of the relation of the gem "amethyst" to "the fruit of the vine," as explanatory of its secret virtues, the brilliant idea of our immortal bard Shakspeare—"Sermons in Stones,"—will be beautifully exemplified and realized.

I am, my dear brother,

Yours affectionately,

JOHN MAIR.

---

### LETTER XXII.

My Dear Sir,

We have still another argument drawn from prophesy, tending to show that "the fruit of the vine" was designed by Jehovah to be the antidote of alcoholic intemperance. We refer to Isaiah lxv, 8, where it is written: "As the new wine is found in the cluster, and *one* saith, destroy it **not for a** blessing *is* in it; so will I do for my servants' sakes, that I may not destroy them all." But previous to entering upon the examination of this passage, we may be permitted to **say a few words as to the** origin of this inquiry.

Our first idea of an antidote to alcoholic intemperance, arose in this manner: On our voyage from Canada to England, with invalid soldiers, in the Resistance Troop Ship, in 1850, we fell in with a pamphlet bearing this title: "An Earnest Appeal on behalf of the Total Abstinence Reform; addressed to Ministers of the Gospel, and other Religious Professors, on Scriptural Authority: by John G. Marshall, Esq., of Nova Scotia." The array of Scriptural evidence adduced by him, to show that there were two kinds of wine—one intoxicating, and the other not—recognized by the inspired writers—made a powerful impression on **our** mind, and we could not rest till we had investigated the subject, and drawn our conclusions fresh from the fountain-head of Divine truth. In the course of our inquiry, thoughts of the peculiar power of vaccinia, or the cow pock, in preventing small-pox, as discovered by Jenner, occurred to us, and somehow or other, blended themselves with ideas derived from the interesting narrative (Deut. xxxii, 14-33,) concerning "the pure blood of the grape," the drink of God's people, and its opposite, "the cruel venom of asps," the drink of His enemies; the one seeming to bear some analogy to "vaccinia," and the other to "variola,"—or "the cow pock," and "small pox,"—and it became our endeavor to seek for a stable foundation upon which to rest our hope that an analogous antidote of alcoholic intemperance might be discovered in the word of God. Sooner or later, while our mind was occupied with this train of ideas, the following remarkable passage (Isaiah lxv, 8,) attracted our attention: "Thus saith the Lord, as the new wine is found in the cluster, and (one, in italics omitted,) saith, destroy it not for a blessing (*is*) in it; so will I do for my servants' sake, that I may not destroy them all." It seemed to us to cast a ray of light upon this obscure subject, and to intimate that a preventive of alcoholic intemperance might be discovered in the Bible.*

In June, 1853, we committed the following remarks to paper: "The Devil must not have it all his own way; he has been tampering fearfully with the souls of men, in regard to the use of fermented, vinous potations. Can it be supposed that there is no equivalent on the side of holiness and virtue, to counterbalance 'the red wine,' which snares so many to their ruin?

---

* The following motto to my Thesis, or "Dissertatio Medica Inauguralis, De Peste Ejusque Relationibus Morbidis," published at Edinburgh, in 1819, prior to my receiving my degree in Medicine, would have accorded with my state of mind at the time the above sentence was penned, omitting the author's name, in parenthesis, an eminent physician, and changing the words "pestilentis," and "naturæ," also in parentheses—into inebriantis, and Scripturæ Sacræ, respectively thus: "Si quis meam opinionem roget, dicam (cum Julio Palmario,) aliquod certum veneni (pestilentis) inebriantis, antidotum creatum quidem esse, sed illud hactenus in (naturæ) Scripturæ Sacræ sinu, occultum latuisse." "If any one ask my opinion, I will say, that some certain antidote of drunkenness has indeed been ordained, but still lies concealed in the bosom of Holy Scripture."

The 65th chapter of Isaiah, 8th verse, unfolds the mystery and makes it plain, that there is an equipoise, (we should have said, a preponderating power.) It exists in the blessed wine contained in the ripe grape before it is destroyed by fermentation. The Devil says: 'Drink red wine, and every species of intoxicating drink, to the fill.' Solomon says: 'Look not thou upon the wine when it is red.' 'A greater than Solomon,' says: 'Drink ye all of the fruit of the vine.' *This* is the remedy which God has appointed, it seems to me, for innumerable evils. There has been too violent a divorce of the soul from the body of man, and consequently of physical agencies operating upon the body, as if religion had nothing to do with the latter. Now there are physical agents which act primarily on the body, and which have a secondary influence upon the mind, and one of these is *alcohol;* and, till its effects be estimated, and counteracted by wholesome discipline, a most important department of religion will remain uncultivated. No adequate means have been adopted to arrest the evils flowing from the use of intoxicating drinks, because the religious element has been ignored—'the heavenly' view of the earthly thing, for alcohol is of 'the earth, earthy,' and its demoralizing effects can only be combated effectually, by the application of the heavenly restorative. *It* has upon it the impress of Divinity. No human being could have discovered the plan, but when disclosed, it is seen to possess the very requisites for counteracting the effects of alcohol, which were desiderated, **and** which would have operated successfully long ago, if they had been carried into practice."

Let us now endeavor to analyze the important passage, which appears to us distinctly to point to "the fruit of the vine," or as it is there termed, "*the new wine in the cluster*," as the Divinely-appointed *antidote* of alcoholic intemperance.

"Thus saith the Lord, as the new wine is found in the cluster, and (*one*) saith destroy it not for a blessing (*is*) in it; so will I do for my servants' sakes that I may not destroy them all." We have here:

1st. The Lord's own statement respecting His own wine, "the new wine in the cluster," in air-proof bottles of His own construction—*unfermented* and *unfermentable*, while these bottles remain uninjured—the model wine, the nearer to which we can approach in our manufacture of wine, **the nearer we shall approach to perfection.** For equivalents, look to Canticles i, 2: "Thy love is better than wine;" v, 1: "I am come into my garden, my sister, my spouse; I have drunk my wine with my milk: eat, O friends, drink; yea, drink abundantly, O beloved." Prov. ix, 1, 2, 5: "Wisdom hath builded her house; she hath hewn out her seven pillars; she hath killed her beasts; she hath mingled her wine. Come eat of my bread, and drink of the wine which **I have mingled.**" And in the New Testament for words of similar import: Matt. xxvi, 28, 29: "For this is my blood of the New Testament which is shed for many, for the remission of sins. But I say unto you, I will not henceforth drink of this fruit of the vine until the day when I drink it new with you in my Father's kingdom;" **reference** here, being made to the fruit of the tree of life, which **grows** abundantly on each side of the river of the water of **life,** (as previously spoken of.) Similar **references might be made to** the other Evangelists who have treated **of the Lord's supper,** but what has been said may suffice to explain our meaning. Upon the subject of communion wine, the learned author of "Tirosh Lo Yayin," thus expresses himself: "As it was the **common** practice to bring the bunches of grapes to the table,*

---

* "The **two great sacraments** of baptism **and** the Lord's supper are constantly represented and alluded to **in the paintings of the catacombs, but no** others. Thus the administration of the Lord's supper is depicted by **a** sketch of seven, or in one instance twelve Apostles, sitting on one side a table, on which is placed a dish containing loaves of bread, and *grapes*, sometimes **a fish."**—*The Family Treasury*: Part xiv, p. **178.**

and then and there to squeeze them into a cup or drinking vessel, is it not probable that Christ so used them on that occasion, (the Passover and the Lord's supper.) And might he not thus have spoken of the contents of the cup with reference to the bunch of grapes he had only the moment before been pressing?"\*

2d. We have here, the prayer of the new wine in the cluster personified, presented to its Creator, imploring that it may not be suffered to be destroyed, "and saith, destroy it not." It is said by a learned writer in the Abstinence Journal, for December, 1854, with reference to this passage: "The same word that is translated wine, occurs with this distinct explanation: 'Thus saith the Lord, as the wine is found in the cluster, and one saith, destroy (literally, ferment or corrupt,) it not for a blessing is in it.'" If this explanation be correct, the new wine views destruction and fermentation as synonymous, and deprecates both alike, and thus "Wisdom is justified of all her children." Are we not here taught a most useful lesson— *even* this, to avoid fermented, alcoholic, intoxicating wine, by the word of the Lord? For was it not the Lord that dictated this prayer? Surely, such a passage as this, (and it is by no means a solitary one having the same import, and bearing the same Divine impress,) ought to prove a stumbling-block in the way of those who will have it that alcoholic wine was prescribed by the immutably, eternally-holy Jehovah, (who gave utterance by His prophet, Isaiah, to these words,) to be the precious sym**bol** of His blood, to be partaken of by all true communicants,

---

"The fish has long been a significant emblem under Christianity. The Greek name 'ιχθυς is composed of the first letters of the words Jesus Christ—Son of God—Saviour:

Ιησους Χριστος Θεου 'Υιος Σωτηρ."

*Biblical Cyclopædia,* by John Eadie, D.D. Article—Fish. Might not the fish here have been intended to be the emblem of the Lord Jesus Christ, as the bread, of His body, and the fruit of the vine, of His blood?

\*Tirosh Lo Yayin: p. 132.

at the Lord's supper till His second coming, without sin **unto** salvation.

3d. We have here, the reason assigned **for the new wine's** prayer to its Creator and Preserver, to be kept from undergoing the vinous or alcoholic fermentation, *"for a blessing in it ;"* or a blessing exists in the unfermented wine, or will exist; or does and will exist a *twofold blessing*. It is good for food and drink in its fresh state, but we apprehend, there is wrapt up in it mysteriously, the blessing of the prevention of drunkenness—a far greater blessing than that depending on its nutritious qualities! O that all Christians had been **as** wise and pious **as** "the new wine in the cluster," and had always offered up the same prayer, what a different world, sin-stricken though **it be,** would **this world** have proved! **How much** of peace, joy, health, wealth, soundness of mind and body—in short, of physical and spiritual prosperity might thus have been secured, now lost forever to the fallen **race** of Adam!

What do you suppose is the spiritual blessing to be found in "the new wine in the cluster?" It is written, Judges ix, 13: "And the vine said unto them, Should I leave my wine (*tirosh, the produce of the vine,*—Stubbin,) *which cheereth God and man, and go to be promoted over the trees?*" Where can anything be plainer than that this language of the dumb vine, like that of the dumb ass, is intended to teach man a **lesson not** to kick against God or His anointed? (Numbers **xxii, 22, 23.**) Does it not correspond with the very word of Immanuel, when at His last supper with His disciples, **before** His crucifixion, He thus addressed them: "**Drink ye all** of it, for this is my blood of the New Testament, **which is** shed for you for the remission **of sins**: But I say **unto you,** I will not drink henceforth of *this fruit* of the vine, until the day when I drink it new with you in my Father's Kingdom:" (Matt. **xxvi, 27–29.**) The fruit of the vine, and the produce of the vine, mentioned in these two passages, are the same thing; and the very same

17

word, *tirosh*, used in Judges ix, 13, is that used in the portion of Scripture **we are** now considering. What, then, can be more evident than that it was for qualities possessed by this " fruit of the vine" in its natural state, *un*fermented and *un*intoxicating, that the Lord Jesus Christ selected it to be the sacred symbol of His blood. If so, does not the identity of language used by the inspired writers from whom we have quoted, (literally of the terms in Judges and Isaiah, and substantially in Matthew,) indicate a common train of thought existing in their minds, or at least, a common blessing to which they pointed in connexion with the fruit of the vine, (though with ignorance of its nature on the part of the Old Testament prophets,) which would make it peculiarly precious to mankind. May not the blessing in the new wine, then, in the passage under consideration, have reference to *that* "which cheereth God and man," (Judges ix, 13,) and to that which may be the thing there referred to, the use of that "new wine," or "unfermented fruit of the vine" to represent the sin-atoning blood of the Redeemer? (Matt. xxvi, 27–29:) and is there not something corroborative of this idea in the following passage : (I Cor. x, 16:) "The cup of blessing" (or the unfermented fruit of the vine—the cup standing for its contents—) "which we bless," (the eucharistic or thank-offering which itself personified, thanks God for not permitting it to be fermented or turned into alcoholic, poisonous liquor,—we also thank God *for*, or acknowl**edge** the goodness of God in giving it to us, to be the perpetual memorial of the unspeakable love of Jesus to our souls, **in** offering Himself up a sacrifice for us.) Referring to Judges ix, 13, **the** learned and ingenious author **of** " Tirosh Lo Yayin," p. 49, says: "**Had** not the enemies of temperance contended so fiercely **for the** application of this passage to an inebriating wine, as the only species by which man could possibly be cheered, and the reckless blasphemy involved in the application of it, whether in that sense or any other, **as a** material food for an immaterial being, it would scarcely have been necessary to intimate that it could only be by way of sacrifice **offered up with** humility, sincerity and prayer, that it could have cheered **the** Almighty." And is it not offered **up as a** sacrifice of thanksgiving at the Lord's supper, by every one who partakes thereof with "the unfermented fruit of the vine"—believing that *it* is the only Divinely-appointed symbol of the blood of Immanuel to be dispensed at that sacred feast? How could the deadly poison alcohol, or any drink tinctured with it, be an acceptable thank-offering to the Holiest of all holy beings, who *alone* can make men holy? Why might it not rationally be conjectured then, that "the new wine," in this petition, prayed that it might not be corrupted into alcoholic wine, but might be preserved good and proper, in the fulness of time, to represent the blood of the Messiah, about to come into the world to save sinners, and to be the antidote of alcoholic intemperance, to obtain a far nobler and more illustrious position than that of "king over the trees,"—to be inseparably identified with Him who is King of Kings and Lord of Lords,—and the blessed instrument in His Almighty hand, of saving innumerable souls from perishing under the fearful delusion of alcoholic wine being the sacrificial emblem of His sin-atoning blood?

> "I, Jesus, am the vine—of life, the only root,
> And those good works alone can shine,
> That from my branches shoot.
> My precious blood Divine, when I to death *was trod*,
> Produced so rich, so rare a wine, *it cheers both man and God.*"
> —Delta.

4th. We have *here*, the gracious promise of the Almighty to grant the prayer of the suppliant, "*so* will *I* do;" or, in other words, *I* will not destroy the new wine, or permit *all* **of** it to be *fermented;* there shall be enough left to **accomplish** the special purpose I have determined upon, **even** the offering up of a suitable drink offering to me: (Joel ii, 14, compare i, 8–13.) This language (if our interpretation be correct,) would accurately correspond with the whole testimony of Holy Writ, which we have endeavored to show uniformly forbids the use of alcoholic liquors in man's normal state of health, and would imply that if "the new wine in the cluster" were destroyed, it would be an enemy of God and man, who would perpetrate the unlawful deed. Taking this view of the passage, we have italicised the words *so* and *I*, to signify that they are emphatical. Moreover, from the light which we *now* have, (if our views be at all in accordance with the mind of the Spirit,) we can see how the preservation of the "new wine in the cluster," to be an acceptable drink offering to God, as the symbol of the blood of His only begotten Son, to be drunk of at His supper, would have the effect, when thus offered up (at however distant a period,) of opening the eyes of the blind to the sin they had committed, in using alcoholic wine for sacred and secular purposes contrary to God's express commandment so often repeated in the oracles of Divine truth,—and prove the antidote of alcoholic intemperance.

Moreover, may not prophetic allusion be made (Malachi i, 6–8–14,) to the awful desecration of the Lord's supper which has gone on in the church for centuries past, and which has at length in our day reached the climax of profanation, in the substitution of atrociously adulterated, impoisoned wine for "the unfermented fruit of the vine," the emblem chosen by our Lord to represent His precious blood? The words are well worthy of being pondered by every lover of the Lord Jesus Christ, and are as follows: "A son honoreth his father, and a servant his master: **if**, then, I be a father, where is mine honor? and if I be a master, where is my fear? Saith the Lord of hosts unto you, O priests that despise my name, and ye say, Wherein have we despised Thy name? Ye offer *polluted* bread upon mine altar; and ye say, Wherein have we polluted Thee? In that ye say, *The table of the Lord is contemptible*. (Mark the language, *the table of the Lord*. Is not this with reference to the *abuse* of the Lord's supper in future times?) And if ye offer the blind for sacrifice, is it not evil? And if ye offer the lame and sick, is it not evil? Offer it now **unto thy Governor, will he** be pleased with thee, or accept thy person? Saith the Lord of hosts. . . . . But cursed be the deceiver which hath in his flock a male, and voweth and sacrificeth unto the Lord a *corrupt* thing; for I am a great King, Saith the Lord of hosts, and my name is dreadful among the heathen." Still more: May not the 11th verse of the same chapter refer to that blessed revival of true religion, which we believe will be consequent upon the return of the church to the use of "**the unfermented fruit of the vine**" at the Lord's supper? The remarkable words are: "For from the rising of the sun, even unto the going down of the same, My name shall be great among the **Gentiles**: and in every place, incense shall be offered unto My name, and *a pure offering:* (not **a corrupt** and corrupting one, such as alcoholic wine is,) for My name shall be great among the heathen, Saith the Lord of hosts."

5th. We have here, the persons for whose sakes the gracious promise was given: "for my servants' sakes;" or, in other words, for the benefit of the children of God. Here we have opening out to us an extensive and inviting field of inquiry— much too large—for us to do more than glance at. One thing appears to be implied in these words coupled with the context, "that I may not destroy them all," viz: that even God's own children, for whom Christ died, would be in imminent danger of making "shipwreck of faith and of a good conscience," from the reckless, anti-Scriptural use of "the wine, wherein is excess," as the symbol of Immanuel's blood, at His supper. So that, if possible, the very elect should be ruined **by it, and** cast away!

But let us come to close quarters with the enemy, and grapple resolutely with him, in the hope of slaying him, and cease to cast missiles at him from a distance, which may fall short of the mark. In simple language, let us endeavor as perspicuously and briefly as we can, to show under the following heads:

1st. That the practice of the professing church of Christ, in making use of alcoholic wine as the symbol of His blood, at His supper, necessarily arising from the belief that it was appointed by Jesus, for that purpose,—is contrary to God's law, plainly set forth in many parts of Scripture, and in a variety of forms;—that it must be followed by the belief of this other falsehood, that the Bible contains no law against the use of such alcoholic wine, or other alcoholic liquor, and that its use is placed under no other species of restraint, by Divine authority, than is imposed upon the use of wholesome food or drink; while the twofold belief of these untruths affords a most powerful incentive to obedience to them, viz: the use of alcoholic liquors by *all* those *so* believing, and the ruin of soul and body in many.

**2d. That** the belief of the church of Christ, founded upon the clearest Scriptural evidence, that "the unfermented fruit of the vine" was dispensed by the Lord Jesus at His supper, and commanded by Him to be used as the sole symbol of His blood, at that ordinance, till His second coming,—must necessarily lead to the exclusive use of the same *there*, by the persons so believing, and to the farther belief, founded upon equally valid Scriptural evidence, that the law of God forbids **the use** of alcoholic wine, and all other alcoholic liquors by man in his normal state of health; while the twofold belief of these truths with the enjoined practice of the use of unfermented wine at the Lord's supper, will afford a most powerful stimulus to hearty obedience to the more comprehensive law of entire abstinence from alcoholic liquors, upon evangelical principles.

1st. That the practice of the professing church of Christ, in making use of alcoholic wine as the symbol of His blood, at His supper, necessarily arising from the belief that it was appointed by Jesus, for that purpose,—is contrary to God's law plainly set forth in many parts of Scripture, and in a variety of forms,—that it must be followed by the belief of this other falsehood, that the Bible contains no law against the use of such alcoholic wine, or other alcoholic liquor, and that its use is placed under no other species of restraint, by Divine authority, than is imposed upon the use of wholesome food or drink; while the twofold belief of these untruths affords a most powerful incentive to obedience to them, viz: the use of alcoholic liquors by *all* those so believing, and the ruin of **soul** and body in *many*.

"If the light that is in thee be darkness, how great is that darkness:" (Matt. vi, 23.) "Woe unto them that call evil good, and good evil; that put darkness for light, and light for darkness; that put bitter for sweet, and sweet for bitter!" . . . . **Woe** unto them that are mighty to drink wine, and men of strength to mingle strong drink:" (Isaiah v, 20, 22.) If that which you believe to be true be a lie, how great is that lie. Theirs is a pitiable case who think they are walking wisely and well, in the light of God's countenance, when they are pursuing the path of lies and destruction according to the devices of the great adversary of souls—blinded by him at his will. Such are they who are "mighty to drink wine, and men of strength to mingle strong drink." But they did not all at once become so abandoned. They began with littles, and by degrees drank deeper and deeper, until alcohol at last became their idol and their destroyer. What **was** their first sally? Some one or more of them may have acquired a liking for intoxicating wine, first at the Lord's supper. That "simple" youth may first have sipped it at the table of the Lord. **No** bad thing could be given him there. "It must be 'a good creature of God,' or it would not have been appointed by Jesus, to be the symbol—the representative of His precious, sin-atoning blood." Thus, the unsuspecting lad would naturally reason, (if he reasoned at all upon the matter, and did not merely partake of the poisoned chalice, as his fathers did before him, as a thing of course,) and thus he could see no harm, but rather good in tasting of the intoxicating cup upon such a sacred occasion, and if good there, how could it be bad elsewhere, if partaken of with thanksgiving. Thus he would be disposed to look upon "the wine when it is red—giving his color in the cup," as a blessing, rather than a curse. By and by he might become a slave to the habit of drinking intoxicating drinks, and at last fill a drunkard's grave. What a pity he did not rather partake of the sacred feast, of which Divine wisdom says: "Come eat of *my* bread, and drink of *the wine* which *I* have mingled:" (Prov. ix, 5;) of which "wine," the same Divine wisdom, even Jesus, in another place, has said: "Eat, O friends, drink; yea, drink abundantly, O beloved:" (Canticles v, 1;) and, in another *still*: "Drink ye all of it, for this is my blood of the New Testament, which is shed for many for the remission of sins:" (Matt. xxvi, 27, 28.) But, alas! he had not been taught by his religious teachers, that there ever was such a wine as is here described—without any poison in it—and that it was the wine which was used by Immanuel, as the telling emblem of His pure blood, at His last supper; the idea, probably, never entered into *their* minds that there ever was such an innocent wine, and so he was lost, **because** of the culpable ignorance of his instructors, upon a point which they ought to have made themselves acquainted with, and concerning which, they should have informed him. The fact (we believe,) is, that not in a solitary case, or tens, or hundreds—but in thousands, and tens of thousands of instances, the belief of the false doctrine, that the Lord Jesus Christ commanded alcoholic, intoxicating wine to be used at His supper, has proved ruinous to both soul and body, in time and in eternity. For how could it be otherwise? Sincere belief in Jesus, as the wisest and best of beings, must be followed by obedience to His commandments under the conviction that they are certainly conducive to man's welfare, both here and hereafter; and the more sincere and unshaken the belief, the more prompt and unwavering will be the obedience; so that thus, the best man will, (*cœteris paribus*,) be most likely to encounter the greatest danger, just because his strong faith prevents him from having any suspicion of imposture, and his tender conscience is implicitly submissive to his faith. But another element in the mischief must be mentioned here, although often noticed before. We mean the fact, that alcohol (the *sine qua non* of communion wine,) is a most seductive and highly dangerous narcotic poison, which, besides having the approbation, (as the simple youth ignorantly believes) of his Lord and master on its side, has the strongest tendency to produce a continually increasing appetite for it, terminating in an irremediable corporeal disease, added to the invincible mental habit which cannot be overcome—all the remonstrances of friends, and all the expostulations and prayers of ministers notwithstanding. And the almost universal belief, that Jesus used, and commanded to be used, intoxicating wine at His supper, is not productive of injury to the church only, ("the pillar and ground of the truth,") but to the world also, which is sure to follow her as a leader, in every respect agreeable when she inculcates a doctrine,—and recommends it by a practice,—so pleasing to "the carnal mind," which "is enmity against God."

In conclusion, here let it be remarked, that we ought not to be "ignorant of Satan's devices,"—of his impostures, sophistries and lies;—and that we ought ever to search the Scriptures to find out "what is truth," and not trust to the reports of others, however able or excellent; and, when we are sure we have found "the truth," never to sell it for anything the world can tempt us with. "Buy the truth and sell it not; also wisdom, instruction and understanding:" (Prov. xxiii, 23.) "Ye are of your father, the Devil, and the lusts of your father ye will do. He was a murderer from the beginning, and abode not in the truth, because there is no truth in him. When he speaketh a lie, he speaketh of his own, for he is a liar and the father of it:" (John viii, 44.)

2d. That the belief of the church of Christ of the truth, founded upon the clearest Scriptural evidence, that "unfermented fruit of the vine" was dispensed by the Lord Jesus Christ at His supper, and that it was commanded by Him to be used as the symbol of His blood, at that ordinance, till His second coming,—must necessarily lead to the exclusive use of the same, by the person so believing, and to the farther belief, founded upon equally valid Scripture evidence, that the law of God forbids the use of alcoholic wine, and all other alcoholic liquors, to man in his normal state of health; while the twofold belief of these truths (with their associated truths,) will **afford** a most powerful stimulus to hearty obedience, or entire abstinence from alcoholic liquors, upon evangelical principles.

"Sanctify them through thy truth: thy word is truth:" (John xvii, 17.) "It is invariably and eternally true, that the belief of truth will lead a man right, and secure his temporal and eternal interests."—(*Philosophy of the Plan of Salvation*, p. 99.)

Time will not allow us to enter into a full consideration of the principles laid down under this head. It cannot but be **evident,** to all intelligent, reflecting, inquiring persons, that if the belief of lies—"according to the constitution of things, the **character of** God, and the nature of man"—must be wrong, and **lead to** wrong conduct, and prove injurious to those so believing; **in like** manner, the belief of truth must be right, and lead **to right** conduct, and prove beneficial to those who so believe, in relation to the things believed.

As it is impossible for a believer in the doctrine that the Lord Jesus Christ dispensed alcoholic wine at the institution of His sacred supper, and commanded the same to be used in all future time, till His second coming, to *disbelieve* the correlated truth that there is *no* law of God which interdicts the **use of** alcoholic liquors upon all occasions, in man's normal state of health; so it is impossible **for a** believer in the doctrine that the Lord Jesus Christ dispensed unfermented wine at His supper, and commanded it to be used at that ordinance in all future time, till His second coming, to *disbelieve* the correlated doctrine, that there is a law of God which interdicts the use of alcoholic liquors upon all occasions, in man's normal state of health. As soon, then, as an intelligent, conscientious Christian man, upon Scripture testimony, carefully examined, shall have ascertained to the satisfaction of his judgment, that the Lord Jesus Christ dispensed *only* "unfermented fruit of the vine" at His supper, and commanded the same species of liquid to be used at all future celebrations of that feast, he will be at once led to drink of the same, if he have an opportunity, in fellowship with his brethren, in remembrance of His Lord's death for him, according to His commandment; and the glaring inconsistency will strike him, of using *un*fermented, *un*intoxicating wine *only* at that supper, and fermented, alcoholic, intoxicating wine at other meals, &c.; and this feeling, confirmed and deepened by the remembrance of the appalling, ruinous effects of the use of alcoholic liquors, will force upon him the conviction that the Lord Jesus Christ, the only begotten Son of God, the greatest benefactor of the human race, and their Saviour from sin, could not have been propitious to it—but if not propitious to it, neither can the moral law, revealed by Him, in all its length, breadth, depth and spirituality, and receiving from Him its highest sanctions, be favorable to it. Thus, he will be led to search the Scriptures, where he will find that his views, deduced from the benevolent character of Immanuel, are fully borne out and amply confirmed by the moral law, which is unmistakably against it, as plainly declared in a variety of ways, and in the most positive terms, throughout the Old and New Testaments. Thus, it was the belief that Jesus commanded "unfermented fruit of the vine," or wine, to be used as the symbol of His blood, at His supper, that removed the veil from his eyes; and, that the **law** of God against alcohol, before invisible, became luminous to his mental vision,—and what, then, could the practice of the Christian thus believing, (if consistent with his principles,) in future be, but total abstinence from alcoholic liquors, in his normal state of health—a doctrine which we have endeavored, in the course of these letters, to illustrate and confirm by sufficient Scriptural data.

But we all know that to be convinced of the existence of a law having Divine authority to make it binding upon us, is one thing, and to be obedient to that law from love to its author, is another and a very different thing. "For we know that the **law** is spiritual: but I am carnal, sold under sin. For that which I do, I allow not: for what I would, that do I not; but what I hate, that I do." But if its author be a Divine and humane friend, above every friend; if He died **to save** us from our sins; if He has rescued us from the grasp of the roaring lion; **if He has** wrought out for us an everlasting righteousness, and secured for us never ending felicity in heaven, by the everlasting covenant sealed with His blood, and attested by His word and Spirit, shall we not be constrained to love Him? and if we love Him, shall we not make strenuous efforts, trusting **in** Divine grace, wisdom and strength, to keep this and all **His** other commandments. Jesus has done all this, and much more than tongue can tell, or the most perfect created intellect can comprehend, for us, that we might be saved. The claims of duty and gratitude, then, are irresistible, and must constrain us to obey the holy, just and good law, which forbids the use of alcoholic liquors whenever they can prove dishonoring to **God, or hurtful to us** or our fellow creatures—given to us by our precious heavenly Father, and ratified by the blood of His only begotten Son.

It is here, as a resistless motive to obedience, that "the fruit of the vine," the everlasting symbol of the blood of the Lamb, with all its heaven-born associations, comes into practical operation.

We have, very imperfectly, endeavored to sketch some of the blessed truths which cluster round the fruit of the vine, and which cannot fail to act in the way above pointed out, upon every blood-bought soul, renewed by the Holy Spirit.

It will at once be perceived, from the tenor of these letters, that "the truth" has an immense advantage over error; all the motives in the one case, being "pure, lovely, and of good report;" in the other, "earthly, sensual, devilish!" May all God's children, in His own good time, be led to drink of "the cup of salvation, and call upon the name of the Lord."

I am, dear sir,

Yours most affectionately,

JOHN MAIR.

---

## LETTER XXIII.

My Dear Sir,

The facts which have been stated by us, glorify God, as mirrors reflecting His image. They do this by glorifying Jesus, primarily, and in glorifying the Son they must glorify the Father also. For thus saith Jesus: "I and my Father are one:" (John x, 30.) And in another place it is written: "Who being the brightness of His glory, and the express image of His person, and upholding all things by the word of His power, when He had by Himself purged our sins, sat down on the right hand of the Majesty on high:" (Heb. i, 3.) If these facts (and evidences of design,) glorify God the Father, and God the Son, they must do so by the purpose of God, or by chance; but not by chance—for if so, they would be taken out of the sphere of God's providential government, which would be contrary to the truths revealed, Coloss. i, 16, 17: "For by Him were all things created, that are in heaven, and that are in earth, visible and invisible; whether they be **thrones**, or dominions, or principalities, or powers: all things **were** created by Him and for Him: and He is before all things, and by Him all things consist." And, Luke xii, 6, 7: "Are not five sparrows sold for two farthings, and not one of them is forgotten before God? But even the very hairs of your head are all numbered. Fear not, therefore: ye are of more value than many sparrows." We confidently conclude, then, that the arrangements to which we have referred, were designed of God:

1st. For *His* glory in the highest:

2d. For peace on earth:

3d. For good will toward men:

and these two last objects, in subserviency to the paramount design: "the glory of God in the highest."

### 1st. "*The glory of God in the highest.*"

The blood of Jesus, and the shedding thereof—our redemption price—are aptly set forth by "the pure blood of the grape," and its *expression;* His incorruptibility and immutability, by its being preserved uncorrupted, or unfermented, by the positive command of God;—the soul's blessings of pardon and sanctification by its pleasant and nutritious qualities, in relation to the body: "For my flesh is meat indeed, and my blood is drink indeed:" (John vi, 55.) Thus, by all these adaptations, God the Father, and God the Son, are glorified. Moreover, they are glorified in a still more signal manner, by the exquisite, Divine adaptation of "the fruit of the vine" to be the antidote of alcoholic intemperance. The reverse of all this follows from the Church's generally received interpretation of the language used by our Lord, at the institution of His supper,—her understanding of the nature of the symbol of His blood,—and her acts, proceeding from her doctrines in the celebration of that ordinance. These must be traced to an opposite source, not to Christ, but to Belial.

## 2d. *"Peace on earth."*

What object in nature is more pleasant to the eye, more agreeable to the taste, or more ready to recall to the imagination delightful pictures of peace and plenty, than a cluster of grapes fully ripe? Alas! that it should ever have been blended in thought with the cup of the drunkard,—as having any sympathy therewith,—to which it is diametrically opposed! But let " **the fruit** of the vine " **be viewed as the Divinely-appointed symbol of Immanuel's blood,** and how much more lovely does it appear? It acquires, by this association, a virtue not before possessed by it. It becomes pre-eminently the love-token of our Great High Priest, to those whom He purchased with His precious blood, and the happy emblem of peace restored between the offended Majesty of Heaven, and His apostate, rebellious creatures! But again—when looked upon as the heaven-appointed antidote of alcoholic intemperance, what **new powers of attraction** does it acquire, and what ineffable value attaches to it!

Let it be borne in mind, that the vine existed **in Eden before** the fall, as "the tree of life;" **that it will flourish in the New** Jerusalem forever, fresh and fair,—growing by "the river of the water of life," producing its fruit every month—indissolubly related to the Lamb, as it had been slain—"with leaves for the healing of the nations;" and this wondrous combination of peaceful elements will be seen admirably to qualify it for diffusing peace and love amongst individuals, families and nations, emanating from the Prince of Peace; where discord, hate, turmoil and war,—the infernal progeny of alcohol, and its sire, Satan,—were before rampant. For, is it not true, that alcohol has been one of the chief causes (if not the chief,) of broils, bruises, ruffianly assaults, inhuman barbarities, and unheard-of atrocities amongst those of the same kindred, as well as strangers? What says Solomon? "Who hath sorrow? who hath contentions? who hath babblings? who hath wounds without cause? They that tarry long at the wine: they that go to mix red wine." And what is the cure enjoined by him? "Look not thou upon the wine when it is red, when it giveth his color in the cup, when it moveth itself aright; at the last it biteth like a serpent and stingeth like an adder." But this was not sufficient to effect the desired object. A greater than Solomon,—even Jesus, the Saviour of sinners,—was required to discover and proclaim the sovereign remedy, needed to accomplish the mighty reformation; and He has accomplished in a manner most simple, yet most sublime, His own stupendous design, in His ratification of all that is written in "the law and the prophets" against wine and strong drink, by His selection of "the fruit of the vine" to be the symbol of His own most precious sin-atoning blood, naturally associating itself with all that it is fitted to make the deepest, most tender and lasting impressions upon the human heart, and wean it forever from the love of "wine, wherein is excess," by the expulsive power of a new affection!

3d. *"Good will toward men."*

The last grand object to be subserved by the adaptations which we have had under review, is the "good will," "loving kindness," or "grace of God," in leading the disciples of our Lord, and others, totally to abandon alcoholic wine,—an end so difficult to be achieved, in consequence of its peculiar seductive qualities, that (as we have endeavored to show, in previous communications,) extraordinary means have been used by the Almighty for its accomplishment; means, which though hitherto ineffectual, (because misunderstood and neglected,) are destined yet to prevail, when cordially embraced, because they are not human, but Divine; and, therefore, must be "mighty to the pulling down of strongholds."

The sentiment we wish to convey, may be appropriately expressed in the following words of inspiration: "The grace of God that bringeth salvation, hath appeared to all men, teaching us that denying worldly lusts," (Titus ii, 11, 12,) (including liquor drinking and not excluding other unlawful gratifications,) "we should live soberly," or deny ourselves the use of alcoholic, intoxicating drinks, &c., except for the legal purposes so often pointed out in preceding pages. Who will deny that such a blessed consummation as this, would be an illustrious triumph of Divine grace and truth,—a resurrection of "life from the dead," to thousands and tens of thousands of poor, infatuated human beings, now "taken captive by the Devil at his will," which would cause the angels in heaven to shout aloud for joy, and Satan with his rebel hosts in hell to scoff and shriek in most horrible anguish and despair, because deprived of the chief instrument of his rancorous hate and vengeance, coupled with the conviction that "the time" of his final doom "is at hand?"

In conclusion,—what is to be done by "the church, the pillar and ground of the truth," in regard to anti-alcoholic temperance—to hasten on the millennium?

The vine, we have found, has spoken wisely and well, to mankind, upon more than one occasion, in the Old Testament: (Judges ix, 13: Isaiah lxv, 8.) Might it not give good counsel in the present case, if its words and example were attentively pondered, and faithfully followed, by all who seek the glory of God and the good of mankind in the department of temperance?

Let us again turn our attention to Isaiah lxv, 8: "Thus saith the Lord," (so that we see the counsel cometh from the Supreme Law-giver, if we can only comprehend and apply it aright,) "As the new wine is found in the cluster, and saith, Destroy it not, for a blessing in it: so will I do for my servants' sakes, that I may not destroy them all;" showing the vine, or its ripe cluster, **to be a** believer in the virtues possessed by its fruit, as is plain from the petition it offers up to the Almighty, not to destroy it: "Destroy it not for a blessing in it;" or, do not let **it be** fermented. What, then, does the vine teach us, and all interested in the advancement of Christ's kingdom upon earth, and the removal of that great barrier to it, alcoholic intemperance, if not the following lessons?

1st. To believe **in "the fruit of the vine"** as a striking emblem appointed by our Lord to represent His blood—indissolubly associated, and, if we may say so, identified **with** "the sufferings of Christ and the glory that shall follow," and thereby fitted to be the antidote of alcoholic intemperance.

2d. **To** pray, as the vine does, to Jehovah, that "the new wine **in** the cluster" may not be fermented, or turned into a liquid containing alcoholic poison—the bane of human nature.

3d. **To** interpret, as **the vine** does, the Holy Scriptures, in relation **to** intemperance, and temperance: "To the law and to **the** testimony, if **they speak** not according to this word, it is because they have **no light in** them:" (Isaiah viii, 20:) "Search the Scriptures, for in them ye think ye have eternal life, and they are they which testify of me:" (John v, 39.) The vine invitingly says, by its beautiful pendent clusters: "Drink of me, I will refresh and nourish you;" wisdom says: "Come eat **of my** bread, and drink of the wine which I have mingled:" (**Prov. ix, 5**;) and Jesus says, once and again: "I have drunk my **wine with** my milk: Eat, O friends, drink; yea, drink abundantly, **O** beloved:" (Canticles v, 1:) "Drink ye all of it: For this is my blood of the New Testament, which is shed for many for **the** remission of sins:" (Matt. xxvi, 27, 28:) while our great adversary, the Devil, through his dupes, exclaims in frantic bacchanalian songs or in soft whispers, as may best suit his purpose: "'Drink, O friends, drink; yea, drink abundantly, O beloved;' not of 'the fruit of the vine,' which has no spirit in it, and cannot drive away dull care,—but of me, **the quintessence of happiness**—the sparkling juice of the **grape,** 'when it giveth his color in the cup, when it moveth itself aright;'—a balm for every wound—a solace for every sorrow—in me you **will** find a panacea **for all** the ills that flesh is heir to—quaff of me till you glide gently and softly into an elysium of bliss!" But beware! beware! it is the voice of an arch impostor, **loud or low.** "Be not ignorant of his devices:" (II Cor. ii, 11:) "Resist the Devil, and **he will flee** from you: Draw nigh to God, and He will draw nigh to you:" (James iv, 7, 8.)

4th. **To trace** out **and fill** up, as the vine would have it, **the** matchless **moral portrait of the Lord** Jesus Christ, especially that part **of it (hitherto, so** often, inaccurately depicted,) which represents His temperance at His supper, according to the vivid likeness given by the Holy Spirit, in the oracles of Divine truth, till the copy in all respects, both of outline and finishing, corresponds with the Divine original representation.

5th. To act according to the example of the vine, in preserving its juice pure and nutritious for man's use, **in the** vessels prepared by **our** Heavenly Father **for that purpose,** manifestly teaching us to **do** in like manner, **by the best chemi**cal and mechanical means we can devise and **employ** for that purpose;—encouraged still more **to do so, by the perfect** example of our blessed Lord and Saviour, **who, at the** institution of His own supper, the night **in which he was** betrayed, "took bread **and** when He had given **thanks, He brake** it, and said, Take, **eat:** this **is my** body, which is broken for you: this do in remembrance **of me.** After the same manner also, He took the cup, when **He had supped, saying,** This cup is **the New** Testament in my **blood:** this do ye, **as often as ye drink it,** in remembrance of me:" (I Cor. **xi,** 23, 24.)

6th. To vindicate the character of Jesus,—("Wisdom," signifying Jesus, as understood by the best commentators—Prov.

viii, 1—and the vine being one of her progeny,) from the unjust aspersions cast **upon it,** according to the saying, " wisdom is justified **of all her** children:" (Luke **vii,** 35,) by opposing those who **would** destroy "the fruit **of the** vine," or basely **insinuate, that** Immanuel could have made use **of** "**wine, wherein** is excess,"—to represent His blood,—have commanded **it to** be used for that purpose,—**or** could in any way, by His word and Spirit, have countenanced its unlawful employment.

7th. To glorify God, **as does the** vine, by keeping His commandments. "Herein is my Father glorified that ye bear much fruit, so shall ye be my disciples:" (John xv, 8.) "Think not that I am come to destroy the law, or the prophets: I am not come to destroy, but to fulfil. For verily I say unto you, Till **heaven** and earth pass, one jot or one tittle shall in no wise **pass** from the law, till all be fulfilled. Whosoever, therefore, **shall break one** of these least commandments, and shall teach **men so,** he shall be called the least in the kingdom of heaven: but whoever shall **do and teach them, the same** shall be called great in the kingdom **of heaven:**" (Matt. v. **17-19.**) "Ye are my friends, if ye do whatsoever I command you:" (John xv, 14.) "Come eat of **my** bread, and drink of the wine which I have mingled:" (Prov. ix, 5.) "And as they did eat, Jesus took bread, and blessed, and brake *it*, and gave to them, and said, Take, eat: this is my body. And He took the cup, and when He had given thanks, He gave it to them: and they all drank of it. And He said unto them, This is my **blood of the** New Testament, which is shed for many. **Verily I say unto** you, I will drink **no more** of **the fruit of the vine, until that** day that I drink **it new in the kingdom of God:**" (Mark xiv, 22-25.)

———

I began these **letters** some nineteen months ago, confident that the Bible must **be** the strong-hold of Christian temperance if ever it was to be established upon an immovable foundation; and feeling that **if** the doctrine of total abstinence from alcoholic liquors, was part of the revelation of God to man, it ought no longer to be shrouded in darkness, or corrupted by tradition, but to be universally displayed in all its heavenly effulgence, so that the honor hitherto claimed by man, as if the discovery had originated with him, might be transferred to Jehovah, to whom alone it is due.

The course of these letters has often been interrupted by events, which, when they occurred, seemed untoward, but which, in the good providence of God, have ultimately proved propitious, by enabling me to review what I had written,—compare it again and again, with the sacred records,—supply defects,—and correct errors. I now commit them to your care, conscious of their numerous imperfections,—cordially thanking you, for having so patiently borne with me in all my shortcomings,—for your prayers, and the kind, encouraging voice with which you have cheered me onward, so that although often faint, I have yet by the mercy of God, been enabled to pursue, and at length reach the goal.

For whatever of error may be found in these pages, I only am responsible; and, it is my sincere desire, that it all may be discovered, exposed, and rendered harmless.

All the truth they contain, has emanated from the God of truth. May it be made effectual by the teaching of the Holy Spirit, to the propagation of anti-alcoholic temperance to earth's remotest bounds, to the praise of His glorious grace!

I am, my dear friend,
Yours most affectionately,
JOHN MAIR.

# ADDENDA.

### LETTER I.

My Dear Friend,

Having endeavored, to the best of my ability, to accomplish the work primarily laid out for me, I am still required to express my views upon certain important topics, which have been only incidentally and slightly, if at all, touched on, in preceding letters. But, before attempting this, let me say, how deeply I am indebted to the noble band of philanthropic men, who, many years before I gave my attention to the subject, had by their observations, experiments and researches, collected a vast amount of important facts regarding alcohol, and deduced valuable conclusions from them. That I may have drawn materials out of the general fund of temperance literature, in some instances without adequate acknowledgment, is possible, (if so, I now acknowledge the debt,) but I trust I have not injured any one by wilful trespass upon his domain.

While I would render "honor to whom honor is due," *always* —no one will think ill of me for singling out the venerable Dr. Nott, as "worthy of double honor." It would be vain and presumptuous in me, to attempt a commendation of the works of one whose praise is in "all the churches," and whose name is identified with the temperance movement throughout the world. I leave this alone; but, I may be permitted to indulge the pleasure of recording my admiration of the man, who uttered the following sentiment: "To think and speak, and act on his own responsibility, and not to do the bidding of

another, **is** alike the privilege of a free man and a Christian;"\*
and who, **for the** warning of youth, in all ages, has said: "A
friend of **mine gave me** the number and the names of a social
club of temperate drinkers, which once existed in Schenectady,
and of which, when young, he himself was a member; and I
have remarked, how bereft of fortune,—how bereft of reputation,—bereft of health, and sometimes even bereft of reason,
they have descended, one after another, prematurely to the
grave; until at length, though not an old **man**, that friend
alone remains, **of** all their number, to tell how he himself was
rescued from a fate so terrible, by the timely **and** prophetic
counsel of a pious mother. And I have marked too, how those
pupils of my own, who, in despite of warning, and admonition,
and entreaty, persisted in the use of intoxicating liquors, while
at college, have, on entering the world, sunk into obscurity, and
finally disappeared from among those rival actors, once their
companions, rising into life; and when searching out the cause,
I have, full of anxiety, inquired after one and another, the
same answer has been returned: 'He has become or gone a sot
into the grave.'

"Among these cases of moral desolation, I remember one of
peculiar aggravation: It was that of a gifted and aspiring
individual, and a professed Christian. Crossed and humbled
by domestic affliction, he sought, as many still seek, relief in
alcohol. His friends foresaw the danger, and warned him of
it; that warning he derided; he even denied the existence of a
propensity, which, by indulgence, was soon thereafter rendered
uncontrollable; when suddenly shrinking from the society of
men, he shut himself up in his chamber, and endeavored to
drown his cares in perpetual inebriation. His abused constitution soon gave way, and the death scene followed. But Oh!
what a death scene! As if quickened by the presence of the

---

\* Dr. Nott's Lectures on Temperance: p. 16.

King of Terrors, and the proximity of the world of spirits, his reason suddenly lighted up, and all his suspended faculties returned in their strength. But they returned only to give to retribution a severer aspect, and render the final catastrophe more instructive and more terrible. For though at intervals he seemed to pour his soul out in confession, and to implore forgiveness in the most thrilling accents, shame, remorse and despair, were predominant: and there was at times an awfulness in the paroxysms of his agony, **which no words** can describe, and which can be realized only by those who witnessed it. 'There,' said he, pointing to his bottle **and his** glass, which he had caused to be placed beside his death-bed, 'there is the cause of all my misery; that cup is the cup of wretchedness; and yet—fool that I have been!—I have drank it, drank it voluntarily, even to its dregs. Oh! tell those miserable men, once my companions, who dream of finding in inebriation, oblivion to their miseries; as I have dreamed of this; tell them,—but it were vain to tell them—Oh! that they were present, that they might see, in me, the dreadful sequel, and witness in anticipation, the unutterable horrors of a drunkard's death.' Here his voice faltered—his eye fell upon the abhorred cup—and as his spirit fled, a curse, half articulated, died away upon his quivering lip! . . . . This is not poetry, but history. Nor is this the whole. To say nothing of the untitled dead; the heads of families; the members of families, whose number has not been summed up; but—to say nothing of these—how many clergymen, how many physicians, how many jurists, in this and the neighboring cities, have, during the existing generation, fallen victims to the destroyer? Who, of my equals in age, does not remember those venerable men, all moderate drinkers, who once held in Albany, **their** meetings at noon-day? And who does not remember, **too, the** results of those meetings?—aye! and of those other meetings, held at a later hour by their sons—those young men of promise, that were, but are not?

"Over all classes, in that beloved city, intemperance hath cast its withering influence. Nor over these only. There is no city, or town, or hamlet, known to the speaker, where it is otherwise. Of all the avenues to death, the world over, this is the broadest, steepest, most frequented. The sword hath indeed slain its thousands, but alcohol its ten thousands!"\*

Take another terrific sketch, from the Enquirer, (p. 144,)—enough to curdle one's heart's blood, to listen to its withering details: "Suddenly, Amos roused himself from one of his lethargic fits—'the demons are after me,' cried he. 'There they are, grinning, grinning at me, and gnashing their teeth. I see their eyes of fire, and their horrible looking visages. They seek to chastise me with their red-hot, iron scourges. Oh! how they scowl and hiss! while a stream of livid fire issues from their mouths! And now they rush toward me,—Away! away! I will not be taken and thrown among the loathsome, venomous reptiles, in that deep and dark pit! Keep off! I will not go with you!'

"Saying this, and uttering screams of terror, this unhappy being, exerting a preternatural strength, burst from the bands which had confined him during the night, and, in spite of Samson's exertions, threw himself from his berth. He sprang to the forescuttle, and pushed the cook, who sought to prevent his leaving the forecastle, with violence against the bulkhead. He rushed up the ladder, and in a moment was upon deck, fully impressed with the idea that a legion of devils were in close pursuit, bent upon torturing him to death! His appearance at that moment was singularly wild and terrific; he was clad in no garment except a shirt; his long, black hair hang in elf-locks on his shoulders; his eyes were lighted up with the

---

\* Dr. Nott's Lectures: p. 27.

fires of insanity; his teeth were firmly set, and his lips apart—exhibiting a ghastly grin; his visage was haggard—bearing the stamp of unutterable woe,—and his voice was clear and shrill, and unearthly, as he cried out: 'Oh, help me! for God's sake help me! Save me from these devils, who are clutching me! Away—away—away! Ah! they have got me now. I feel their burning breath on my shoulders. Oh! mother—mother—help your son! I feel their talons buried in my throat,—and thus, and thus, I dash them to the earth!' Here the hapless sailor escaped the hands of Mr. Culpepper and Ned Hopkins, who had seized him as he was running aft, after having, with almost incredible agility, leaped over the windlass and fife-rail. He sprang upon the beak of the quarter-deck, and was instantly within the powerful grasp of Capt. Branchbill—but, notwithstanding his great strength, he was unable to arrest the career of the madman to destruction. Amos caught the captain by the windpipe, and compressing it with all the fury of madness, threw him, as if he had been a dwarf, with tremendous force against the binnacle, and in a moment after, the maniac was standing alone on the taffrail, unincumbered and free. With one hand he pointed to the fathomless deep, which seemed to yawn beneath his feet, and he fiercely shook the other at his fancied pursuers,—exclaiming in a hollow but exulting tone: 'Accursed fiends! I have escaped from your withering grasp. I am now beyond your reach, and I defy you! Ha! ha! ha!' And his maniac laugh swept over the face of the waters, and sent a chill to the bosom of his shipmates.

"A rush was made by the crew to the stern of the ship, to save the unhappy man from the fate which he involuntarily seemed to covet,—but ere a hand could be laid upon his person, he sprang high in the air, and alighted in the waters, over which the ship had just passed. He disappeared for a moment, beneath the surface, and then his head suddenly rose high up above the waves. **The** poor fellow uttered a shrill and piercing shriek—a shriek which seemed to be the very embodiment of horror—and **which** rang in the ears **of** his shipmates for days, and months, **and** years afterwards. He then sank beneath the **waters,** and was never seen again.

"**The** main top-sail was laid aback,—the quarter boat was lowered and manned—Mr. Ringbolt himself sprang into the stern seats and seized the tiller, and the boat was shoved off and pulled in the direction of **the ship's** wake, where Amos was last seen,—but no trace of this miserable victim of intemperance could be found. The waters which had parted to receive him, were now closed over him, and not a ripple remained to mark the spot. Such was the fate of Amos **Chauncey.**"

That any man of intelligence and education should have ventured to give such a definition as the following of temperate drinking, in the year 1843, may well excite astonishment; but, **that it should** have proceeded from the **lips of a** man of science, and a physician, seems almost incomprehensible. Nevertheless, "According to Dr. Hun, the drinking just so much as promotes the comfort and well-being of an individual, at any particular time, of which each person must be his own judge, is *temperate drinking.*" "According to Dr. Sewall, the taking a glass of mint-sling in the morning, of toddy at night, or two or three glasses of Madeira **at dinner, is** in common parlance termed *temperate drinking.*" According to **the London press,** the "**Standard,**" "**The** taking of half a **dozen glasses of** wine, a glass **of brandy** and **water, or two** glasses **of ale** daily, is temperate **drinking. Edward C.** Delavan maintains, (as Dr. Hun remarks,) **that** there is no such thing as temperate drinking; that alcohol, in all its **forms, is** poisonous; that alcoholic drinks, when taken (in health,) are always injurious; consequently, there can **be** no temperance in the **use of** these drinks (as a beverage in health,) any more than of arsenic; or, in other words, all use (as a beverage in health,) is abuse." \*

To this last summary of temperance truth, I heartily set my seal, and say amen; and, if my labors are worth anything, in the cause to which I am so warmly attached,—and if I have not gone far astray, in my persevering efforts to find out the doctrine of the Holy Scriptures, in regard to alcoholic liquors, it corresponds with this summary. On the same subject, the Rev. Dr. Nott thus expresses himself: "The question, so far as good wine is concerned, is a question of expediency, and only of expediency, and abstinence becomes a duty only when indulgence would be injurious. But abstinence from bad wine, is always a duty." †

I am, my dear friend,<br>Yours most affectionately,<br>JOHN MAIR.

### LETTER II.

My Dear Friend,

I concluded my last letter to you, with the following quotation from the Rev. President Nott's Lectures: "*But abstinence from bad wine is always a duty.*" The question now arises: "What is good, and what is bad wine? not according to the judgment formed of wine, by the drinkers of Christendom, in the present day, but according to the Bible standard."

The Greek and Latin writers made a clear distinction between intoxicating and unintoxicating wine, and much useful and interesting information upon this subject will be found in Dr. Nott's Fourth Lecture, in "Bacchus and anti-Bacchus,"—in Dr. Lee's works, &c. But it is not my intention to enter upon

---

\* The Enquirer. Note by the Executive Committee: p. 144.
† Dr. Nott's Lectures: p. 130.

this theme. I confine myself to the Scriptural and physiological view of the question; and, I adduce the following arguments, to show that there is a distinct line of demarcation drawn **between** "good and bad wine," (or wines which it is lawful and unlawful to use in man's normal state of health,) in the Bible; and, that this line runs parallel with physiological and pathological observations and experiments:

I. The first and most direct, and decisive argument, is derived from the following passage, which has often been matter of reference, viz: "Look not thou upon the wine when it is red, when it giveth his color in the cup," &c.: (Prov. xxiii, 31,)—where the process of the vinous fermentation is accurately and **beautifully** described. This **is** one of the most express and comprehensive of **all** the statutes, against the use of intoxicating **wine**, to be found in the Bible; and, **I** have surmised, that the teetotalism of modern times may have been unwittingly derived from it.

II. **The second** argument is like the foregoing, and is drawn from **the** Gospels **of** Matthew, Mark and **Luke**, where the celebration of the Passover, and the institution of the Lord's supper, are recorded. I have shown, in the plainest manner, (Letter 18,) that only "unfermented things" were allowed to be made use of, upon both these occasions; so that the employment of unfermented things, including unfermented wine, by **our** Divine Redeemer, at His model supper, was a confirmation **of the law** previously enunciated by Solomon, limiting the use of **wine to that** which is unfermented **and** unintoxicating.

The following arguments spring out of the laws of man's physical organization:

III. The peculiar affinity or attraction of the brain for alcohol, by which—first, the high intellectual and moral powers,—**next,** the motor and sensory,—and last of all, those essential **to life,** are injured or destroyed, **(Letter** 7;) the fact **that** a taste for weak alcoholic liquors gradually and insensibly leads to a desire for those containing larger, and still **larger proportions** of alcohol; and the facts stated by Dr. Beaumont, from examination of the stomach of **St. Martin, after** indulgence **in** intoxicating liquors, **thus:** "On examining St. Martin's stomach, after he had been indulging freely **in ardent** spirits for several days, Dr. B. found its mucous membrane covered with crythematic (inflammatory) and aphthous (ulcerous) patches, the secretions vitiated, and the gastric juice diminished **in** quantity, viscid and unhealthy; *although St. Martin still complained of nothing, not even of impaired appetite. . . . . The free use of ardent spirits, wine, beer, or **any intoxicating** liquor, **when** continued **for some days, has** invariably **produced these morbid changes.**"\*

IV. The impossibility of laying down any other definite, intelligible rule, applicable in all cases, by which the evils arising from the use of **"wine** and **strong drink"** in man's **normal** state of health, could be prevented,—in consequence of the great diversity of constitutional peculiarities, age, climate, &c., (and the laws of alcohol adverted to in the last paragraph,) which would require corresponding diversities in the quantity and quality of the alcoholic liquor suited to each, (even upon the scripturally disproved hypothesis of the least **quantity being** ever safe and allowable,) and innumerable persons capable **of** adjusting the precise measure of liquor, and the exact proportion of alcohol adapted to the case of each individual.

The following remarks of Mr. Goodell are to the point, and command my assent: "The ancient wine, which God explicitly pronounced 'a mocker,' contained no mixture of distilled spirits; for the **art of** distillation **was unknown,** till centuries after **the** pen of inspiration had penned the condemnation of **that liquor.** Where, then, is the line of demarkation? Do **we not** all know where it is? Who at this day does not know, that *previous* to

---

\* The Physiology of Digestion. By A. Combe, **M. D.: 5th ed., Edin.,** p. 145.

the vinous fermentation, no juices of wholesome fruits or grains are in the least degree intoxicating? Who does not know that all the alcohol on earth, whether existing in wine, beer, cider, rum, brandy or gin, or anything else, is produced solely and exclusively by this same process of fermentation?

"Distillation produces no alcohol—not a particle—nor does it alter the nature of the alcohol previously existing. It only separates the alcohol previously produced by fermentation. . . . . Having learned from the Bible, **that God** expressly prohibits the use of certain wines, while He speaks **of** other wines as a blessing; and, having learned that *vinous fermentation*, and *that* alone, can draw the dividing line between 'the mocker' and the 'blessing,' we possess ourselves, do we not, **of** the true Scripture doctrine on the subject? The Bible prohibits *intoxicating* wines. It allows and sanctions those that are *unintoxicating*. Both these kinds of wine we know have **existed**, and have **been extensively used in the** East, from the earliest periods to the present time. 'Look not thou upon the wine when it is red, when it giveth **his** color in the cup, when it *moveth* itself aright; at the last it biteth like a serpent, and stingeth like an adder:' (Prov. xxiii, 29–32.) What a graphic description of a *fermenting* liquor! The reader sees it move and sparkle. The most scientific definition of the modern chemist could not have been equally demonstrative, forcible, **and** universally intelligible! How total the prohibition, 'look **not.**' The temperance societies have only said: 'touch not, taste **not,** handle not.' Let the Bible carry things farther. 'Wine **is** a mocker.' Yes, the thing *itself*. Not its abuse, as some say. '**Because** he transgresseth through wine:' (Hab. ii, 5.) Not through the abuse of wine. 'Be not among wine-bibbers:' (Prov. xxiii, 20.) To bib, or *sip* wine, is certainly a **very** 'moderate' way of using it 'as a drink.' But God forbids us not only to drink, but to *sip*—not only to **sip, but even to** be among those who do so." *

As for argument **on the other side, I would simply** say, that if hoary age can sanctify error, **or the tenacity with** which it is grasped, convert it into truth, then I yield submission to the only powers which (it seems to me,) can be brought to bear against the law which I believe to be in the Bible, against alcoholic, or in other words, fermented wine, in **man's normal** state **of** health.

But some may be heard to say, **in** contradiction **to these** views: "This doctrine is too high for us; we cannot attain to it. We cannot get **such wine as** you so positively assert **the** law of God requires us **to use."** "Think again, dear friends. Have you ever attained yet, to the perfect keeping of any of the Commandments of the Decalogue? **If so,** you must be more than human,—you must **be Divine. For** "it is written, there is none righteous, no not one. There is none that understandeth, there is none that seeketh after God. They are all gone out of the way, they are together become unprofitable; there is none that doeth good, no not one :" (Romans iii, 10–12.) "If we say that we **have no sin,** we deceive ourselves, **and the** truth is not in us:" (I **John i, 8.)** "For in **many things we** offend all:" (James iii, 2.)

"But have you honestly *tried* to get *unfermented* **wine** ; and, **after** hearty, persevering efforts, have **you failed in your** attempts? Have you been as much upon your guard to avoid the use of intoxicating wine as you have been to shun lying, or stealing, or sabbath-breaking; and, has it been your assiduous desire, especially to succeed in obtaining unfermented fruit **of** the vine to represent your Saviour's blood at His supper? If so, I venture to affirm, without much fear of contradiction, that you have not been compelled to drink fermented **or** alcoholic

---

* The Enquirer. Appendix: p. 16.

wine, to any considerable extent, anywhere; and, that the only insurmountable objection to your sitting down at the Lord's table, in the church to which you belong, has arisen, not from the impossibility or impracticability of getting unfermented fruit of the vine to show forth the Lord's death, but from the disinclination of your fellow Christians to receive it, because they prefer intoxicating wine as the emblem of His sin-atoning blood, and do not care to search the Scriptures to find out 'whether these things were so.' Moreover, brethren, let it be remembered by you who oppose this doctrine, that it is not obligatory, by command of God, upon you or any one to drink of wine *at all*, either inebriating or *non*-inebriating, (any more than it is or was binding upon you to get married,) except at the sacred ordinance of the Lord's supper; and surely, upon reflection, you cannot find it very difficult to procure grapes, either dried or fresh, or preserved by some chemical process, uncorrupted—as often as you resolve to bring to mind your Saviour's blood-shedding for your sins, 'according to the Scriptures,'—and what *more* is wanted of you, but a small supply of pure water, one of Heaven's choicest, and yet most abundant blessings, wherewithal to make an infusion of the precious fruit, which Jesus has so highly honored by selecting it to be the symbol of His life's blood poured out on the Cross at Calvary, to atone for our sins,—and a believing, loving heart, to partake of it?"

The best practical rule for Christians to adopt, would be, never to drink of wine or any other liquor, when alone, in the family, or society, unless convinced of its being unintoxicating; and to make doubly sure of *that* which is about to be dispensed at the Lord's supper, being without the slightest taint of alcohol, or other poison.

Believe me, my dear brother,<br>
Yours most affectionately,<br>
**JOHN MAIR.**

## LETTER III.

My Dear Friend,

Next to the groundless supposition, to which professing Christians so generally adhere, that intoxicating wine was given by our Lord to His disciples at the institution of His supper, in the upper room at Jerusalem,—perhaps no event, in His most memorable life, has been more confidently urged, or with less reason, as a plea against teetotalism, than His turning water into wine at the **" marriage in Cana, of Galilee."** The simple and beautiful narrative, as contained in the 2d chapter of John's Gospel, is as follows:

"And the third day there was a marriage in Cana of Galilee, and the mother of Jesus was there. And both Jesus was called, and His disciples to the marriage. And when they wanted wine, the mother of Jesus saith unto Him, They have no wine. Jesus saith unto her, Woman, what have I to do with thee? mine hour is not yet come. His mother saith unto the servants, Whatsoever He saith unto you, do *it*. And there were set there six water-pots of stone, after the manner of the purifying of the Jews, containing two or three firkins apiece. Jesus saith unto them, Fill the water-pots with water. **And they filled** them up to the brim. And He saith unto them, Draw out now, **and** bear unto the governor of the feast; and they bare it. **When** the ruler of the feast had tasted the water that was made wine, and knew not whence it was, (but the servants which drew the water knew;) the governor of the feast called the bridegroom, and saith unto him, Every man at the beginning doth set forth good wine; and when men have well drunk, then that which is worse: but thou hast kept the good wine until now. This beginning of miracles did Jesus in Cana of Galilee, and manifested forth His glory; and His disciples believed on Him."

With the light which has been shed upon the subject of anti-alcoholic **temperance, in** preceding letters, I apprehend there will **be** no great difficulty in setting at rest the question, " Was the wine, which Jesus made in Cana of Galilee, intoxicating or unintoxicating ?" Without hesitation, but after much thought, I say *unintoxicating*, because the action of Jesus could not **have** been in opposition **to His own** law,—and it was His law (as has, I trust, been satisfactorily proved by incontrovertible facts and arguments, in the course of these letters,) that men should not drink of intoxicating wine, or other intoxicating liquor, except for necessary medicinal purposes. There is not the shadow of a reason, for holding the opinion that the wine which Jesus made at this marriage was inebriating. It is founded upon the groundless assumption, that because Christian men, in large numbers, will have it, that there is only one kind of wine, and that *intoxicating*,—and that there never was any **other;** *therefore*, all the Scriptures, which either positively or by implication, forbid the use of wine, must apply to it, not in all quantities, and of all degrees of alcoholic strength, but only to the *immoderate* use of it, contrary to the obvious meaning of the following, and many similar passages of Holy Writ : " Look not thou upon the wine when it is red ;" attention to which, has been given throughout these letters. The disputants upon the opposite sides of this question, may be arranged under the distinctive appellations of, " The Alcoholic School," and " The Anti-alcoholic School."

To the Alcoholic School, belonged the celebrated Missionary to China, the Rev. Dr. Medhurst, some time deceased. It boasts of **the** popular Dr. Cumming, also, as a resolute combatant ; and to it the majority of divines of the present day, zealously attach themselves,—including all those who go no farther than what is called Christian expediency,—and who will not allow that the laws of revelation and physiology equally militate against the use of alcohol in man's normal state of health.

To the Anti-alcoholic School, on the other hand, belong all those who claim for the Bible, the distinct enunciation of a law against the use of alcoholic liquors, by man in his normal state of health; and for Science, the explicit declaration of the same law.

One or two specimens, illustrative of the mode of reasoning of disciples of each of these schools, may now be given.

The Rev. Dr. Medhurst, in his sermon, "Add to your faith —temperance:" (II Peter i, 5, 6,) referred to in a previous letter, thus expresses himself:

"We are now prepared to consider the question relative to the wine made at the marriage in Cana. We have already got the definition of *oinos*, not only from its derivation, but from the meaning assigned to it by our Lord himself. When, therefore, we find that the *oinos* is spent at a certain feast, and that our Saviour produces a liquor which is reckoned, by a tolerable judge, to be good *oinos*; what are we to suppose that that *oinos* was. What, but the identical liquid which is spoken of, in another part of the same book, as fermented wine? We must say, that if the evangelist intended that we should understand by it an unfermented and a non-intoxicating wine, it became him to employ some other term, in order to prevent our being led astray.

"We may further infer, that the *oinos* made on that occasion was fermented wine, from the account given of it by the master of the feast. Referring to a general rule on such occasions, he says, 'Every man at the beginning doth set forth good wine, and when men have well drunk,' or have had a tolerable portion, 'then that which is worse: but thou hast kept the good wine until now.' Now let us try to explain this, on the supposition of its being unfermented wine. Unfermented wine is used only to slake thirst, or to please the palate. If no stimulus

20

be present, as soon as the thirst is quenched, or the taste gratified, there **remains** no more desire to drink; and, not to speak of inferior wine being then offered, even the same sort of wine would be loathed and rejected. Merely sweet beverages soon cloy, and watery potions fill the stomach; so that when men **have** well drunk of these, they want no more. The man, therefore, who would give his good *must*, or syrup, first, and keep that which is inferior till afterwards, would be likely to get the subsequent beverage returned with disgust upon his hands. But, on the supposition that the *oinos* referred to was fermented wine, the speech of the master of the feast accords with common sense and experience. Fermented wine is used as a stimulant and as a cordial; being of an exciting nature, it can be taken into the stomach long after thirst has ceased; there is still a relish for it, when considerable potions have been swallowed down; and such a relish as would induce men to drink it, notwithstanding the subsequent liquor were somewhat inferior to what was formerly given. The man, therefore, who would keep his inferior fermented wine till afterwards, would be likely to have it accepted, and thus to save his superior beverage; particularly, when the acute sense of taste was so far blunted, as that the difference was not readily perceived. In this, we have been merely discussing the speech of the master of the feast, as to the general practice on such occasions. The evangelist does not say, that the guests at the marriage feast **of** Cana had well drunk; he merely says that *usterantos oinou* —'they wanted wine,' or the wine was done; while the mother of Jesus said to Him, 'they have no wine.' It was, therefore, to supply their need, and not to provide them with superfluities, that Jesus turned the water into wine. The quantity, also, will not appear great when we consider that there were at such feasts, sometimes, hundreds of persons, amongst whom, even six water-pots full of the light wine commonly used in Judea, would not have been too large a supply."

It appears evident to me, that Dr. Medhurst has mistaken the points of contrast, brought out in bold relief in the address of the governor of the feast to **the** bridegroom. It was not, in my opinion, *more* intoxicating wine, **or** wine containing a larger percentage of alcohol, made by the miraculous power of Jesus, which the governor intended to contrast with *less* intoxicating wine provided for the guests at an earlier period of the feast, but the *custom* of "every man"—(i. **e.**, men **in** general— as "*tout le monde,*" or "all the world," is a term applied to a great and indefinite number ;) at the beginning setting forth good wine, and, when the guests had well drunk or used a **good deal** of liquid for a considerable space of time, supplying them with wine of an inferior quality, **which** he intended **to contrast** with the *exceptional* conduct of the bridegroom upon this occasion, in keeping the good **wine in store** till late in the feast, and then presenting it to the guests *contrary* to established custom! If this view be correct, then the nature of the wine is not to be judged of from the speech of the governor, which **conveys** no information as to what was esteemed good in his day, nor from the habits of the people, but from the character of Him who made it, even the Saviour of sinners, who, as has been stated already, could not have broken His own **commandment, but** must have acted in conformity with it, **in converting the water** contained in the firkins into unfermented, unintoxicating wine.

The foundation upon which Dr. Medhurst built his reasonings and conclusions, was this: He judged of the nature of the wine miraculously produced by our Saviour, from the notion that because unfermented wine was not recognized by the churches of Christ, or by him in his day, **as** a distinct entity; *therefore,* it could not have been recognized by Jesus, or the Jewish people as such, and approved of by Him and them, **when this** miracle was performed, although there was nothing stronger than the following allegations to sustain his position, viz: that men would not want sweet beverages which soon cloy, or watery potions which fill the stomach, after having well drunk; therefore, they would be likely to refuse an inferior kind of must if offered to them—whereas having their taste blunted by the **previous** use of intoxicating wine, (implying a somewhat advanced stage of drunkenness,) a wine less intoxicating might **be** relished by them; thus making prior intoxication, poisoning **or** drunkenness, a necessary condition to the stability of his hypothesis, upon which hypothesis alone he could have built his doctrine that **Jesus "manufactured" wine** more intoxicating than that previously used by the guests, at the marriage of Cana of Galilee, for their use when intoxicated.

I have already shown that the points of contrast in the governor's speech, were not differences in the quality of the wines used, as intoxicating or unintoxicating, as has been assumed without the least shadow of proof, but supposed differences in the doings **of** the bridegroom at the marriage of **Cana, and** other bridegrooms at marriages generally, in respect to wines for **the use of** the guests, as good or bad, better or worse ; **the** point mooted being, *not* whether **the** guests preferred the last presented wine to the other upon ordinary occasions,—received or rejected it; but simply the difference between this bridegroom and others, in his supplying good or superior wine towards the end; whereas, it was the ordinary practice to give inferior wine last. It is very possible, nay probable, **that** the guests may not have relished the last wine so much as **the first** (if the same persons throughout,) upon such occasions, **and it** can hardly be supposed that they would, if there was much **disparity** between them, (an event very likely to occur in consequence **of** exhaustion of the servants from continuous and protracted **labor,** and their consequent inability rightly to prepare the wines **if** inspissated,) and all this would tend to enhance the character of Immanuel, by comparison, in the eyes of all who knew **the** law of God to be against alcoholic liquors ; but the creation of alcoholic wine on the other hand, so to *depress* it, as to shear Him of the rays of Divine glory. The alcoholic hypothesis must, *therefore*, be rejected, not **only** as utterly without foundation, but in the highest degree impious and atheistical.

How different the doctrine **which we** maintain. It is no groundless, gratuitous supposition—no chimera—no castle in the air—no figment of the imagination—but a noble, compact, indestructible edifice, **built upon the foundation of the word of God.**\*

---

\* Let it be clearly understood, that the criterion by which we are to judge **of** the quality of the wine as good **or** bad, better **or** worse, spoken **of** by **the** governor of the feast upon this occasion, is not **to be** derived from **anything** said by him, or **from any data furnished by modern opinions of wine, founded** upon established usages, **which have exalted alcohol to a** high place **in popular** estimation, as "a good creature **of** God," **to be used** as a drink for man. Let it be further clearly understood that the criterion, by which we are to judge, is to be derived solely from the Holy Scriptures, and the character of Jesus, as perfect God and perfect **man,** "in two distinct natures, in one person forever;" rendering it *impossible* that He, the only mediator between God and man, who covenanted to keep the whole law, (of course including **all** its parts,) (Matt. iii, 15: v, 17, 18,) and endure its penalty, (I Peter ii, 24,) could, in any instance, or in the least iota, have deviated from it; and, as it has been proved that total abstinence from alcoholic liquors, is a part **of** the Divine law in man's normal state of health,—*therefore*, it behoved the Lord Jesus Christ to abstain from these liquors as His people's surety, to complete "the righteousness of God which is by faith **of** Jesus Christ unto all **and** upon all that believe:" (Romans iii, 22.) **Dr. Lees** broaches an ingenious speculation: "that the marriage **of Cana of Galilee,** was left to be recorded by St. John, whose Gospel is last **in** order **in the** Sacred canon, that **he** might successfully oppose a doctrine then prevalent, that of Manicheism, or of two **principles, Ormuzd and** Ahriman—the former representing the good Spirit, and **father** of light; and the latter the evil, the creator of the material world, but **the** enemy of light and truth.

"This general notion," says the learned Dr., "we can readily comprehend, would receive an emphatic application, when directed to the vine — the *supposed* source of an intoxicating agent, whose connexion with **evil** had been apparent in every age and country, wherein it has been consumed as human beverage. A Turkish proverb says: 'A devil lurks in every berry of *the vine*.' Here, then, was a doctrine and principle which divorced the outward, physical and organic universe of God—the mirror of His perfection,

Hear what the learned and ingenious author of "Tirosh Lo Yayin" says, in relation to this groundless hypothesis which we have been fighting against: "The proofs which we have **already given of the** existence of unfermented **wines in anti-**

**and** the instrument of His will—from the spiritual essence and mental powers enshrined within the living temple of the body,—a doctrine of abstinence indeed, yet a very spurious off-shoot from the oldest and most genuine truth **of** temperance, founded upon just and natural distinctions,—a doctrine moreover, of such **a baleful tendency in its** relations both to morals and religion, that we for our part, find in the **direct and** unmistakable antagonism to it, of the miracle at Cana, a wonderful significancy and depth of meaning: Could Christ in this beginning of miracles at Cana, to show forth the Father's glory, have selected any mode of teaching more fitting than one which, in practically reclaiming to the sovereignty of the One, both the realms of matter and spirit, was at once an illustration of the falsehood, and a prophecy of the final extinction of oriental dualism? It is a remarkable confirmation of the preceding view, that the *record* of this miracle should be found only **in the latest** of the Gospels, that of John—a Gospel which, to every scholar, bears evident marks of *adaptation*, both in form and matter, to the philosophy and errors of the last years of the Apostolic age."—[*Kalon Oinon: p.* 30.

I am disposed to view this opinion of Dr. Lees with favor, as carrying with it an air of probability, and as consistent with the doctrine I have endeavored to establish upon Scriptural data, that "the fruit of the vine is the Divinely-appointed antidote of alcoholic intemperance." But I believe there were and are, other reasons besides this, which ought to be weighed in attempting to account for this miracle being reserved to be recorded by the disciple whom Jesus loved; and, I would say,

1st. That one reason for this was, (speaking with humility and reverence becoming this sacred and sublime theme,) that he was not required to enter into the particulars of the Lord's supper, in which "the fruit of the vine" occupies **so** conspicuous a place, and which were narrated by all the other Evangelists.

2d. That **he** was the beloved disciple *par excellence*; therefore, it was most seemly **that he should** be the recorder of the first miracle, and one of the most remarkable **of all; so** intimately related to the success of his Master's work upon earth, **and the** manifestation of *His* glory.

3d. If this miracle of the conversion of water into wine, had been left out of the Holy Scriptures, there would have been a deficiency of the materials so important to strengthen the broad and indestructible foundation of Anti-alcoholic Temperance, by affording a living, truth-telling, soul-inspiring motive, along with those before touched upon, especially to newly married quity and in the Saviour's days, and of the popular taste and predilection for them even in heathen countries, offer to the choice an interpretation consonant to the Divine character.

persons and their future progeny, **to** abstain *always* from alcoholic liquors in their normal state of health; and, if it had *not* been recorded by St. John, (the disciple whom Jesus loved,) who afterwards had these impressive words addressed to him by his Master, when hanging on the Cross, "behold thy mother," as Mary had these words addressed to her, "behold thy son," it would have lost much of the power which it derives from the Divine, maternal and filial tenderness, love, and home-sympathy, which must ever be associated with it, and render it the most precious, heart-expanding, soul-strengthening of miracles to the humble follower of "the meek and lowly Jesus," who sees through the mystery of "the fruit of the vine," and believes it to be the Heaven-appointed remedy of Alcoholic Intemperance.

Mark well the effects of the opposite hypothesis, of the Alcoholic School, which not only neutralizes the efficacy of all these beauteous associations for body and soul-saving purposes, "by one fell swoop;" but in their place, under homage to the Prince of this world, "the Spirit that now worketh in the children of disobedience,"—by endorsing his lie, that Jesus ever made, used or patronized alcoholic wine; in the most effectual manner, carries out his designs for the destruction of the human species!

4th. Another reason to be assigned for the place which this miracle occupies in the sacred records, and for John being the sole narrator of it, is the following: John is the Evangelist who most fully explains the doctrine of the new birth in the never to be forgotten discourse of our Saviour with Nicodemus: (John iii, 1–21.) He is also the only Evangelist who records the first Passover which was attended by our Lord, in connexion with the ejection of the sellers of oxen and money changers from the court of the Gentiles. Take these facts placed in juxtaposition in the Bible with the miracle of the conversion of water into wine at Cana of Galilee, and I ask, if there be not ground for believing that this apposition was designed of God, and not accidental, and that it was designed in order to afford prompt means for establishing something important? Now the question is, how could the facts of the new birth,—the conversion of water into wine,—the ignominious expulsion of the desecrators of the Temple therefrom,—and of the occurrence of the first Passover, at which Jesus was present, have been reconciled in the mind of John, their narrator, or in the minds of the other Apostles present, with the assumption that Jesus converted the water into alcoholic, intoxicating wine? If it had been alcoholic wine, would not John and **the** other disciples of John the Baptist (supposing them to have been present at the marriage,) have instantaneously perceived, and been appalled by the incongruity of their

*"With such an alternative, how can we presume to entertain the thought that the Lord of Life could, at the commencement of His public ministry on earth, have created a liquor containing alcohol, an element so adapted to destroy life? or, that He*

**new** Master, Jesus, presenting to them intoxicating wine, produced by His miraculous power,—*that* wine which they had been taught by the example of **their** former master to eschew, and the seductive, dangerous nature of which, they must have been acquainted with? Would not their astonishment and dismay have been still greater afterwards upon reflection, when they thought of the impossibility of reconciling such a miracle with the doctrine of the new birth, to which, intoxicating liquor must be so great an enemy,—and of the inconsistency of expelling the money changers, and sellers of oxen and doves, from the court of the Gentiles, after having given to His friends, a short time before, *intoxicating wine* to drink; (which must have appeared to them a greater violation of the Divine law;) and especially, when they had compared that fact with the fact of His partaking, soon after, of *unfermented, unintoxicating wine* at the **Jewish** Passover? Such anomalies would have been **to them** stumbling blocks which they could not get over. If such intoxicating **wine as** the Alcoholic School believe in, had been the product of the miraculous **power of Jesus at Cana,** can you conceive it possible that John, and others **who had been the** disciples of John the Baptist, would have remained with him; or, that the disputed miracle would have been recorded by the beloved disciple who leaned upon Jesus' bosom at meat? You cannot believe it. He would have been **deserted by them.** But this was not the case,—therefore the wine made by Jesus, was unintoxicating.

Another class of reasons may be assigned for the belief that the wine, created by Jesus at Cana, was *unintoxicating*—derived from a consideration of some of the chief ordinances of our holy religion, viz: Marriage,—Sabbath **or the** Lord's Day,—Baptism,—and the Lord's Supper: all links of the same **sacred** chain which binds heaven to earth—so that when one link gives way, **the** continuity is dissolved,—the celestial influences are interrupted,—the sensual and terrene operate with full force, and the progress downwards is rapid and certain. **But what is** it which **most tends to corrode** the links of this celestial chain, **if not alcohol?** Thus, let two members of the church begin, by having their marriage solemnized with alcoholic liquors, under the countenance of the officiating **minister, and** what is likely to follow from the initiation of the bride and bridegroom into alcoholic usages (if not before tainted with the love of alcohol,) but that **they will** continue to use "wine or strong drink" in their family,—soon acquiring a liking for it,—and command their children and household after them, not according to the example of faithful Abraham, "the Friend of God," so that their children should do "justice and judg-

*who came into the world to save souls, could have offered it to others, to dethrone the reasoning faculty, or that immortal part of man, the soul, wherein alone he resembles his Creator? or, that He could have sanctioned by His presence, the drinking*

---

ment,"—but after *that* of some luxurious, pampered, obese worshipper of Bacchus, leading them by precept and practice to become drinkers of intoxicating wine from their youth, as if in doing so they were presenting a "spiritual sacrifice acceptable to God by Jesus Christ."

Again, let the starting point of the evil habit be Baptism, and similar effects will follow; for what is more natural than for the parents to **think** or reason thus: "Jesus used alcoholic wine at the marriage of Cana, (so I believe, **for so I have been taught by my sabbath-school teachers and ministers,) and also at the institution of the sacrament of the Lord's supper. He must have been right in doing so. I must be right in following His** example at a ceremony of religion equally binding, and **equally sacred."** Who could **find** fault with him for reasoning thus, and acting accordingly? **Or,** let the Lord's table be the starting point, the same consequences will follow. The use of alcoholic liquors will be consecrated in all religious families. While the belief remains, the practice must follow, except amongst the small and despised sect of teetotalers. Moreover, if the habit has commenced at the Lord's table, alcoholic wine being identified with the precious blood of the Lamb, may be deemed a true friend of man, under all circumstances, as Jesus certainly is; and, therefore, be applied indiscriminately and with equal partiality in health and disease—lassitude and excitement—cold and heat—joy and sorrow; in short, in **diseases** of mind and body, however contradictory, as a certain remedy for **them all!** Once more—the Lord's day being most intimately and indissolubly **associated** with the Lord's supper—no marvel if people think they should be more liberal in their potations upon that day than any other! Whether they have been so or not, let the keepers of taverns and police courts testify!

On the other hand—let the truth as it is in Jesus—upon this most important question—prevail, and the results will be blessed indeed. Instead of one religious festival and ordinance after another, becoming a snare to entrap,—a tyrant to enslave men's souls,—a deadly venom to corrupt and destroy their bodies,—and an inlet to all kinds of crimes,—they all of them would be what their All-wise and benevolent Designer, with perfect wisdom, intended they should,—channels to transmit gracious streams from the river of the water of life into the spiritual mind, making it like "a well watered garden—filled with the fruits of righteousness which are by Jesus Christ to the praise and glory of God;" while the body, preserved in health and vigor to a good old age by the same means, would unite with it singing the praise of their beneficent Creator, Preserver, Redeemer and Sanctifier—Father, Son and Holy

of a liquor possessing properties of a character similar to that which He rejected at His dying hour?* It has often been a subject of grief, no less than of astonishment, that serious people, and even religious people should have manifested such eagerness to prove the Saviour the creator of an intoxicating wine, and for persons already (as they contend,) intoxicated, at a marriage feast, or the boon companion of the glutton and the drunkard. *How weak, how wicked must they be, who would thus (reflectingly,) break down* **the foundation** *of their hope of redemption; for if such were really the character of the Christ that hath come, then hath the true Messiah not yet come, and all their hopes and expectations are in vain!"*
—[*Tirosh Lo Yayin:* p. 152.

---

Ghost, in this world, till their separation at death, and in the New Jerusalem forever and ever, when re-united at "the resurrection of the just."

To conclude: *Marriage* may be viewed as the Divine model-institution for regulating and preserving *pure* intercourse between the sexes:

*Baptism*, as the Divine model-institution for teaching the necessity of internal spiritual purifying by the Holy Spirit, and the connexion between inward and outward purity:

*The Lord's Day*, as the Divine model-institution for the sanctification of time: and

*The Lord's Supper*, as the Divine model-institution for teaching the necessity of the washing away of human guilt with the sacrificial blood of the Lamb.

"The Fruit of the Vine," with all its holy associations, has been wisely designed and admirably adapted by Divine Providence, as an instrument for the sanctification of believers, in connexion with all these ordinances; and, I believe, was dispensed by our blessed Redeemer at the marriage of Cana and **at His own** supper, (for this, with other reasons,) to give us an "example that we should follow His steps."

The poison alcohol, the product of corruption, is opposed to the pure purposes to be subserved by all these institutions, and is, *therefore*, forbidden by the Almighty in the domestic circle, (the house of man,) of which marriage is the source and guardian; in the church, (the house of God,) of which "the blood of the Lamb," symbolized by "the pure blood of the grape," at the Lord's supper, is the price and the purifier; and at all repasts, and upon all occasions, (except in disease,) connected directly or indirectly with these blessed ordinances.

Hear, also, what your learned and talented friends, the Rev. Dr. Nott, Professor Moses Stuart, and the sainted Dr. Justin Edwards have said upon this subject: "Had Pliny, Columella, Theophrastus, Plutarch, and other ancient sages, some of whom were cotemporary with the Apostles, presided at this festival, the question at issue as to the kind of wine miraculously supplied, would have been decided; for these men have sat in judgment on the quality of wines, and pronounced the weaker, unintoxicating wines, the better wines. But these men did not preside at this festival, and whether the master of the feast, who did, agreed with them in their opinion concerning the relative goodness of wines, we are not informed, and will not presume, therefore, authoritatively to decide; but, on the contrary, leave the question, whether the Saviour of the world miraculously supplied on this occasion, *deleterious*, *exciting*, *intoxicating wine*, or *sober*, *moral*, *unintoxicating wine*, to be passed on by the enlightened reason and conscience of others. For ourselves, however, we may be permitted to say, in view of all the circumstances of the case, we incline to the opinion that the wine, declared by the master of the feast to be 'good wine,' was *good wine*—good in the sense that Pliny, Columella, or Theophrastus would have used the term 'good,' when applied to wine; that is, good, because nutritious and unintoxicating; and of which the guests, even at such an hour, might drink freely and without apprehension,—because it was wine, which though it would refresh and cheer, would not derange, demoralize, or intoxicate."\*

"But the *wedding* at Cana of **Galilee?** How comes it that wine was miraculously supplied, in case it be not proper to drink it? Truly it is impossible to suppose this, and yet leave the character of the holy Saviour unscathed. But as the ruler of the feast pronounced the wine, that had just been made, by far the best; and as it is clear that the ancients regarded the

---

\* Dr. Nott's Lectures on Temperance: p. 143.

*unfermented* wine as bearing this character: what hinders us from supposing this to be the kind of wine which the condescension and comity of the Saviour, towards His friends, supplied? Nay, I may well ask: When *His spotless character, and hatred of sin and all defilement are taken into view, and to this is joined the character of the guests on this occasion, what allows us with any propriety to suppose that alcoholic wine was furnished by miraculous power?*" \*

"'*Every man.*' This is the statement of what was usual on such occasions. Pliny, who lived **at that** time, says: good wine was that which was destitute of spirit:—Book iv, chapter 13. Plutarch calls *that* the best wine which is harmless; *that* the most useful, which has the least strength; and *that* the most wholesome, in which nothing was added to the juice of **the grape.**" †

**Let me** draw this letter to a close, by quoting largely from a most interesting article contained in "The Abstainer's Journal," edited by the Rev. William Reid, December, 1854, entitled "Unbelievers and the Bible;" the extracts from which, I hope, may tend to open the eyes of some, in other respects, devout and conscientious Christian ministers and laymen who have, hitherto, occupied a most unenviable and perilous position in advocating the doctrine, that Jesus *manufactured* intoxicating wine at the marriage of Cana, and otherwise patronized it:

"Modern experience and science have now clearly determined *the essentially deleterious character of alcoholic drinks.* **From this there can be** no successful appeal; and men can only shut out **conviction** by shutting **out** evidence. Taking this ground, the immovable ground of physical truth, the modern sceptic revives the objections of the English deists of the seventeenth and eighteenth centuries, but revives them with a terribly-increased power, subtlety and conclusiveness. Dr. Strauss, in

---

\* Scriptural View of the Wine Question. By Professor M. Stuart: p. 53.
† Family Bible with Notes. By Rev. Dr. J. Edwards: John ii, 9.

Germany, and the *Reasoner*, the organ of atheism in England, are even now busily engaged in reproducing those objections to Holy Writ, which, in relation to the marriage at Cana, and the temperance question **generally, are** intended either to discredit the miracle of the transformation of water into wine, or to place the sanction **of** Scripture in antagonism to the verdict of morality, experience and science.

"Referring **to** the last edition of the *Leben Jesu* of the German sceptic, and having our attention called to an article on 'the Bible and Teetotalism,' **in No. 12** of the *Reasoner* for September last, we have been **shocked to find that the chief** weapons of the unbelievers are drawn from the armory **of** Christian divines; and, that the sceptic mocker **of the Bible, and** the professional expounder of Holy Writ, are ranged side by side against the school of temperance reformers which maintains the *harmony* of the divine word and works. There is not a principle of interpretation—not a single assumption of any importance, which the infidel assailant of the Bible requires for his purpose, which is not borrowed from the books of the orthodox believer! Surely, this is a fact which should startle the Christian drinker into reflecting, whether it is not possible that he may have been thoughtlessly occupying, not only **a** dangerous, but a thoroughly *false* position? **In the spirit of** perfect toleration, and of Christian humility, **we** beseech a renewed and impartial examination of this important topic. A few passages will illustrate the unity of conception, and the identity of stand-point, between the revilers of revelation and the common expounders of it:

1. "'*Wine*,' says the Christian drinker, '*is not wine unless it be fermented*.' So objects the arch-infidel of all time, **Dr.** Strauss, 'The wine at Cana was *no wine*. 1st. Unless **other** elements were put *into* the water. 2d. Unless it **was** organically *individuated* to the vine. 3d. Unless it had gone through the natural *processes* of growing, blooming, ripening, etc. 4th.

Unless it had been artificially *pressed out*. 5th. Unless it had been accelerated by the further natural *process of fermentation*.' The German professor is more subtle than the British drinker, who makes the *last* process essential to his notion of 'wine;' **but** omits the former. Neander rightly objects, 'That we are **not** justified in inferring that the water was changed into *manufactured* wine; but that Christ substituted His creative power for various natural and artificial processes; that He *intensified*, so to speak, the powers of water into those of wine. Indeed,' he adds, 'this latter view of the miracle, conforms better to its spiritual import, than the former. It is the peculiarity of the work of Christianity *not* to destroy what is *natural*, but to ennoble and transfigure it, *as the organ of Divine powers*.' The idea of this passage is excellent, but imperfectly carried out. The simple water *is* ennobled by a transmutation into *natural wine*—' the wine in the cluster '—while the ' wine ' that **'is a** mocker' is *not* the organ of Divine, but rather of demoniac power. He who wishes to be full of the Holy Spirit must not be full of wine. Hence the Apostle (Ephes. v. 18) places them in antithesis. (See Olshausen.)

2. "It is common for divines (take Dr. Cumming by way of example,) in their explanations of Scripture, *to assume that 'wine' and 'alcoholic wine' are necessarily synonymous phrases;* and they illogically put the latter for the former. **The** writer in the *Reasoner* does so likewise. It is the same fallacy as if he were to change everywhere the word 'spirit' into '*evil* spirit,' or the word 'man' into '*black* man.' No **allowance is** made **for the** generic meaning of the word, or for the context, which is nevertheless, an important element in **a** just exegesis. Thus when Solomon *ironically* refers to the evil custom of drowning dull care with strong drink—as much **as** to say, Give strong drink to such, if you will, but let not **the** really wise and great, or the kings and princes, to whom judgment is committed, even *drink* such things, lest they pervert

justice—the *Reasoner*, like the tippler, quotes it as grave counsel—adding, 'If this be not a license for a degrading vice, to drink until you are oblivious of care, I know **not what is.**' And what answer can the drinker give?

3. "Even in condemning the **explanations of** the teetotalers, the drinking believer and infidel **are at one; they** both pronounce the harmonising views to be '*flimsy and unsupported by fact.*' Of course, they both fall into **the pit of** confusion together, commingling texts in the conflict, **in which** the words of the original are altogether different! Instead **of** 'rightly dividing the word of truth,' *hemer* is confounded with *yayin*, *ausis* with *tirosh*, *tirosh* with *gleukos*, and any one of **them** with *shemarim*, *eshishah*, or *sove*! The distinctions of Holy Writ are virtually trampled upon; **by the** one party, **to** support a sensual appetite; by **the other, to bolster** up an infidel opinion.

"In Judges ix, 13, says the *Reasoner*, *wine* is spoken of as '*cheering God* and **man,**' and an irreverent comment is added which we cannot quote. Now, **the very same** word (translated cheering) is applied **to** *corn* in Zech. ix, 17; so that it cannot mean 'intoxicating;' while in Isaiah lxv, 8, the same word that is translated wine, **occurs with this distinct** explanation: '**Thus** saith the Lord, As the WINE **is found** *in the cluster*, **and** one saith, Destroy (lit. ferment **or** corrupt,) it **not, for a** blessing **is** in it.' Will the *Reasoner* have the honesty **to** apologise for his misrepresentation of the truth? We shall see.

4. "As to *facts*, the sceptic and **the** drinker assume whatever are required. From the simple **word '***wine***,'** in Paul's advice to Timothy, they make it out that **Paul** recommended Timothy '**to *stimulate* his stomach with** the moderate use of *alcohol!*' If they **would dip into Pliny**, or even into Thompson's *Materia Medica*, Moore's '**Letters** from Italy,' or Russell's '**History** of Aleppo,' they might find *facts* of a quite other sort. In wine countries, the use of grape juice, both **fresh** and boiled,

is a common cure, called *the wine cure*, for dyspepsia and debility. But what are facts to those who don't want them?"

I am, my dear brother,

Yours most affectionately,

JOHN MAIR.

---

LETTER IV.

MY DEAR BROTHER,

Another **vexed** question has been, **the** mode of celebrating the Lord's **supper** in the primitive church at Corinth. This controversy seems to me, to have turned upon the meaning attached to a single word—"*methuei*," which, in our version of the Bible, is translated "is drunken." It is strange what an affection truly good men have manifested to **this and such** like palpable mis-translations, **as** if their salvation depended upon them. It can only be accounted for by the fact, that they have **been** the victims **of "wine"** which "is a mocker," **and** "strong drink" **which "is** raging," and thoroughly blinded thereby. The venerable Arch-deacon Jeffreys has well observed that, I **Cor. xi**, 21,—the last clause,— "'One is hungry **and another** is drunken,'—should have been translated, 'One is hungry and another is full;'" and, that "the antithesis absolutely requires this rendering, for the other translation totally destroys the antithesis, and presents a sentence so ugly, and contrary to the rules of good composition, that it is barely good grammar. We shall best illustrate our meaning," he continues, "by placing the following antitheses together:

"One is old, another young.

"One is rich, another poor.

"One is hungry, another full.

"'But one is hungry, and another is drunken,' is an ugly **sentence**, in which the second member **of** the antithesis is broken off, and the word 'drunken' is thrust in without any reason, connection or meaning whatever. But what is worst of all, according to the present translation, the horrible vice of drunkenness at the Lord's table is introduced in a most off-hand, indecent, careless manner. It has not so **much as one entire** sentence dedicated to it. For if that one word, mis-translated 'drunken,' be changed, the awful sin of drunkenness at **the** Lord's supper is absolutely struck out of the whole chapter; for there is not so much as another allusion to it, nor anything to suggest the idea, in the whole chapter." \*

According to this view, the charge of the Apostle Paul against this church, was not that the members of it got drunk at the Lord's table, but that the rich *feasted*, while the poor were obliged to *fast;* not being allowed to partake of the viands which had been provided for themselves exclusively, by their selfish neighbors; thus, turning aside the holy ordinance from its original intention of its being a spiritual repast, promotive of love to God and man, into a heartless meal, indicative and provocative of pride and selfishness on the one part, and of discontent and envy on the other; while all the time the paramount design of remembering **the Saviour's** death, seems to have been altogether neglected! Such a state of things would have been amply sufficient to justify the Apostle Paul in administering the gentle reproof contained in the 22d verse, in these words: "What? have ye not houses to eat and to drink in? or despise ye the church of God, and shame them that have not? What shall I say to you? Shall I praise you in this? I praise you not." And one, taking even this more favorable view of the case, is disposed **to wonder** how the Apostle could have passed over this offence with so slight a chastisement, and can only satisfactorily account for it, by observing what is said in the 20th verse, viz: "When ye come together, therefore, into one place, this is *not* to eat the Lord's supper;" implying that they

---

\*Arch-deacon Jeffreys, in the Oriental Spectator.

had altogether misunderstood the nature and design of the ordinance; and, therefore, were not guilty of the same awful crime with which they would have been justly chargeable, if they had wilfully acted in despite of the Lord's commandment. And this view I am the more inclined to take, because it comports well with the immediately following recital by the Apostle of his commission, received immediately from his **Lord** and Master, respecting the nature **and** right mode of observance of this sacred ordinance,—which seems to have been so strangely forgotten by them.

Upon the whole, from a careful examination of the entire passage, it seems to me that the conclusion may legitimately be arrived at, that it was the disorderly manner in which the feast was conducted, and the unhallowed states of mind of the guests, and not the substitution and use of fermented, intoxicating, *for* unfermented, unintoxicating wine, as the symbol of Christ's blood,—ending in the inebriation of some of them,—which drew forth the censure of the Apostle; although, it is not unlikely that sorts of food not enjoined in the Divine rule, may also have been introduced and partaken of by individuals of the company.

If we could conceive of St. Paul being delegated by Divine authority to visit this world on a special mission of philanthropy, the object of which should be, to look into and correct the abuses prevailing in the churches of Christ, as regards the administration of the Lord's supper with intoxicating wine: how are we to suppose he would act in applying a remedy? Probably one of the first things he would do, would be to ascertain whether the corruption was universal, or whether there were any churches where unfermented, unintoxicating wine was dispensed to the communicants. He would find that, in one of the United States, **New** York, in 1841, there were, according to "The Enquirer," vol. i, p. 4, about eight hundred churches in which unfermented fruit of the vine had been substituted for alcoholic liquor, at the Lord's table. What the number in the whole Union now is, I have no means of knowing—neither do I know whether the number of churches in your State is still as considerable as it was in 1841, in which alcoholic wine is excluded. **Perhaps** you may be able to give some reliable information on this important question.* I observed,

---

* The startling exposure made some twenty years since, of the adulterations then prevalent in the wines of commerce, whether furnished for social use at the domestic table, or for sacramental use at the table of the Lord, made a deep impression on the public mind, especially on the religious mind throughout the United States,—and that it was the duty of the churches to substitute, as speedily and to as great an extent as practicable, "the pure blood of the grape," in place of the fabricated, deleterious, intoxicating poisons, then so generally in use, was beginning to be felt.

The reform in this direction, (believed to be the right direction,) was making rapid progress, when opposition to it began suddenly to manifest itself. Men of learning, and even clergymen of exemplary piety and elevated station, mistaking this movement against the fabricated or fermented wines of commerce, for a movement against the Scriptural wines of the cluster, the vat and the press, felt it to be their duty to bear their testimony through the medium of the public press, against the movement, as infidel in its tendency, calculated to interrupt the existing harmony among churches, and disturb the meditations of devout minds while surrounding the table and commemorating the death of their ascended Lord.

This opposition produced its effect in arresting the progress of reform. False issues were introduced and an impression made on the public **mind,** that the object was to exclude the use of wine from the sacramental table, and substitute in its place, water, molasses and water, tamarind and water, and other like unauthorized and revolting mixtures.

Still, and notwithstanding these misrepresentations, a salutary impression had been made by the discussion, upon the public mind, and seed was then sown that has subsequently produced, and is still producing, its legitimate effects. It is worthy of remark perhaps, in this connection, that a diminution in the quantity of wine made use of on sacramental occasions, was observable in certain churches after this discussion, in relation to the kind of wine to be used, took place. An officer, in one church with which I was acquainted, containing from five to six hundred members, informed me that, previous to this agitation, he usually provided five gallons of wine for the celebration of the supper—that afterwards, on like occasions, a quart only was required; and I doubt whether a sixth of the quantity of wine is now used on sacramental occasions, that was used before this discussion took place.

not many months ago, a number of communications to the editor of the Manchester, (Eng.,) "Alliance Weekly News," in reply to a correspondent desirous of ascertaining what churches used unfermented wine at the communion? As accurately as I can remember, only eighteen churches were returned as using **such** *innoxious* wine to celebrate their Lord's death, in the United Kingdom; and, of these—two, one at Leeds, the other at Nottingham, part of the communicants used *intoxicating*, and part *unintoxicating* wine, at different tables.

A distinguished surgeon, and well-known temperance reformer, John Higginbottom, Esq., in a letter dated Nottingham, July 8, 1860, addressed to the editor of the "Alliance Weekly News," pleads strongly for the introduction of unfermented wine into the churches, in the following words: "The word 'wine' is never mentioned by our Redeemer in reference to the Passover.

---

There can be no doubt that the opposition, made at that time to the substitution of the pure, unfermented, unintoxicating fruit of the vine, as the same exists in the cluster, the vat and the press, in place of the enforced, fermented, intoxicating wines of commerce, arose from a mistaken apprehension, that nothing could rightfully be called wine in the Scriptural sense of the term, that was not in its nature intoxicating.

Whether any of those learned and excellent men, who are yet alive, continue to hold these opinions, I know not; but, should the abundant proofs to the contrary, which have since been furnished, have reached them and produced a **conviction** in their minds that the pure blood of the grape, as expressed from **the cluster,** is a **more** appropriate and Scriptural emblem, and therefore a **more** befitting memorial of the death of the son of God, than the enforced, fermented and drugged substitutes then resorted to in place thereof, it would be a **happiness** at a crisis like the present, if **the evidence** of that change of opinion **could** be furnished the public, and a corresponding change introduced into their respective churches.

I have thought **it** particularly incumbent on the Church of England, as well as the Episcopal Church of this Continent, that they should look well as to the *kind* of wine procured for communion purposes, they both having the rule in their respective prayer books, that all the wine remaining after communion, shall, immediately after **the** blessing, be reverently drank by the minister and other communicants. E. C. D.

ALBANY, *January* 6, 1861.

It is written 'the cup,' and 'the fruit of the vine,' both in the original Greek and in our translation. It occurred to me that there is no similitude whatever, between 'the fruit of the vine' and the alcoholic wine commonly used at the Lord's table. The fruit of the vine is rich in flavor and taste; nutritious from its containing mucilage, albumen and sugar,—and as such, thought worthy to be a type of the blood of Christ. The alcoholic wine is deleterious, and destitute of nourishment. The port wine, *so called*, used often at the Lord's table, is frequently a mixture of cider, brandy, alum, &c., and coloring matter, nauseous, and fiery to the taste, and very objectionable to the healthy, pure taste of any individual. . . . . I may add that the Jews use no fermented wine at the Passover, but an unfermented wine. The wine they use at this feast is made by steeping bloom raisins in water near the fire till the flavor is extracted, and it is then used in the unfermented state. The unfermented wine I have been accustomed to take, has been prepared in the proportion of one pound of bloom raisins with two pints of water, put in a covered vessel and placed in an oven to simmer for about thirty-six hours, or until only a pint of fluid remains. Boiling for a few minutes hastens the making and improves the wine. It is then poured off to cool and is fit for use. . . . . I write this paper from a sense of duty, for two classes of persons—first, for those who have not yet considered the question, and are ignorant of the nature of the wine used at the ordinance of the Lord's supper; and secondly, for the benefit of my poor teetotal brethren, who are reformed drunkards, and are now sincere Christians; they *dare* not touch the fermented wine at the Lord's supper; the taste to them would be dangerous, as it would lead them again into the temptation to enter the paths of the destroyer of both soul and body. *It is sinful to deprive them of so great a Christian privilege.* . . . . In conversation with an excellent clergyman, and a person of considerable influence, he said he should be very glad to use the unfermented wine in his church at the Lord's supper; and, I believe many of the clergy and dissenting ministers unite with him in this feeling." \*

After this long digression, let us return to the philanthropic mission of the Apostle Paul. We have supposed that he would institute an inquiry into the number of churches using unfermented wine, and even here there would be cause found for censure in the fact, that in two of the eighteen, reported in Great Britain, there was a division,—part using *intoxicating*, and part *unintoxicating* wine, at different tables; a state of things not very unlike that which called forth the Apostle's rebuke in the church of Corinth, thus: "For first of all, when ye come together in the church, I hear that there be divisions among you." What would the Apostle say to this in the 19th century, when so much is known of the injurious effects of alcoholic liquors upon all classes of men, in almost all manner of ways,—of the great damage done thereby to the cause of Christ, and the dishonor put upon His name? How painfully it would affect his tender and enlightened conscience, to find only eighteen congregations, out of many thousands, using unfermented wine, in the most highly privileged of all the nations of the earth, and two of these churches at variance, in regard to a plain Scripture doctrine, upon which perfect unanimity should have reigned long ago.

In the 30th verse of the 11th chapter of I Corinthians, it is said: "For this cause, many are weak and sickly among you, and many sleep;" that was because they misunderstood the spiritual nature of the Lord's supper, and observed it in a selfish, sensual, carnal manner. What would St. Paul now say of the disastrous effects of the vicious mode of commemorating

---

\* Passover or Sacramental wine, unfermented and unintoxicating, prepared from finest Lisbon grapes, and preserved *in vacuo*, at the suggestion and under the direction of Dr. F. R. Lees, by Freeman and Wright, chemists, Kensington, London: Price 36s per dozen.

His Lord's death with the most destructive of poisons, which is all but universal, in that land of clear Bible light and perfect religious liberty? Is there not reason to believe that he would impute a great part of the disregard to sacred things among the masses,—of the coldness, carnality and lukewarmness, of many of the members of churches,—and especially, of the expulsions therefrom, of nine-tenths of those who are excommunicated, (from drunkenness or sins resulting **from it,**) to the use of intoxicating wine as the symbol of our Saviour's precious, sin-atoning blood, at His supper—instead of "the pure blood of the grape," so plainly enjoined by Him at its institution? What remedy would the Apostle apply? **In** answer **to** this question, I can only surmise as a thing not improbable, that he might speak of the accumulated **experience** of ages, **as to the** pernicious effects of alcoholic liquors upon man, as a physical, intellectual, moral and religious being,—of the multiplicity of crimes of the deepest dye, which had resulted from their use,—of the fearful desecration of God's ordinances,—of the violation of His Sabbaths,—of the hindrance to the spread of the Gospel amongst heathen nations, and the followers of the false prophet who deemed it unlawful to drink of alcoholic liquors,—of the impious association of the thrice holy name of Immanuel with "the poison of dragons and the cruel venom of asps,"—above all, of the perversion of the plain doctrine of both the Old and New Testaments, which distinctly forbids the use of wine and strong drink in man's normal **state of health; and**, putting base falsehoods into the mouth of his beloved Lord, who has so explicitly expressed His will, that "unfermented fruit of the vine" shall be used at His supper; and thence infer and enforce the duty of *instantaneous* repentance and return to the use **of that** fruit as the sole symbol of His blood to be used at His table. That he would refer to the original institution as recorded by Matthew, Mark and Luke, there can be no doubt, as well as to the revelation made to himself, and say: "Thus it is written, 'Drink ye all of it—*the unfermented fruit of the vine;*'" and he might shew (as has been done in a former letter,) how frequently and emphatically *this* command issued from the pure lips of Him of whom it was said: "Never man spake like this man;" "Who did no sin, neither was guile found in His mouth."

Is it not possible that he might refer to the expulsion of "those that sold oxen, and sheep and doves, and the changers of money from the temple," by our **Lord**; and, in doing so, show how much greater the sin with which they were chargeable was, than that of which those men were guilty.

In meditating upon this subject, and giving reins to my imagination, I have sometimes thought that a closer analogy would have been displayed between the cruel practice of dispensing a loathsome, poisonous liquor to communicants at the Lord's supper, as the symbol of Christ's blood,—if, instead of the case being as it was enacted, and is recorded in the sacred Scriptures, when Jesus drove the defilers of the temple from its sacred precincts, *that* filthy creature, the sow—the type of idolatrous worship—had been immolated as a sacred victim, by the priests, upon the altar of burnt offering at Jerusalem!

I may now advert to the views of Professor Moses Stuart, and Mr. Stubbin, of Birmingham, upon this subject,—and with them, conclude this letter: "But Paul's account of the Lord's supper at Corinth, (I Cor. xi, 18–34,) clearly shows that *intoxicating* wine was employed,—'One is hungry and *another is drunken.*'"

Truly it does, if our translators have hit the mark. But allowing for a moment that they have, does Paul *approve* of the Corinthian practice? He says expressly that he *condemns* it. We might rest the case here, then, without farther animadversion. But I am not persuaded that our translation does justice to the Corinthian church; very strange—passing strange it would be, if a church so gifted and so famous went to the sacramental table in order to celebrate the orgies of Bacchus. The simple state of the case seems to be, that the Corinthians kept a love-feast on sacramental occasions. Thither some carried plenty of provision **and drink, and** ate and drank to the full; while the poor in the church could not do this, and were thus put to shame by the richer class. *One is hungry*—this is the poor man; another, *methuei*, drinks to the full—this is the richer man. That the word *may* mean *gets drunk*, I do not deny. That it must mean so, I do deny. Its etymology shows the real meaning. *Methu* means *sweet wine*, and most naturally, therefore, *unfermented* wine. *Methuo* is a denominative verb formed from it, and means to *partake of methu*,—and, very naturally, **in** the second place, to *partake freely* of it. But **as** to being *drunken*, that is another question. A free partaking of the *sweet wine* would make no man drunk. The indecorum complained of, lay in the feasting on the one hand, and the starvation (so to speak,) on the other. Paul lays his hand upon the whole proceeding, and prohibits public love-feasts, as connected with the Lord's supper.*

"The best explanation which the author has seen of the passage, is in an edition of the Greek Testament, with English notes, by the Rev. S. T. Bloomfield, D. D., F. A. S. He says: '*To idion deipnon*, denotes the supper which each **one had** brought, as his own contribution to the common meal. *Prolambanei*, has reference to the eagerness with which each one (of the richer sort, we may presume,) snatched up the food **which he had** brought (and **that, no doubt, a** plentiful portion,) and **filled himself** therewith, before **the** poorer sort could well touch **it**: which would cause *them* (who had brought little or nothing,) **to** fare very scantily. And as this (which is to be understood of the *agapai, accompanying*, and at times preceding the Lord's supper,) was not a *common meal*, **it was a** viola-

---

* Scriptural View of the Wine Question, in a Letter to the Rev. Dr. Nott, by M. Stuart, Professor in the Theological Seminary, at Andover: p. 54.

tion of *propriety*, as well as *Christian charity*, so to act; for though each brought his own supper, yet when it had been thrown **to the** common stock, it ceased to be his own. Thus, the plenty of some, shamed the want of others; which would occasion heart-burnings, and so defeat the end of the Lord's supper. It is remarked by the ancient commentators, **that the** *ratio oppositi* requires the word *methuei* **to be** interpreted of *satiety*, in both drinking and eating. We need not understand any *drunkenness* or *gluttony;* nay, the **very words of the** verse following—*me gar oikias* . . . *pinein*—forbid this. The fault with which they are charged, is *gross selfishness* at a meal united with the eucharistical one, and formed on such principles of Christian charity and brotherly communion, as would be a proper supplement or introduction to it." *

It is the opinion of these eminent men, and of other learned commentators, that it was a love-feast to which the Apostle referred. It does not become me to speak dogmatically upon the subject after them. The decision either way, whether for the feast referred to being all that was deemed by the Corinthians as the Lord's supper, or for its being a love-feast, preceding or following that ordinance, will not materially affect the cause of anti-alcoholic temperance. If it was a corrupted Lord's supper, and all that stood for the true one, as I am inclined to believe, (for I see not a word about a love-feast in **the** chapter, or in any other part of Scripture except Jude,) **there is** nothing **to** show that intoxicating wine was used at it**, as manifested** in **the conduct of** the guests or the language **of the Apostle,** but the **reverse;** and, if it was a love-feast, there is the same lack of evidence **of** which the Alcoholic School could avail themselves, in support of their doctrine. Perhaps the opinion, that it was a love-feast *with* wine, but *not* alcoholic wine, (and it is almost certain that wine would be used at it preparatory to, or after the Lord's supper,) would be more in favor of the reign

---

* Tirosh Lo Yayin: p. 154.

of total abstinence principles amongst the respectable inhabitants of Judea, than the other opinion—which seems to me the more probable.

    I **am,** my dear brother,
      Yours most affectionately,
        JOHN MAIR.

---

### LETTER V.

My Dear Brother,

  By some it has been objected to Teetotalism, that it demands too much of its disciples, by others not enough. The former plead for *moderation* in the use of alcohol, which we have found to be a phantom; the latter opine that if men abstain from alcoholic liquors they will fall into some other course of sensual indulgence, such as the use of opium, or some other narcotic drug equally destructive of health, and ruinous of reputation, if not so productive of crime. Again, the charge has been brought against Teetotalism by that most influential paper the London Times, that "It won't do to come before a jovial drinking community with a new commandment, 'Thou shalt not drink wine.' This is no age for prohibitions. Mahomet understood men better. He was a Teetotaler, but his was no mere negative doctrine. He provided plenty of compensation for that one denial—sense, ambition, fancy, and even reason **had** their gratifications. What are the positive attractions of the Temperance cause? They have yet to be shown." We **do** not intend entering the lists of controversy with one or other **of** these objectors. The two first we would point "to the law and to the testimony," and say, "if, after diligent and prayerful search (we address ourselves to Christians) you do not find Teetotalism in the Bible, attach no great importance to it; if you do, disregard it at your peril." To the Times **we would say,** "You are somewhat inconsistent, for while you appear to sneer at Teetotalism in the passage quoted above, in your paper of 11th March, 1857, you remark (as previously noticed) that " opium is in the same category as wine, or gin, or tobacco. Are our distillers enemies to their race—are the planters of Virginia and Cuba to be denounced—are France and Spain no longer to send in the produce of their vineyard because the people drink more than is good for them ? If the moderate use of these is to be allowed, **why should we** pour invectives against those who sell the production, which is the equivalent of them (opium) to 300,000,000 of men?"* To the Times, thus speaking, we would address ourselves in the following terms : " In principle you seem to be one with us. You have your doubts about the rectitude of the moderate use of tobacco, gin and wine, as indicated by your use of the conjunction *If*. We have more than doubts. We are convinced that it is wrong, in **man's** normal state of health. You talk in a strain somewhat ironical; yet you admit that alcohol, the intoxicating principle of gin and wine, is a poison, although you do not explicitly say so, for you include it in the same category with opium, which all admit to be a poison. We call alcohol the type of a large class of poisons named emphatically and expressively brain poisons, because they are peculiarly distinguished from other poisons by exerting a deleterious influence upon the brain, and through it upon the mind of man. The Bible has given us reasons for the interdict of wine and strong drink : in other words, alcoholic liquors in **man's** normal state of health. It is not because certain things are termed wine and strong drink that they are forbidden in **the** Bible, but because the things called wine and strong drink possess certain qualities rendering them hurtful, particularly endangering and tending to destroy the noble faculties which distinguish man from the lower animals, such as reason, conscience, &c. But

---

* The Times, in advocating Mr. Gladstone's wine bill, admitted that wine was a poisonous drink, but less so than gin.

if it be not on account of the names given to these substances, but their deleterious qualities, that they are forbidden in the Bible, must it not be evident to every one capable of right thinking and judging, that other substances possessing like qualities must, from the nature of the case, be interdicted by the same paramount authority, just because they possess similar qualities? for it was on account of the qualities, and not the names that the wine and strong drink were primarily prohibited in the Holy Scriptures. We conclude, then, that alcohol, because of its peculiarly seductive and destructive qualities, has been specially interdicted in the Bible, as the type of all brain poisons, and that it affords us not only an admirable index to other poisons of the same class, such as opium, tobacco, belladonna, &c., from the fact that its deleterious effects are most fully and graphically described in Holy Writ, but also presents itself when viewed in the light of revelation in its most criminal aspects, as a friendly monitor, to guard us against imposition from similar crafty foes; so that God, in his infinite wisdom and goodness, thus educes good from evil, and extracts salutary nourishment from deadly poison."

We trust it will now be plainly perceived that the Anti-alcoholic Temperance of the Bible, as we have taken the liberty of calling it, is far superior to the Teetotalism of the world. Indeed, it would now seem that a name still more comprehensive might be given to the grand principles of Bible Temperance, which we have endeavored to trace from small beginnings to a mighty system of truth. But if it be understood that alcohol is the type of all brain poisons, and that the name *Anti-alcoholic Temperance* is intended to convey the meaning that they are all forbidden in Holy Writ, it will suffice.

Who has any just cause of complaint against this God-like system of truth? Is it *now* seen to be too restrictive of an appetite which, when at all yielded to, is so apt to end in ruin of both soul and body? Or is it *now* seen to be too limited in its range, when, according to the showing of the Times, it comprehends within its embrace both tobacco and opium? and we contend that all brain poisons are included under it. Again, what of the melancholy wail of the same mighty journalist, respecting want of compensation for self denial, in contrast with the liberality of the false prophet! Does that self denial amount to much, which seems to him so hard to bear? while "sense, ambition, fancy and even reason had their gratifications" under the Mahommedan creed.

What are the positive attractions of the Temperance cause? We do not now speak of the attractions of Teetotalism apart from the Bible. We apprehend it is not possessed of many. But we have no hesitation in proclaiming the truth, that the system of Temperance which we maintain—that of the Holy Scriptures—is possessed of innumerable precious attractions, flowing from divers sources with which those of the Koran cannot compare. Surely there are gratifications to be found in a sound mind, a pure heart and a clear conscience; and who will take upon himself to say—that abstinence, *not* from alcoholic liquors *only*, but from all other brain poisons also, has nothing whatever to do with securing these blessings? But even on the low ground of sensual gratification, I will ask the popular journalist if there be not more real pleasure, with less pain, in drinking of "the pure fruit of the vine," squeezed into water, than in gulping down the stuff called wine with twenty-two per cent of alcohol, besides other nameless poisons? and this pure fruit of the vine is what we would recommend on Bible authority as a beverage where it can be had, or the preserved fruit when it cannot. But there is a higher class of enjoyments still than even that held out to us, of a sound mind, a pure heart and a clear conscience. It is intimate, holy communion with our reconciled Father in Christ Jesus—it is ascent into the highest heavens upon the wings of faith, and rejoicing in the contemplation of redeeming love, with angels and the spirits of just men made perfect, in the presence of Him who loved us and gave Himself for us. "But we are come unto Mount Sion and unto the city of the living God, the heavenly Jerusalem, and to an innumerable company of angels, to the general assembly and church of the first born, which are written in heaven, and to God the Judge of all, and to the spirits of just men made perfect, and to Jesus the mediator of the new covenant, and to the blood of sprinkling, that speaketh better things than that of Abel." These are some of "the positive attractions and *gratifications*" which are associated with partaking of "the pure blood of the grape," as the emblem of the Redeemer's blood, instead of "fire water;" and which are intimately connected with the system of anti-alcoholic Temperance, to be found clearly revealed in the Holy Scriptures; and we ask the Times, if they do not surpass any or all "the attractions and gratifications" which a Mahommedan paradise can present to stir up to emulation the most zealous Mussulman, at least in the estimate of a humble disciple of the meek and lowly Jesus?

To illustrate what a horror the sensitive, sin-hating soul of the renewed man has of strong drink, let us narrate the following anecdote, in connexion with revivals in Ireland: "One youth I knew of, went down upon his knees as usual to pray before going to bed. His mind had been somewhat impressed, but a friend had persuaded him to join in some strong drink in a very moderate way. As he was praying, or at least repeating the language of prayer, the thought struck him, can I speak to God with the smell of strong drink upon my breath? No! From that hour **he** wholly abandoned it." \*

I could quote from the Enquirer several most remarkable cases of fearful conscientious struggle in persons obliged to partake of intoxicating wine at the communion (with the effects

---

\* Irish Correspondent in New York Independent.

of relapse into drunkenness in some who ventured), or deny themselves a high Christian privilege, but time and space forbid.

I take this opportunity, however, of entreating you to republish the thrilling narratives to which I refer. They ought to be universally read, and pondered by every Christian man and woman every where.

Some of the blessings of total abstinence may be judged of from the following testimonies of eminent ministers of the Gospel. The Rev. Mr. Jay says: " I am thankful that all through life I have been a very temperate man, and for more than twenty-five years generally a teetotaler; but for the last six years I have been one constantly and entirely. To this (now I am past 70) I ascribe, under God, the glow of health and evenness of spirits, and freshness of feeling, and ease of application, and comparative inexhaustion by public labors I now enjoy. The subject of teetotalism I have examined physically and morally, and Christianly, and after all my reading and reflection, and observation, and **experience, I** have reached a very firm and powerful conviction, that next to 'the glorious Gospel' God could not bless the human race so much as by the abolition of all intoxicating spirits." *That* would not be in the order of God's providence, but He enjoins upon man the duty of preventing fruits from going into the vinous fermentation, as it appears to us (except for medicinal or extra vital purposes), or if they have done so without his helping hand, to avoid using the alcoholic product, and thus man's forethought and ingenuity are exercised, and his faith and submission to the divine authority tested. The Rev. R. Knill said: " I wish your correspondent may reap as many advantages from teetotalism as I have done, and still continue to do. There is scarce a day passes but I bless God for the plan I have adopted; and I trust I shall bear my testimony to the advantages of teetotalism, even upon a dying bed. I believe few men labor so much, so constantly, and with so little fatigue. I thank the Lord for an ability to work; and if my life is spared, I intend to work more **than ever**; and I am persuaded that teetotalism will, through the Divine blessing, help me to perform it."

The Burke murders in Edinburgh and the murder of the Italian **boy in London,** for anatomical purposes; the Essex poisonings of infants by their mothers, for the sake of the funeral expenses, to be recovered from benefit funds to which they had subscribed; the frequent cases of poisoning of persons by their husbands, or other near relatives, possessing policies of their insured lives, are melancholy proofs of awful demoralization, **scarcely to be** paralleled for atrocity in the **annals of** the most barbarous tribes, where the light of Christianity never dawned!

We are inclined to trace them up to their source in a misinterpretation, misunderstanding, and consequent neglect of the Bible law of Temperance, which we have endeavored to show, is clearly laid down in a variety of intelligible **forms in** the Holy Scriptures, and to the merciless substitution of intoxicating (impoisoned) wine for the pure fruit of the vine, the appointed symbol of Jesus' blood, and the true **antidote of** Alcoholic Intemperance!

To the same prolific parent we also trace up the opium curse in China, and much of the deadness, lukewarmness and indiffe**rence** to religion amongst the masses, in addition to the chief part of the offences (before referred to), for which expulsion of members from churches and depositions of ministers from the sacred office take place! These are, no doubt, appalling events (and we have merely touched upon a few, for their name is legion), but they need not excite much wonderment when it is remembered what a flagrant violation, or rather an uninterrupted succession of gross violations of the Divine law, forbidding the use of alcoholic liquors, and especially at the Lord's table, has been committed for ages past (with hardly a single exception till within the last twenty years) in all the churches of Christendom. It rather should have been cause for astonishment if numerous falls amongst ministers and members of churches, **and** innumerable crimes **had** not occurred, when alcoholic liquors have been all *but Deified*, instead of being treated as **under** the ban of God's holy law.

We have no hope whatever of any general Temperance reformation until such time as intoxicating liquors are for ever banished from the house of God, as insulting to His Divine Majesty, and productive of the greatest evil to mankind.

May God hasten this blessed consummation so devoutly to be desired, in His good time.

I am, my dear brother, in gospel bonds,

Yours most affectionately,

JOHN MAIR.

### LETTER VI.

MY DEAR BROTHER,

The next question to be touched upon is a thoroughly practical one. I refer to the possibility of supplying unfermented wine for domestic and religious purposes. Not long ago a highly-esteemed minister of the Gospel, in a letter to a friend of mine, threw out the doubt—whether wine could be preserved unfermented, in a warm climate, such as Judea? To this suspicion I would simply reply, by referring to the writings of Columella, Cato, Pliny, Theophrastus and other ancient authors, who have discoursed more or less copiously upon the means of preserving wines free from fermentation, and have abundantly proved that it was practicable to do so in their days; and if the ancients could provide themselves with unfermented, unintoxicating wines, ignorant as they were of chemistry, surely it would be a reproach to Christendom if, with vast stores of information upon all the arts of life, her chemists and wine producers could not accomplish the same object. But the respected gentleman, of whom I have spoken, could not have consulted the standard **writers of modern** times upon the subject, otherwise he would **have** learned **that unfermented** wines have been and can be obtained in the nineteenth century, if the necessary pains be taken in any part of the globe.

Graham, in his Elements of Chemistry, says: "The action of yeast and all other ferments is destroyed by the temperature at which water boils, by alcohol, by acids, salts of mercury, sulphurous acid, chlorine, iodine, bromine, by aromatic substances, volatile oils, and particularly empyreumatic oils, smoke and **decoction of** coffee, these bodies, in some instances, combining with the ferments, or otherwise effecting their **decomposition.**" I believe that a rich reward would attend the labors of any operative and scientific chemist who should devote his attention **to** the investigation of **the various methods by** which **the juice of the** grape might be preserved untainted, with its fine flavor, and free from fermentation, for **a period** of time, anticipating the blessed era when the world shall be filled with "the knowledge of the glory of the Lord, as the waters cover the sea;" and when it is impossible that "the wine which biteth like a serpent and stingeth like an adder" can any longer be admitted into the sanctuary, or be patronised by the church of Christ. The preceding remarks were in manuscript before these letters were commenced. I have been glad to find that some progress has been made in the preparation of unfermented wine since they were committed to paper. I have already referred to the advertisement of Freeman and Wright of unfermented wine for sacramental purposes, in a foot **note, and I** have now much pleasure in referring to a note **of** Dr. Lees, in his pamphlet entitled the "Rotheram Discussion," **to** the following effect: "We were favored with the possession of three bottles of this wine (from Mr. Delavan). **This** day, December

28, 1858, nearly twenty years after 'the wine was made,' we have had **the last bottle** opened, and find it just as pure and unchanged as it was sixteen years ago. It is *vino cotto*, or inspissated wine."

It affords me additional gratification to bring **before** you the following very interesting and important suggestions of my excellent friend, Mr. Bonwick, the highly respected Inspector of Schools of the colony of **Victoria**, now on a philanthropic mission on the continent of Europe, in regard to wines and other fermented and alcoholic liquors. He is in Switzerland, at the vintage season, or as he beautifully terms it, "the very land of harmony, the region of popular choral sounds," when, with the utmost *naiveté*, he thus speaks :

"It is a joyous season, this *egrappage*, or stripping of the vines. All hearts are merry. Even the children sport about in unusual friskiness, and smiles beam from faces everywhere. No fruit has ever been so admired in all eyes as the grape. The Bible especially places it and its produce among the choicest of blessings. **Those of the** cold and sterile north **have** little appreciation of the charms of this cooling fruit beneath the scorching of a more elevated sun, and the delight with which its advent is hailed by the country peasant or the city lord. Smiles beget smiles, and I feel my heart expand with gladness in the pleasure of those around me.

"Then comes the reaction upon me. Though I know I am **not** among a people so delighting in potent **liquor** as my own countrymen—though I know that their **very** frugal habits are opposed **to** dissipation—though I know that the vast majority of the **wines** produced for home consumption here will be little worse than the small beer of England—yet, when I see the introduction of alcohol, that fierce destroyer of life and joy, in any guise, in any quantity, I know it is so seductive in nature as to give honey to the lip, but gall to the heart; and sadness comes over me then amidst the laughter of the vineyard, and

I am almost tempted to applaud the stern monarch of olden days who laid waste the vine hills of his people.

"Then comes another thought. What if these gushing purple streams were to be converted into the real offspring of the grape! What if, when the saccharine liquor came oozing from beneath the press, so joyously luscious in its prime, it should be preserved in the best sense of the term! What if instead of permitting, under the warm temperature and its more liquid condition, fermentation as a rotting, decomposing agency, to set in, the sweet juice were preserved in its normal, safe and nutritious state for the food and delight of man! What if, instead of being dreaded and feared by the good, and taken so carefully by the sober, it should be so that we might have again the drink for tender infancy, as wholesome and as welcome as milk; and again the invigorating, strengthening and beautifying draught, the "new wine for maids!" How, then, should we all be gladdened when the fair bunches plump forth their sweetness, and sing praises to our father for his gift of the vine!

"And why cannot this be? What prevents the indulgence of this pleasant dream? Is it difficult to manufacture such a wine? Not at all. We have but to follow the ancient system—either reduce the liquidity, or keep down the temperature—and the produce is there. Why, then, is this not done, when its flavor is confessedly so good, when medical men all agree that it is so nutritious, and when the youngest may partake of it with no more need of parental caution than when he raises to his lips a bowl of milk? The secret is this—the wine makers must regard the taste of the wine buyers, and these have no fancy for the juice in its natural condition. It is not something nice and wholesome only they require, but that which is stimulating to excitement. The liquor must inflame the brain; it must give a glow to the frame; it must rouse the animal nature; it must raise the impulsive feeling; it must enkindle the fire of those lower passions, in whose gratification our greatest mere earthly pleasure exists. It is found that above all substances, all poisons, that which is most productive in these results is alcohol. The mere brutal man will have it in its more undisguised form. He will burn his intestines with whiskey, gin, brandy. Others, who want the pleasure extended, who will have quantity with quality, and who prefer flavor in addition, will be content with alcoholic beer and alcoholic wine. Some may be satisfied with but a slight percentage of the spirituous element, and desire only an agreeable drink. These take the light beers and wines. But with these there is still the fear, from the entrancing nature of that alcohol, that in the increase of taste, or in the growth of years, they may rise in the scale of strength, till they plunge into the cup of ardent spirits. **Hence it** is that wines must be fermented now.

"But is there no probability of returning to the primitive system, or of adopting the unfermented juice of the vine? I think there **is.** But then, this must be done in a wine country, and for a people who are what are now denominated "Teetotalers." On the continent I see little chance of such a drink being made for themselves. Yet were there a demand for it in Britain, the wine growers would be too happy to provide a supply for the rich islanders. There is no fear but they would soon know how to prepare it, and that in the best manner. The cold French grape is not suitable. It must be the richer juice from the warmer hills of Italy and Spain. The limestone slopes of Palestine, once so renowned for its grapes, would again be clothed with the clustering tendrils, did such a market arise. Instead **of Mr.** Gladstone being the great lover of his species, in procuring **the** introduction of cheap French wines, that man would be the true patriot of Britain who should be the means of bringing to **the** cottagers of his country so harmless, and **yet** so luscious a drink as we Teetotalers could take. To do this we know a taste **must** be awakened **for** it. Now is the time. The Temperance success has given us ample materials. It is idle to say, as many do, there is no occasion for it, and that a substitution for alcoholic drinks is unnecessary. I contend that there is occasion for it, and that a substitute is, with our growing taste for luxuries, absolutely necessary. **As I have lived nearly twenty years in a warm climate, I know the craving for something more than water,** especially when it is too often the case in warm latitudes that the water is **so indifferent as to compel one to adopt some means of altering its flavor.** Hence it is that in our colonies so much tea is consumed, the cups being introduced at every meal. But one is not always prepared for hot drinks, and **the convenience for procuring them is not always at hand. Hence, as on the continent, the** cheaper wines are so largely used; while, in Britain, it is **the beer,** or the spirit put in to *kill* the **water.**

"If, then, there is this natural **craving,** or, it may be an educational want, is it wise for us Temperance Reformers sternly to rebuke the people for their lustful propensities, or move philosophically and benevolently, to seek to satisfy **this** feeling in such a way as to promote social enjoyment, without any risk to virtue?

"The next thing is, how is it to be done? **The drink must be** cheap as well as agreeable. It must be easy of access to the consumer. To accomplish this, capital is requisite. **The** organization must be strong and effective. Relations must be judiciously entertained and maintained. **The produce** field will be, as I have said, the shores of the Mediterranean. Spain, Italy, Greece and Syria are all easy of reach by our steamers. Their present wines, from their very sweetness, are unpalatable to our English lovers of well-toned port; but they prove that the grape has pre-eminently the quality to produce **the** luscious tonic and wholesome beverage whose interests I plead.

"I bring forward these views from the vine-clad borders of Lake Geneva, in the hope that some united and vigorous effort will be made to satisfy what I believe to be a *want* of the present day."

That some danger is admitted in the use of the most moderate of modern wines will appear from the following testimony **of a Swiss** writer upon wines in the last century:—He says: "As the property of the spirit in wine is to rarefy in the different parts to which it is carried, and to rarefy the liquids which it finds there, it follows that when it is in too great abundance it dilutes the parts beyond measure. They act no more with the same ease as before; so much so that the equilibrium which governs the solids and fluids would be deranged. This is what one sees happening to those who drink too much wine; their head becomes heavy, their eyes are troubled, their limbs tremble, and their phrenzies prove only too much this disorder. But without drinking wine to this extent, it always happens, **when** one drinks much, that the membranes and vessels of the brain are more extended than they ought to be, sinking at last, by that reiterated effort, into a relaxation which will no more permit them to recover their first action; that which would necessarily interrupt the secretions and carry much mischief to body and mind." It is with such a caution that Citoyen Reymondin, of Lausanne, introduces his subject of the manufacture of wines. If such care be needed in the use of these light grape wines, what should be said of those strong narcotic excitants called wines, but without the aid of the grape, in **common** consumption with our countrymen?

**It is** therefore on the highest of moral grounds that I urge the **adoption** of that wine which is associated in Isaiah with the blessings **of the** Gospel, in contradistinction to that other wine even then associated with what was vile and degrading. Instead, however, of entering upon this vexed question of Scripture wines, let us be at least content to follow such learned authors **upon** wine-making **as Pliny** and Columella, and prepare, according to **their** recipes such drinks as cannot, from the nature of things, be intoxicating, and yet be both agreeable to taste and satisfactory to health. Let friends of Temperance, and friends of humanity, seek to work out this problem, so interesting to the real happiness of our social state, and to the moral progression of our people.\*

If these suggestions are cordially received, and energetically acted upon, they will tend powerfully, with the blessing of God, to remove the prejudices which now exist against the use of unfermented wine as the symbol of Christ's most precious sin-atoning blood at His table, and thus greatly facilitate the spread of the Gospel amongst the followers of Mahomet, Brahma, and Buddha.

I am, my dear brother,
Yours most affectionately,
JOHN MAIR.

### LETTER VII.

My Dear Brother,

I should wish, before concluding, to say a few words on "the place and power" of anti-alcoholic temperance in the Christian System. It is a hackneyed phrase among the teetotalers of expediency, that teetotalism is not Christianity; and among the extreme teetotalers of the secular stamp, hardly anything will take but teetotalism, as if it were **the sum total** of religion.

The teetotalism of expediency is certainly, as taught by its professors, far, far remote from Christianity. It is founded upon false principles,—does not possess Divine authority over conscience,—lacks evangelical motives,—has not the expansive energy of true religion,—and does not recognise the threefold duty of abstinence from alcohol in relation to **God**, self and neighbor. (See Letter I.)

---

\* The Alliance Weekly News, November 17, 1860.

It is equally remote from the truth, that secular teetotalism is the whole of Christianity, or that it is sufficient of itself to enfranchise a man from the thraldom of sin and Satan, although superior to the other in this respect,—that it acknowledges **alcohol** to be a poison to be avoided by man in his normal state of health. Indeed, it cannot be received as a part of **the** Christian System any more than the former, because Christ is not acknowledged as essential to its existence, or His law to its success. Let us endeavor to ascertain

*First.* What is the Place; and

*Second.* What is the Power of Anti-alcoholic Temperance in the Christian System:

1st. *The Place of Anti-alcoholic Temperance in the Christian System.*—The place held (or rather to be held,) in the Christian System, by anti-alcoholic temperance, is an important and well defined **one**.

Under the head of precepts or commandments, it may be **viewed** in **different** phases:

(1st.) In relation to God,—ranging itself under the first table of the Law.

(2d.) In relation to the individual,—ranging itself under the second table of the Law.

(3d.) In relation to the species,—ranging itself under the second table of the Law.

Again, under each of these heads, there are special relations **to** be considered; as e. **g.**, under the 1st to God, as "the only true **God**," (1st Commandment,) whom we are bound to worship and **glorify as** such,—abstinence from alcohol being conducive to such **worship**, and the use of it opposed to it; to the worship of God by images, &c., (2d Commandment); to the taking of God's name in vain, (3d Commandment); to hallowing the Sabbath, (4th Commandment); to the due observance of all of **which** in like manner, abstinence from alcohol is conducive, and the use of it opposed; and, therefore, such abstinence is enjoined, and such use forbidden in man's **normal state of health.**

We might proceed to point out the relations subsisting between the anti-alcoholic law **and all the** commandments included under the second table, in **reference to** the individual, and the species,—and show that it has an **evident bearing upon** each; and also, upon the sum of the commandments of the first **table,** (through the second,) every sin against the creature being also a sin against the Creator,—a truth most strikingly brought out in the fifty-first psalm, where David in an agony of remorse, exclaims: "Against Thee, **Thee only have I sinned,** and done *this* evil in thy sight."

But **anti-alcoholic temperance or total abstinence from alcoholic liquors in man's normal state of health, may also be viewed** *doctrinally;* and, it is in this aspect, as well **as in the aspect of a law of God, that the Bible System we have endeavored to** direct attention to, **is so remarkably distinguished from** the teetotalism **of expediency, and** that of secularism.

We hold, then, not only that abstinence from alcoholic liquors and all other brain poisons **is a part of** God's revealed Law; but, also, that it is a doctrine of the **Bible, that** when that law is believed on as emanating **from God, and acted on from evangelical motives, a grace of the Holy Spirit is exercised, well-pleasing to God through Jesus** Christ our Lord. In short, we believe that such anti-alcoholic temperance forms part of the temperance referred to **Gal. v, 23, in the following** words: "Meekness, temperance: against such there **is no law.**"

2d. *The Power of Anti-alcoholic Temperance in the Christian System.*—It **is a power that will** "remove mountains;" just because it **is the power of God, as** is the power of every grace of the **Spirit.** What mountains? Mountains **of** men's prejudices and passions,—mountains of men's **diseases** and crimes,—mountains of delirium tremens, and spontaneous combustion,—mountains of family broils, onslaughts and murders,—

mountains of revels, poisonings, Sabbath and sanctuary desecrations,—mountains of scandals and excommunications of church members and of depositions of ministers,—mountains of curses, oaths and blasphemies which pollute the atmosphere, from the **mouths** of drinkers,—mountains of animosity against the truth **as it** is in Jesus, amongst Brahmins, Mahomedans—and other teetotalers—(one-fifth of the population of the globe,)—mountains of money, gold and silver, squandered away upon alcoholic liquors,—mountains of wholesome food transformed into deadly poison,—mountains of conflagrations of men, houses, ships, manufactories, &c.,—mountains of poverty, squalor, wretchedness and woe! But where should we stop? We might go on *ad infinitum*, heaping mountains upon mountains; for who can tell the sufferings of those doomed to eternal misery in the fire which never shall be quenched, whose destruction has been caused by alcohol? Suffice it then to say, that we have no doubt whatever, that when the Bible doctrine of anti-alcoholic temperance shall have thoroughly permeated the church, it will extend itself to individuals, families and states; that it will become a constituent principle of all sound jurisprudence; in short, that it will bring about a wide-spread reformation of morals,—exercise a most beneficial influence upon health,—tend greatly to promote the comfort and well-being of all classes,—and above all, give the glory to God in Christ, which has been so long withheld from Him.

I am, my beloved friend,<br>
Yours ever,<br>
JOHN MAIR.

### LETTER VIII.

My Dear Brother,

In your letter to me, of date February 14, **1859,** you say: "I feel that we can make but little progress **further,** until the church cuts loose from the poison. I have said so to Mr. Dow, and others,—leading friends of total abstinence."

Has the church been awakened to a sense of her duty since that time, in America or Europe, in regard to the crying evils of alcoholic intemperance, so as to seek out and apply the only effectual remedy which can be found for them, as it is revealed in the Holy Scriptures? I apprehend not, to any considerable extent. It is true, that in Canada, the year before your letter was penned, the Synod of the Presbyterian Church "called for the Report of the Presbytery of Cobourg, on the Petition of Dr. Mair, of Kingston, remitted to that Presbytery by last Synod, on the subject of the use of intoxicating wine at the Lord's table. The report was given in and read. On motion made and seconded, the Synod agreed to receive and adopt the report, in so far as it states that the agitation of this question does not tend to edification; and further recommends to the office-bearers of the church to endeavor to procure, for sacramental use, the purest wine within their reach." \*

In 1852, the Conference of the Wesleyan Methodist Church in Canada, passed the following resolution:

"*Resolved*, That this Conference enjoins upon each of the preachers not to use, in the administration of the Lord's supper, any kind of mixture as a substitute for the generally acknowledged port wine of the country; as no mixture, which is not acknowledged by authority as wine, can be regarded as one of the elements in the holy sacrament; **and, as** the legally acknowledged port wine in the country, (*whether pure or impure*,) is the most expressive symbol attainable, of the precious blood of our Lord **Jesus** Christ."

In 1858, if I **am not** mistaken, this strange edict was rescinded by another Conference, and leave granted to preachers **to use** pure wine, the produce **of the** Province (i. e., I believe fermented

---

\* The Minutes of the Synod of the Presbyterian Church of Canada, June, 1858: p. **19.**

grape-juice, unenforced by alcohol.)* What is the significance of these events? Do they tend to show a disposition to yield to the arguments and entreaties of earnest men who cannot, for conscience sake, drink of intoxicating wine at the Lord's supper; or, a fixed determination to cleave to "the cup wherein is excess," and not listen to statements of facts or reasonings against it? *Whether or no*, it amounts to the same **thing as** far as true-hearted, Bible-taught abstainers from alcoholic liquors are concerned; for it is a grand *principle* they are contending for, and they are as much shut out from the table of their Lord by the use of wine with one per cent as twenty per cent of alcohol.

It is certainly hard work to rouse the dormant churches to a sense of their duty and their danger. One would imagine that **the** light you, Mr. Bonwick, and others, have thrown on the drunkenness to be found in wine countries, from wine drinking—in addition to the astounding disclosures from various quarters respecting the horrible adulterations of what are called wines, from divers poisonous substances—might have had an effect in making them at least eager to investigate the subject thoroughly, so that they might find out the truth, and follow it. I know little of their having done so. The following facts seem to lean rather to the opposite side of the question:

In the Address of the Personal Abstinence Society, to the Ministers of the United Presbyterian Church in Scotland, I find their pledge to be as follows: "I hereby promise to abstain

---

* Since the above was written, I have laid my hand on the following resolution of Conference:

"*Resolved*, That, whereas this Conference heretofore passed a rule requiring the use of the port wine of commerce, in the sacrament of the Lord's supper; and, whereas there is now made in Canada a pure wine from the cultured grape, the Conference now alters the aforesaid law so as to allow the wine made in this country from its own produced grape, when such is preferred by any of the churches.—[*Minutes of several Conversations, &c., at the Thirty-fifth Annual Conference, from 2d to 11th February*, 1858.

from all intoxicating liquors, *except in the ordinance of the Lord's supper*, or when required as medicine." Then come these words: "The propriety of this attempt to imbue the temperance movement with more of a Christian spirit, and enlist in its behalf Christian men, cannot be called into question; nor has the attempt proved unsuccessful." Afterwards the statistics of membership of this and kindred religious associations are given; the recommendation to office-bearers of the United Presbyterian Church of Canada to become total abstainers on the ground of *Christian expediency*, is referred to, and the evils brought upon the church, by the dissipation of its members, lamented. Then comes a pithy saying of Mr. Vanderkiste, the author of "A Six Years' Mission among the Dens of London:" "We may build churches and chapels, and multiply schools; but, until the drunken habits of the lower orders are changed, we shall never act upon them as we ought. While the pot-house is their church, *gin their sacrament*, and the tap-room their school-room for evening classes, how can we adquately act upon them for the conversion of their souls?" The question for us to ask, is this: Is the *gin sacrament*—here spoken of with so much disgust and abhorrence—to be wondered at, when we find a little lower down in the same report, the following piece of reasoning, in justification of teetotalism: "It is not overlooked that numerous objections have been advanced to total abstinence. Without entering upon an attempted refutation of these, it appears sufficient for those who desire, by the means we recommend, to wipe away a reproach from the Christian profession, and remove a stumbling-block from the path of the weak, that as *the Bible nowhere requires the use of intoxicating liquors*, there can be no evil done by abstaining; for 'where no law is, there is no transgression.' The question I solemnly put to the president, secretary, and two hundred and eighteen ministers who signed this address, is simply the following: 'How can you pledge yourselves, or ask other ministers to pledge themselves, to drink of intoxicating liquor at the Lord's table, and nowhere else, except medicinally, when you positively declare that the Bible nowhere requires the use of intoxicating liquors; and why do you not substitute *unintoxicating* wine, for intoxicating, at the Lord's supper, when, by your own admission, you are at liberty to do so, and thus remove a stumbling-block out of the way of many conscientious total abstainers, who are excluded from the Lord's table because they cannot defile themselves by drinking of that which they believe their Lord has interdicted, viz: alcoholic wine, in contempt of His holy commandment?" How much good the conclusion of this report is calculated to produce, after the above contradiction, I leave you to judge. The report continues: "In a word, we would add, give us but the universal practice of abstinence, among the followers of the Redeemer, and with the blessing of God, we predict a speedy revival of religion in the church, and a rapid extension of it over the world; give us the energies which moderate drinking paralyzes, and the money which moderate drinking wastes, and the moral influence which moderate drinking destroys,—and with a replenished treasury, and an invigorated piety, we may then, and not till then, set ourselves hopefully to the work of the world's conversion."

In the June number for 1859, of the Journal of the American Temperance Union, which contains the paradoxical report, from which I have so largely quoted, there is to be found a letter, from which the following pathetic, piquant and racy remarks are extracted, relative to the pledge of the United Presbyterian Church allowing a salvo to drink of intoxicating liquor at the Lord's supper: "Now, although I must have often perused the words in which the promise or pledge is expressed, I never till now felt any peculiar mental agitation. But, what I may call the eye of the mind being awakened, I look again and again, at a strange something contained in them. Nay, I felt mingled emotions, between wonder and shame, and shame and sorrow. I said: 'Surely there must be something **rotten in the state of Denmark**,'—something which I hesitated to **call** unchristian, and yet could find **no other** word by which to call it: 'I hereby promise **to abstain** from all *intoxicating liquors*, except in the *ordinance of the Lord's supper*.' A queerness here came over me; I felt as if I had awakened from a dream; I rubbed my eyes and read again: 'Intoxicating liquors, except at the Lord's supper!' Intoxicating liquors—that which is the bane of our country—that which, more than anything else, is ruining both the bodies and souls of men—the cause of crime, disease and death, filling our poor-houses with paupers, our jails with criminals, and our asylums with lunatics—and exclaimed: Is this a thing not **to be abstained from in that ordinance which** commemorates the death of Him, 'who gave himself **a ransom** for us, that He might redeem **us** from all iniquity, and purify us unto Himself, a people zealous of good works? Oh! there is here something about which the serious mind should think with deep impressiveness. I will think about it, and follow the light that an implored and a gracious Divinity may be pleased to inspire me with.

"Intoxicating liquor is used in the ordinance of the Lord's supper—so speaks the pledge—intoxicating liquor, the very nature of which is such that, because of its quality to intoxicate, it is hereby resolved on not so much as to taste it, except when it commemorates an event solemn beyond all that the mind can comprehend—and even, too, the *very object of which was, and is, that every inducement to sin should be avoided, and nothing used that is either directly or indirectly hurtful to man.* Surely, it is something else that should be so employed—something that is not simply innocuous, but highly beneficial. And there is such a something—not the fermented, brandied, intoxicating result of this fruit, but the pure, entire, beneficial juice of it. Gold, therefore, cannot be too dear to buy it for bringing before our minds in a commemorative ordinance, that event—the death of the son of God, whose blood was shed for the remission of sins, and by which, through faith in it, we will not only avoid but loathe not only the means, but the very idea of intoxication."

It is from such indications as this, of the dissatisfaction of individual members of churches expressed in periodicals from time to time, that we derive our hopes of a better state of things approaching, more than from any perceptible movement towards it, in religious organizations or amongst ministers of the Gospel.

In your letter to me of 2d March, 1859, you encouraged me by saying: "Your letters will be read with interest, and, what is better, without prejudice. May the Lord be with you in this work, and may His Spirit guide you in all charitableness towards those who still look upon our views with contempt." *You* have borne the burden and heat of the day,—with me, it has been a comparatively light matter to study the subject in quiet, undisturbed by clamor, insult or opposition, except now and then a sneer or a cold shoulder. Not one friend, as far as I know, have I lost by my firm adherence to the noble cause. For this I thank God, who has dealt so bountifully with me. If hereafter called upon to fight, may I do so with "weapons not carnal, but mighty through God to the pulling down of strongholds;" and may I manifest that spirit of meekness and forbearance which it becomes the disciples of the Lord to cherish, not only towards those who conscientiously differ from them, but also to their bitterest enemies. I am a novice in teetotalism, compared with you.

That which might discourage many, affords me encouragement. I refer to the all but total absence of the artisans of Great Britain from the Lord's table. In an article in the "Gospel Tribune," for November, 1856, I advert to this fact in the following terms, which I take the liberty to introduce here. The writer referred to, is the Rev. John C. Miller, Honorary

Canon of Worcester, and Rector of St. Martin's, Birmingham, well known and highly esteemed for the warm interest he takes in all practical schemes for ameliorating the condition of the humbler classes:

"This esteemed clergyman, in his lecture entitled 'The Home Harvest,' delivered before the Young Men's Christian Association in London, 1855-6, thus expresses himself: 'Let us look our work in the face; and let us not talk of the working classes, and of the poor so exclusively, as to fall into the error of supposing that they only need our anxious thought and earnest effort. In reference to the former, I shall not rehearse in your ears statistics which, although they have lost none of their terrible importance by repetition and familiarity, are yet known sufficiently for my purpose to every man among us. One test, however, of mournful significancy and conclusiveness may be touched on—the testimony of our Communion tables. Exceptions here and there, in no wise invalidate the fact that the proportion of our communicants among our artisans is absolutely 'Nil,' when set beside their numbers. I do not exaggerate the importance of this test. I do not regard absence, even habitual absence from that Holy table as necessarily conclusive of spiritual death, any more than I regard habitual presence as necessarily conclusive of spiritual life. But surely it is a test, and no unimportant one; and it is a mournful symptom of the spiritual indifference of the masses to their Christian duties and privileges, that the great bulk of them should seem to have no concern with the dying injunction of their Lord—no care for a child's place, and a child's bread at the table of their Father in Heaven.' Had this benevolent clergyman, free from prejudice in favor of an antiquated but unscriptural dogma, penetrated a little deeper than the surface, he would have discovered perhaps, that there was a substantial reason why the bulk of the working men of England should absent themselves from the Communion table. Why they seem to have no concern with the dying injunction of their Lord—no care for a child's place, and a child's bread at the table of their Father in Heaven. It is a matter of notoriety that teetotalism sprang up among the laboring classes of society, and that there it has had its chief triumphs. There is much shrewd sagacity amongst them. They are the pith and sinews of the body politic. Read their masterly essays upon the Sabbath question, if you would judge correctly of their intellectual and moral powers. They are not all addicted to strong drink—far from it. Many of them are sober, industrious, highly respectable men—otherwise what would have become of the manufactures—the commerce—the science—the glory of our mother country? Ichabod would have been inscribed upon her deserted palaces and temples ere now. It is then a melancholy sign of the times that Britain's workmen, her mainstay, have forsaken the assembling of themselves together, and sit not down to commemorate the death of their Saviour at His table. And yet it is in another point of view a consolatory sign. If we were to draw the sweeping conclusion from the premises, that these men disregarded the solemn injunction of the Lord Jesus Christ, to partake of unfermented bread and fruit of the vine in remembrance of Him, because they absented themselves from the Communion table—then indeed, this, their absence would, in our estimation, be the symptom of a fatal heart disease which they labored under; but if, on the other hand, we should have good grounds for believing that they were in the habit of separating themselves from the church at the celebration of 'The Lord's Supper,' because they viewed the mode in which it was observed with highly intoxicating wine as altogether anti-scriptural, then we should be constrained to give them credit for conscientiousness and strict adherence to the precept of their Lord, instead of censuring them for neglect of it. We apprehend this to be the truth, and we found our opinion upon the striking fact that about the end of the year 1847, when three prizes of £25, £15 and £10, were offered by a philanthropic layman, for the best essays on the subject of the Sabbath, written by laboring men; at least nine hundred and fifty were forthcoming, and appeared in 1848, three months after the announcement. This, we say, indicates a healthy state of religious feeling and principle amongst the working classes in regard to the Lord's day; but if they are sound in regard to it, can it be believed that they would, almost to a man, absent themselves from the kindred ordinance of the Lord's supper, if they were not forcibly impressed with the conviction that it was not observed according to Christ's appointment, in the churches to which they respectively belonged? But still farther upon this point:—Judge Marshall, of Nova Scotia, the devoted advocate of total abstinence, in his 'Earnest Appeal on behalf of the Total Abstinence Reform,' based on Scripture, addressing himself to the ministers of the Gospel, thus writes: 'As an additional argument and motive to you, Reverend sirs, it may be well to inform you, of what, perhaps, as yet you scarcely suspect, or at least, it would seem, do not sufficiently know, namely, that by opposing or neglecting the abstinence movement, you are impairing your influence and usefulness, as to religious ministrations, and in various other respects. Many have left and are still leaving your churches, and are declining to attend on your ministry, from dissatisfaction with the course you are pursuing with regard to the movement, and are meeting in private, in the halls or other places, for religious exercises of a public description, or are entirely neglecting them. It is a distressing truth, as all who spiritually and fully examine into the subject ascertain and admit, that the standard of religion as to vital piety and practical holiness is at present very imperfect and **low**. As to a revival from this state, it cannot scripturally be expected for many reasons that might be assigned, but most especially while the drinking of strong liquors so generally prevails, it being admitted by all, that drunkenness is, far more than all others, the cause of individual declensions and expulsions from churches.'

" Now, it is as clear to us as the sun at noonday, that hardly in any other way could the ministers of the Gospel present so formidable a barrier to the cause of Christ, as by their obstinate persistence in the use of highly intoxicating and drugged wine at the Lord's table, in direct opposition to His sacred commandment; and we cannot doubt that many sagacious, far-seeing and conscientious artisans, who have adopted the principles of total abstinence, must have their eyes open to the gross inconsistency of the office-bearers of churches dispensing such abominable stuff at that solemn ordinance, as if it could truly represent that blood which cleanseth from all sin. Under these circumstances, and until furnished with positive evidence that the Christian artisans of Great Britain *en masse*, absent themselves from the Lord's supper for some other reason, we shall feel ourselves justified in believing it to be highly probable that a large proportion of that class of men, who are intelligent teetotalers, do so, because their love to their Redeemer will not allow them to drink of intoxicating wine, or in other words, (and to make use of the language of inspiration,) of 'the cup of devils'—the wine which 'at the last biteth like a serpent and stingeth like an adder'—as the symbol of His precious sin-atoning blood.*

" If these views be correct, we have grounds to look upon the symptom which has been brought before us by Canon Miller, as one, and an alarming one, too, not of disease **of the** class to which he refers, but of a special malady in the visible Church of Christ, **to** which the distinctive appellation of ' alcoholic

---

\* "It may appear startling to some who do not know the progress that true temperance principles are making among young Christians; but yet it is a fact, that numbers are excluded from the church because they cannot conscientiously participate in *one* of its ordinances. They are reluctant to imbibe intoxicating drink, even as a religious rite."—*The Temperance Spectator, Dec.* 1, 1860.

consumption' might be assigned. The church is stupified **by** strong drink. She reels and staggers under its malign influence. She is paralysed, convulsed and eviscerated by it. It preys upon her very vitals. It eats out her piety. It undermines her constitution. I would **much** rather see the communion table deserted by the aristocracy and science of the land, than by the men who earn their bread by the sweat of their brow; for amongst them, if anywhere, true piety is to be expected,—because 'the poor have the Gospel preached to them:' (Matt. xi, 5:) and 'not many wise men after the flesh, not many mighty, not many noble are called; but God hath chosen the foolish things of the world, and things which are despised hath God chosen, and things which are not, to bring to nought things that are:' (I Cor. i, 26-28.)

"But although we have referred the ominous symptom, which we have had under consideration, to 'alcoholic consumption' in the church, rather than to a diseased condition of the working classes, yet the fact must not be ignored, that there is great danger of the disgust with which they view the habitual employment of intoxicating drink at the Lord's table, in the Establishment and other sections of the church—the consequent coldness and nakedness of her divers religious services, and her impotency in arresting the deluge of crime which overflows **the** land and threatens to submerge its most cherished institutions and sweep away its blood-bought rights—ripening in them into settled aversion to all religious institutions, and branching out into some one or other of the proteiform monstrosities of modern infidelity or positive atheism. Nor are these bad, although they be, the only or even the greatest evils to be dreaded. Who can tell when 'the wrath **of** the Lamb' may not be kindled against the people who turn **a** deaf ear to all His tender expostulations—cleaving to 'the cup of devils,' and reject 'the cup of salvation'—bringing upon them swift destruction? The only remedy for the church, is at once, and forever, to banish from the sanctuary, the 'wine wherein is excess,' (the principle of physical and moral ruin,) that filthy thing, which, like Achan's wedge of gold, causes the enemies of God to triumph, and the ranks of Immanuel to despond!"

Once more—let us look to our friend, "The Times," for a leading idea: "The instant," says he, "people determine that a moral and religious principle is involved in a question, they are committed to fight it at all hazards." We have found that a moral and religious principle is involved in the question which we have been so long discussing, and we humbly ask the "Times" to aid us in bringing that principle to bear upon mankind.

We appeal to "the common people" such as heard Jesus "gladly," regarding it.

We entreat you, dear friends, to look into this question with all the ardour, candour and intelligence, for which you are distinguished,—trusting that you will arrive at the same conclusions which we have reached, and that you will contend manfully for the introduction of 'unfermented fruit of the vine' into the churches according to the revelation of God, as the only emblem of the blood of Jesus admissible at His table.

To you, the ministers of the everlasting Gospel, of all denominations, holding the truth in love, and to you, the office-bearers of the church, we respectfully appeal in behalf of anti-alcoholic temperance, and we hope that our appeal shall not be in vain. It cannot be—we will not allow ourselves to harbour the ungenerous thought for one moment, that you, the faithful stewards of the mysteries of God, who possess such critical acumen, are endowed with so much learning, and burn with such love to souls, will lag behind any longer in this noble movement. 'Watch ye, stand fast in the faith, quit you like **men,** be strong;' 'Come out boldly, and separate yourselves from the unclean thing;' cast from you 'the abomination which maketh desolate'—the 'wine wherein is excess.' Let it no more defile the communion table of our Great High Priest, but *there* let 'the fruit of the vine' in its purity represent, henceforth, the precious blood of Jesus which cleanseth from all sin."

**To** our brethren of the healing art, who are already disciples of the Anti-alcoholic School, we would address a few words of encouragement, and say: "Go on, dear friends, in your career of total abstinence, only be sure you take the Bible for your text-book and guide. You cannot err if you keep close to its doctrines and precepts in temperance, as well as every other department of religion and morals. Fight and conquer!"

To those who are still lingering in the ranks of the alcoholic fraternity, **we** would say, more in sorrow than in anger: "Come out from among them and be ye separate. Flee for your lives; **the avenger of** blood is at your heels. Tarry not for a moment; get within the city of refuge, or you may be lost forever. Use no alcoholic liquor, except where it is indispensable for the cure of disease. Study the works of Carpenter, McCulloch, Mussey, Miller, Higginbottom and others. Apply the principles of sound temperance *always*, both in health and in disease. Valiantly

---

NOTE.—A reformed drunkard, now a distinguished clergyman, dares **not** partake of the intoxicating Communion wine he dispenses. He passes the cup, after applying **it** to his lips, fearing the taste might revive his dormant appetite.

A celebrated temperance lecturer, once **intemperate,** now a professing Christian, bows to the cup, not daring to taste, lest **he** fall. While a man continues to be a drunkard, can he be a Christian? If reformed, and he becomes a Christian, should he be tempted back **to his** old vile habits through **the** Communion cup? If for no other reason than benevolence **to the reformed** Christian drunkard, should not the universal church unite **in** discarding the intoxicating Communion cup by substituting the fruit of the vine in a state free from the "mocker," which, at the last, "biteth like a serpent and stingeth like an **adder?**"

oppose the drinking usages at all times,—at all hazards,—and in every place, by deed; and, whenever you have a favorable opportunity, by suitable counsel and exhortation. Much depends upon you. After the ministers of the Gospel, you can exercise the greatest influence in arresting alcoholic intemperance, and rich **will be** your reward if ye continue 'faithful unto death.'

Let it no longer be the disgrace of our profession, that so many of its members make themselves sots and die drunkards! Will you believe it—the Rev. I. Inglis, Reformed Presbyterian minister, positively asserts: "I have now lying before me, a list of all the ministers whom I have either personally or historically known, that have died within the last twenty years in Scotland, and I find most lamentable to write, that *every tenth minister* has died either an excommunicated, or a 'habit and repute' drunkard!—and from a similar list of medical practitioners, that *every third* medical man has died a habit and repute drunkard!—and of both professions, some others were reputed heavy drinkers."*

"We have examined the Statistical Reports on the Sickness, Mortality and Invaliding among the troops at the Mauritius, where Delirium Tremens is more prevalent and fatal than in any other possession of Her Majesty, and we find that one-sixteenth of the deaths of the soldiers in that Island was caused by that disease, within twenty years. It is true, others may have died from other diseases caused by drunkenness, and have been habit **and** repute drunkards,—but still, **it indicates** a heart-sickening degeneracy on the part of the sacred profession of the Gospel—of **those** whose duty it is to set an example of Godly living

---

* Permit me, here, to call your attention to the great benefits which would probably result from the re-publication of Dr. Sewall's Drawings of the Stomach, as affected by **the** use of intoxicating drinks,—from health, to death by Delirium Tremens. If the publishers could introduce them into this work, **as** I understand they are out **of** print, they would afford admirable illustra**tions of** our theme, and practical lessons adapted to all in every age and country, to shun **"the** wine, wherein is excess," as the bane of humanity.

before their flocks,—and on that of the men who ought to be at all times capable of exercising the clearest judgment, and performing the most delicate and dangerous operations—to find that drunkenness prevails to such a ruinous extent amongst them, approximating, if not exceeding that of the profession held ordinarily to be the most dissipated of any, that of *arms*. If either of the professions, of the Gospel or of medicine, in Scotland, can disprove these allegations, it is plainly their duty and their interest to do so. If they cannot, it is high time for them to 'repent and bring forth fruits meet for repentance;' and they may rest assured, that while these facts remain uncontradicted, and therefore presumed to be well grounded, they must suffer in their reputation, and have their usefulness seriously impaired." *

In a speech by E. Dawson, Esq., J. P., Aldcliffe Hall, (near Lancaster,) it is stated that "out of twelve medical men who studied in the same University, as his doctor, not one was living,—the whole having died early in life through drink." †

If these things be so in respect to the doctors, the awful questions arise: How many of their patients died natural deaths? how many filled drunkard's graves? how many are in hell lifting up their eyes in torment? Let us ponder these things, and combine our most strenuous exertions to get this foul blot washed out of our professional escutcheon. Let our crest, instead of the intoxicating cup, (too long our badge,) henceforth be a cluster of ripe grapes, with the Scriptural motto, "Destroy it not, for a blessing is in it."

To you, the learned members of the legal profession, we look with confidence for support in this crusade against alcohol, **for** few have better opportunities than you of knowing what an appalling amount of crime is produced by it. We might refer you to Judges, and other high legal authorities for proof that

---

* The Scottish Temperance Review, February, 1852: p. 64.
† The Alliance Weekly News, September 29, 1860.

two-thirds of the crimes which are committed in England and America, spring from this source.

We point you to the illustrious names of A'Beckett, the Chief Justice of Victoria; to Judge Crampton, in Ireland; to Warren, the Recorder of Hull; Hill, the Recorder of Birmingham; Pope, the Secretary of the United Kingdom Alliance, as holding high rank in the temperance army; but we chiefly wish to draw your attention to that admirable man, Lord Brougham,—himself a host,—who, for the last sixty years, has occupied so prominent a place in the history of his country and of the world—"the observed of all observers." Whether we fix our eyes upon him as a lawyer, orator, statesman, philosopher, patriot or philanthropist, he stands almost unrivalled. **See what he** has done for jurisprudence,—what for government,—what for education,—what for emancipation of the slave,—what for social science,—what for temperance,— and say does he not deserve to be classed, in all these respects, amongst the most illustrious benefactors of his species?

When the daughter of his deceased friend, Sir James Mackintosh, hung over the couch of her dying father, eager to catch some expression which might console her with the hope that he was going to glory, it is said, he gave utterance to the following never to be forgotten words: "Jesus—Love—the same thing."

May Henry, Lord Brougham, have all his earthly excellencies crowned with faith and love which are in Christ Jesus, to the praise of the glory of His grace. May his last days be pre-**eminently** his best days, because devoted to the Saviour. May he yet, by his decided testimony for Jesus, be the instrument of "turning many to righteousness;" and may he shine as a star of the first magnitude and purest lustre, forever and ever!

The following are characteristic specimens of his masterly eloquence in 1839, where he addressed the House of Lords, upon the sale of the Beer Repeal Bill of which he was the mover; and, in 1860, when, as President of the Social Science Congress, at Glasgow, he gave a clear statement of his views respecting a prohibitory liquor law.

Having recapitulated a vast mass of evidence as to the results of the beer-house system in all parts of the country, Lord Brougham proceeds to say:

"With respect to the effects of beer-shops upon the morals of the people, he was in possession of some of the most grievous and distressing facts. Hardly a petition came to him that was not accompanied by a letter either from a magistrate, a grand-juror, an overseer, a high-constable, or a reverend clergyman, all stating facts similar to what he was about to detail, and they were only to be taken as a sample. . . . Examples were given, too shocking for him to read to the House, of the most abhorrent cases of female prostitution, and of such profligacy and crapulous vice as he had never read or heard of before.

. . . To what good, or with what consistency, should the clergy occupy themselves in inculcating piety and morals on the Sunday and visiting their parishioners, in order to tend their flocks and keep them in the right path?—to what good was it, that the Legislature should pass laws to punish crime, or that their lordships should occupy themselves in finding out modes of improving the morals of the people by giving them education?—what, in the name of Heaven, could be the use of all the education they could bestow?—what the use of sowing a little seed here, and plucking up a weed there, if these beer-shops were to be continued, that they might go on to sow the seeds, not of ignorance, but of that which was ten times worse—immorality broadcast over the land, germinating the most frightful produce that ever had been allowed to grow up in a civilized country, and, he was ashamed to add, under the fostering care of Parliament, and throwing baleful influences over the whole community?"

On the same day, in the House of Lords, Viscount Melbourne, the Prime Minister, announced the intention of the Cabinet to resign, in consequence of a hostile vote of the House of Commons on the question of the suspension of the Jamaica Constitution. On this announcement being given, Lord Brougham made the following memorable remarks:

"My lords, after what has fallen from the noble lord, I shall postpone the second reading of the Beer Bill, although I consider that bill to be of more importance, as regards the public morals, than the resignation of any ministry. I do not apprehend that any Legislature will be so wanting in a due regard to what I hold to be the highest functions of the Legislature—namely, superintending the morals, the instruction, and the welfare of the people under their care—as to allow any mere party feeling, any temporary, and, it may be, only momentary, gratification of those feelings, to interfere with what I hold to be the highest duty of the Senate in this country. My lords, I hold this bill, the repealing the Sale of Beer Act, to be of greater moment than **any** party question that can divide either House of Parliament; and I shall persist, whoever holds the office of Minister of this **country,** in my endeavors to obtain the repeal of a measure which **I** believe to be permanently fraught with mischief to the **character** of the country."

On the 3d of June, Lord Brougham moved the second reading of the Beer Act Repeal Bill, and delivered an able and eloquent speech, from which we take the following passages. Referring to the Temperance societies, his lordship said:

"Why should the noble duke (of Wellington,) or his noble **friend** opposite, enter into a society binding themselves not to drink spirits, when they had the perfect power of drinking their claret, **burgundy,** and champagne? He knew plenty of persons who would have no objections to enter into those societies, but they said **they** would not be guilty of such hypocrisy as to declare that ardent spirits should not be drank, when they felt certain that they could continue to enjoy their wine. He himself felt strongly the objection to drinking ardent spirits. They were the parent of crimes of the worst description, as the police reports showed—namely, crimes accompanied with violence."

Lord Brougham, in his reply, adverted to the thin attendance in the House, and the absence of the bishops—only **two of** whom were in their places. This reply was very caustic, but well deserved. He was sorry to see, from the aspect of the House, that the present critical hour had had the effect of sadly thinning their lordships' numbers. Their lordships liked the Beer Bill little, but they liked remaining **in the House** after half-past 7 o'clock less. Their lordships liked **to see a** good state of morality in the country—the tranquil order of society they dearly loved—it was the very apple of their eye; but there was another affection operating upon certain delicate organs **in** the constitution of noble lords, still **more intimately than those** connected with the peace, **order and purity of society, and** reminding them of what had **been called the most** important event of existence—that of **dinner**. . . . There is hardly a bishop whom I have not heard imploring your lordships, from this very place, for God's sake to apply a remedy to that which makes all our preaching **and** teaching vain, to **reform** these nests of drunkenness, to remove these moral plagues—and now that I come forward at their instigation, that I lend myself as their coadjutor, that I put myself as an humble instrument **in the hands of** morality and religion, but two, out of six-and-twenty right reverend prelates, will sacrifice their dinner, their regard for their belly, which is their God.

The noble lord was called to order by the Marquis of Salisbury, who moved that the noble and learned lord's words be taken down. Lord Brougham responded **by** saying, that in order **that** they might correctly be taken **down, he** had better repeat **them,** when considerable confusion ensued, two or three noble lords speaking at once. Lord Brougham explained his meaning, by saying: "Well, well, my lords, to oblige **my** noble friend, (Salisbury,) I will say this, **that** the bench of bishops, at whose instigation I brought this subject forward, have, out of their earnest regard to the morals of the community, sacrificed all personal considerations and have attended during this discussion, by two of **their** body—I can't go further. And I, having the greatest veneration for the bishops, a respect for them, in which **I don**'t yield to my noble friend opposite, I felt peculiar pain **in** not seeing more than two, out of twenty-six, present on this occasion. But my noble friend is content with two only; I, on **the** contrary, would fain see the whole twenty-six here, for if they were here they would all vote for the bill."

The Bishop of Chichester rose to repel the unwarrantable attack that had been made on the bench of bishops, and was called to order by Lord Ellenborough; and after a brisk altercation the House divided. Contents, 36; non-contents, 19; majority for the bill, 17. The two bishops (Bangor and Chichester,) and the Duke of Wellington, were among the contents.

Thus **ended** that remarkable debate. The Beer Act still **curses** the country. Beer-houses are an established pest—a legalized pollution; and the "old man eloquent" is still calling upon the country to apply a remedy. Having lost faith in the bishops, the magistrates and the excise, Lord Brougham now joins with the United Kingdom Alliance in the grand remedy— the giving to the people the power to prohibit their greatest curse and source of misery. If the people WILL to abolish **the** liquor-traffic, who ought to resist that decision? Will the **Bishops,** the House of Commons, or the Government, refuse to yield **this** power to the people? If so, on them the responsibility must rest.

[From Lord Brougham's Address to the Social Science Congress, at Glasgow, Monday, September 23, 1860.]

"At our last Congress, great attention was given to the important subject of Temperance, and especially to the necessity of preparing public opinion for those repressive measures which experience daily proves, more and more clearly, to be **required** for lessening the consumption of spirituous liquors. The great source of pauperism and of crimes has **hitherto** only been attacked by palliatives; and, although these have **had a** certain success, yet if there be any means not **exposed to serious objections** by which the evil may be extirpated, the gain to society would be incalculable. No measure of absolute repression can, **of** course, be recommended until the public mind has been not only prepared, but strongly inclined for it. But the proposal of the Grand Alliance\* well deserves **a careful** consideration—the plan of enabling **a certain** proportion of the inhabitants **in** every district—a proportion considerably above the commercial majority—to **give the magistrates** authority for placing the district under a general repressive act, passed with such modifications as, according to the act's provisions, may be **allowed in** the peculiar local circumstances. A very extensive adhesion has been given to the proposal, in the great districts of Manchester and Birmingham; and this, besides its intrinsic merits, will be quite sufficient to cause a searching examination by our departments, sanitary and of jurisprudence. That it deeply concerns both, need not be added. But which of all **our** departments does it not most deeply concern? Remember **the** memorable expression of that great philanthropist, our eminent colleague, the Recorder **of** Birmingham: 'Whatever **step I** take,' says Mr. Hill, 'and into whatever direction I **may** strike, the drink demon starts up before me, and blocks the **way.**'

"When Lord Melbourne, in the House of Lords, during the debate on **the** Sale of Beer Act Repeal Bill, told their assembled lordships that, do what they might to regulate public **houses,** 'riot and disorder would be found in such places'—that, in fact,

---

\*At this point his lordship, looking up from his written notes, added, "The United Kingdom Alliance;" thus obviating the possibility of misconception of his meaning.

to breed and foster crime 'was the nature of the thing'—he gave utterance to a great philosophical truth, which has been notoriously confirmed by the sad experience of every country under heaven, where the making and selling of intoxicating beverages has had the sanction and been protected by the civil power."

Finally, we commend Anti-alcoholic Temperance, with its Divine precepts, doctrines and motives, as revealed in the Bible, to the attentive study of all of both sexes, of every class, age and country, as fraught with unspeakable blessings to mankind, and as manifesting, in a way hitherto obscurely if at all perceived, the power, wisdom and goodness of God.

And here, let us set up our Ebenezer, saying: "Hitherto hath the Lord helped us."

"We will rejoice in thy salvation, and in the name of our God we will set up our banners: The Lord fulfil all thy petitions. . . . Some trust in chariots, and some in horses: but we will remember the name of the Lord our God:" Psalm xx, 5, 7.

"Her priests have violated my law, and have profaned mine holy things: they have put no difference between the holy and profane, neither have they shewed *difference* between the unclean and the clean, and have hid their eyes from my Sabbaths, and I am profaned among them:" Ezekiel xxii, 26.

"Thou son of man, shew the house to the house of Israel, **that** they may be ashamed of their iniquities: and let them measure the pattern. And if they be ashamed of all that they have done, shew them the form of the house and the fashion thereof, and the goings out thereof and the comings in thereof, and all the forms thereof and all the ordinances thereof, and all the forms thereof and all the laws thereof: and write it in their sight, that they may keep the whole form thereof and all **the** ordinances thereof, and do them. This is the law of the house: Upon the top of the mountain, the whole limit thereof round about, shall be most holy. Behold this is the law of the house:" Ezekiel xliii, 10–12.

"A son honoreth his father, and a servant his master; if, then, I be a father, where is mine honor? and if I be a master, where is my fear? saith the Lord of hosts unto you, O priests, that despise my **name**. And ye say, wherein have we despised thy name? Ye offer polluted bread upon mine altar, and ye **say**, wherein have we polluted thee? In that ye say, the table of the Lord is contemptible. And if ye offer the blind for sacrifice, is it not evil? and if ye offer the lame and sick, is it not evil? Offer it now unto thy governor: will he be pleased with thee, or accept thy person? saith the Lord of hosts. And now, I pray you, beseech God that he will be gracious unto us: this hath been by your means; will He regard your persons? saith the Lord of hosts. Who is there even among you that would shut the doors *for nought?* neither do ye kindle fire on my altar for nought. I have no pleasure in you, saith the Lord of hosts: neither will I accept an offering at your hand. *For from the rising of the sun even unto the going down of the same, my name shall be great among the Gentiles, and in every place incense shall be offered unto my name, and a pure offering, for my name shall be great among the heathen, saith the Lord of hosts:*" Malachi i, 6–11.

" Neither shall any priest drink wine, when they enter into the inner court. Neither shall they take for their wives a **widow**, nor her that is put away: but they shall take maidens of the seed of the house of Israel, or a widow that had a priest before. And they shall teach my people the difference between the holy and profane, and cause them to discern between the unclean and the clean. And in controversy they shall stand in judgment, and they shall judge it according to my judgments, and they shall keep my laws and my statutes, in all mine assemblies, and they shall hallow my Sabbaths:" Ezekiel xliv, 21–24.

*"Thus saith the Lord, as the new wine is found in the cluster, and (one) saith, Destroy it not; for a blesing (is) in it: so will I do for my servants' sakes, that I may not destroy them all. And I will bring forth a seed out of Jacob, and out of Judah, an inheritor of my mountains, and mine elect shall inherit it, and my servants shall dwell there. . . .* For, behold, I create new heavens and a new earth: and the former shall not be remembered, nor come **into** mind. But be ye glad and rejoice forever in that which I create: for behold I create Jerusalem a rejoicing, and her **people** a joy. And I will rejoice in Jerusalem and joy in my people: and the voice of weeping shall be no more heard in her, nor the voice of crying. There shall be no more thence an infant of days, nor an old man that hath not **filled his** days: **for** the child shall die an hundred years old: but the sinner being an hundred years old, shall be accursed. **And they** shall build houses and inhabit them, and they shall plant vineyards, and eat the fruit of them. They shall not build, and another inhabit; they shall not plant, and another eat: for as the days of **a tree, are the** days of my people, and mine elect shall long enjoy the work of their hands. They shall not labour in vain, nor bring forth for trouble; for they are the seed of the blessed of the Lord, and their offspring with them. And it shall come to pass, that before they call, I will answer; and while they are yet speaking, I will hear. The wolf and the lamb shall feed together, and the lion shall eat straw like the bullock, and dust shall be the serpent's meat. They shall not hurt nor destroy in all my holy mountain, saith the Lord:" Isaiah lxv, 8–9: **17–25.**

"There shall **be an** handful of corn in the earth, upon the top of the mountains; the fruit thereof shall shake like Lebanon, and they of the city shall flourish like grass of the earth. His name shall endure forever: His name shall be continued as long **as the** sun, and men shall **be** blessed in Him: all nations shall call Him **blessed.** Blessed **be** the Lord **God,** the God of Israel, who only doeth wondrous things. And blessed be His glorious name forever and ever, and let the whole earth be filled with His glory; Amen, and Amen:" Psalm lxxii, 16-19.

If we should never see each other "face to face" in this world, may we meet in the holy, heavenly Jerusalem, with the multitude which no man can number, and there drink of the fruit of the vine "new," with Him who loved us and gave Himself for us.

Farewell—farewell,—"The Lord bless thee and keep thee; the Lord make His face to shine upon thee, and be gracious unto thee, and give thee peace,"

Is the earnest supplication of<br>
JOHN MAIR.

'At the last it biteth like a serpent and stingeth like an adder.' *Prov. xxiii*, 32.

*From the London Temperance Spectator, February 1, 1861.*

## The Weekly Record's Recantation on the Biblical Wine Question.

It will be in the recollection of our readers, that, about a year ago, we **were** under the painful necessity of taking the *Weekly Record* to task, for the dangerous and inconsistent character of its teaching, on the Scriptural wine question.

The lapse of a year has worked a change, it seems, in the views of our contemporary; or, perchance, some patent eye-salve has given to its optics more clearness and strength of vision. In order that our readers may judge for themselves of the greatness of the change, we bring into juxtaposition the *ipsissima dicta* of the two periods, thirteen months **apart:—**

[***Weekly*** *Record*, Nov. 26, 1859.]

"With respect to the nature or 'quality' of the wine [at Cana,] we would offer no opinion. The plain inference is, that it was such wine as was usually drank, and of the best kind. We think it presumptuous to affirm or deny that it was different to other wines; and the trouble which many persons have taken to prove that this or that wine mentioned in Scripture was not alcoholic, militates rather against than for that total abstinence which they advocate [!?]. From the examples, the precepts, the similitudes, and the denunciations which we meet with from Genesis to Revelation, relative to drunkenness, every plain and unsophisticated reader of his Bible must come to the conclusion, that the ancient wines of Palestine and other countries were alcoholic. We can say for ourselves, that we shall **continue** to read our Bible without a **teetotal** translation; and when we come to the word 'wine,' we shall not stop to inquire whether it was red or white, intoxicating or unintoxicating, as those have done who have shown themselves 'wise above that which is written,' and **have** labored **to** darken counsel by words without knowledge. . . If we wrote daily for the next twenty years, as to its 'qualities,' we should only show, as others have done, our extreme ignorance, not to say our vanity and presumption—we had almost written, our impiety, in passing our judgment on **the** wine which our Lord so miraculously created. We are willing to leave the subject where we find it, and to read that, and every other passage of Scripture where wine is mentioned, just as we did before we were favored with the learned opinions and Hebrew criticism of our teetotal expositors."

[*Weekly Record,* **Jan.** 5, 1861.]

"We are by no means certain that our Lord ever sanctioned, by his own practice, the use of intoxicating liquor **of** any kind; but we are quite sure that **he** did not sanction the kind of wines in common use in the present day. We **are** quite prepared to admit, that not only did intoxicating wines exist in those days, but that many people were the victims of intemperance; but we think it equally certain, that many of the wines of the ancients did not possess the power of intoxication; and, in the absence of clearer evidence, it seems not at all unreasonable to conclude that our Saviour sanctioned the use of the safer and more harmless class of beverages; and, as regards the institution of the Lord's Supper, it should be remembered that all leaven and ferment were scrupulously *excluded at the time of the Passover.* . . **It may,** therefore, be a question, whether our translators have given us the correct idea [as to 'drunken,' in I Cor. xi, 21.] Suppose, however, that our authorized version is the best, the passages under consideration do not say much in favor of intoxicating drinks, *nor ought they to be regarded as giving a sanction of their moderate use.* In conclusion, we are by no means prepared to admit that the Bible gives its high and holy sanction to usages which are fraught with danger to the physical, social, moral and religious interests of thousands of our fellow-men."

"Do we complain, then, that the *Weekly Record* has thus read its recantation? Undoubtedly not. We the rather rejoice that it has yielded to the force of evidence, which, however, was precisely as forcible in November, 1859, as in January, 1861; but we have two very serious causes of complaint against the *Weekly Record*, which we have to urge in a spirit, not of petulance, but of honest displeasure. First of all, why has our contemporary made this grand revolution, without a hint of its being a revolution at all?. Granting it sincere in 1859, and equally sincere now, was it not a duty to have admitted its former error—in short, not to have recanted only, but to have shown repentance by at least a confession of previous error? Could it not have done what the *Westminster Review* has had the manliness to avow? Secondly, in the very act of coming over to those whom it formerly abused, the abuse is persistently continued."

James Miller, F.R.S.E., F.R.C.S.E.; Surgeon in Ordinary to the Queen, for Scotland; Surgeon in Ordinary to His Royal Highness, Prince Albert, for Scotland; Professor of Surgery in the University of Edinburgh, &c., on unfermented wine, remarks: "Some people have great difficulty in understanding how anything can be really called 'wine' which is unfermented, such is the strength of prejudice and custom. They see only the fermented wine now, and they cannot fancy the possibility of any other, either now or formerly. 'How will it keep?' they say. Not long ago, I made the acquaintance of an **extensive** vine-grower, on the Moselle. 'Have you any unfermented wine— **juice of** the grape?' said I. 'Tons!' said he. 'How old?' 'Some of it fully **ten** years.' And then **he** went on to explain two modes of preserving it, in its pure, natural, unfermented state—one by the boiling process; another by the 'sulphur cure'—*both precisely as practised in olden times.* The latter he preferred: **filling the** cask nearly full, then burning sulphur in the empty portion, and **whilst the** fumes were still there, fastening all tightly by the bung. So it was kept unfermented, for mixing subsequently with the fermenting grape-juice, to constitute the sparkling wines peculiar to that district. There need be no difficulty, then, in understanding how not only the recent *juice of the grape*, ere any fermentation shall have had time to begin, may be harmlessly drunk in the grape season, by young or old."

Let farmers try the "*sulphur cure*" with their new cider as taken from the vat, **and see** if they cannot have pure, *unfermented, unintoxicating* cider the year round, for a healthful beverage, or for culinary purposes.

## UNFERMENTED WINE.

**Pure** unfermented wine, manufactured by J. Reynolds, Ripley, Ohio, from the Catawba Grape, by a new method to prevent fermentation, which is perfectly effective, and does not in any respect injure the wine. Experienced chemists **have** given it a thorough test, and find no alcohol.

We have received twelve pages of Certificates from Rev. Dr. Duffield, of Detroit; space only allows giving one:

CINCINNATI, *December 6, 1859.*

We, the undersigned, having examined a specimen of the Unfermented Wine, manufactured by J. Reynolds, of Ripley, Ohio, cheerfully testify that, **in our** judgment, its adaptation to Communion purposes is unequalled.

H. A. TRACY, *Dis. Sec. A. B. C. F. M.*
B. F. MORRIS, *Pastor of the Cong. Church, Lebanon, Ohio.*
H. BUSHNELL, *Pastor of the Storrs Cong. Church.*
MATTHEW GARDNER, *Elder in the Christian Church, Ripley, O.*

# DIAGRAMS

OF THE

# STOMACH AS AFFECTED BY ALCOHOL.

BY THE LATE

DR. SEWALL, OF WASHINGTON, D. C.

Orders for the work will be promptly filled by
            C. VAN BENTHUYSEN, *Albany.*

# THE STOMACH IN VARIOUS STAGES,
## From Health to Death, by Delirium Tremens.

These diagrams are taken from drawings made from actual dissections in 1842, by Dr. Sewall, of Washington, D. C.

Perfect accuracy is not claimed, as no **two** cases would probably present exactly the same appearance; but **it** is claimed that they give a truthful illustration of the ravages resulting from the **introduction of the poison** alcohol into the healthful stomach, and forever settle **the** question that **the injury** commences with the *first glass*—with the moderate (falsely termed temperate) use of this poison.

Before these representations were submitted to **the** public **in** 1842, those celebrated surgeons, Dr. Warren, of Boston, Dr. Mott, of New **York**, and Dr. Horner, of Philadelphia, endorsed them. In 1843, **after a** lengthened discussion as to the principle **more** especially involved in the second stomach in the series, the same distinguished anatomists re-endorsed them, and recommended their universal circulation **for the** instruction of all classes.

---

### WESTMINSTER REVIEW, LONDON.

This influential Review, in 1855, defended the moderate **use** of alcohol in health, as necessary, indeed, as food for the body. Prof. Youmans, and others, of the United States, and learned writers in Great Britain, exposed the fallacy of this position.

Now, in 1860, this same Journal magnanimously acknowledges that recent scientific French investigators of the highest rank, have exploded this doctrine, asserting that alcohol is a poison, and always pernicious as a beverage in health. By the use of alcohol, they say: "*The pathological* alterations are *very vivid inflammation of the mucous membrane of the stomach.*"

"Very lately," **says** Dr. James McCulloch, of Scotland, "Messrs Lallemand, **Perrin** and Duroy in **France, and Dr.** Edward **Smith,** L.L.B., F.R.S., in London, **have** published **a number of** carefully conducted experiments, and most important discoveries, proving **that** alcohol undergoes *no change in the body,* it being **expelled** unchanged by the **lungs, skin** and kidneys;" and that, in the words of **Dr.** Smith, "*it should be prescribed medicinally, as carefully as any other poisonous agent.*"

The *British Medical Journal,* lately in a leader, appears willing to accept **the** improved scientific *status quo* as touching alcohol. It says: "The subject **of the** use of alcohol is daily becoming one of more importance. The question of **its** influence on the body in health is being daily canvassed by the chemist and physiologist; and, *as far as their lights reach*, it would seem that not only is alcohol not of service to the body, but is actually injurious."

# DIAGRAMS OF THE STOMACH IN VARIOUS CONDITIONS.

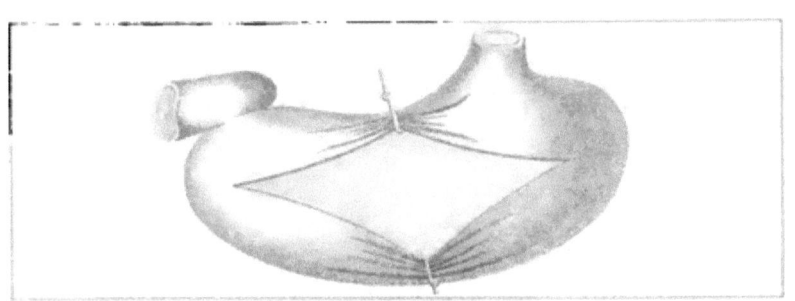

Healthful.

Moderate Drinking.

Drunkards.

Ulcerous.

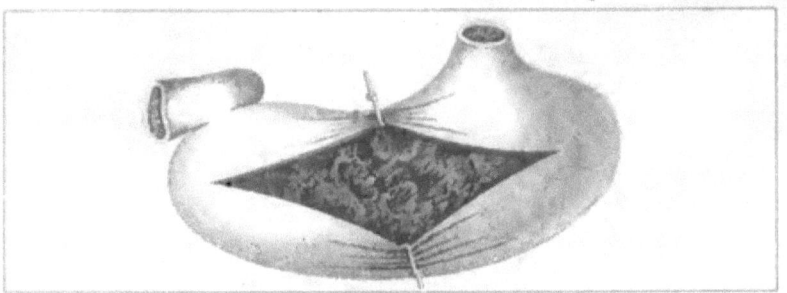

After a long Debauch.

Death by Delirium Tremens.

Eng.d on Stone by A Tolle.

www.ingramcontent.com/pod-product-compliance
Lightning Source LLC
Chambersburg PA
CBHW031249250426
43672CB00029BA/1393